8

FINAL ACTS
The End of Life,
Hospice and Palliative Care

Edited by

Gerry R. Cox
University of Wisconsin-La Crosse

Robert G. Stevenson
Mercy College

Death, Value, and Meaning Series
Series Editor: Darcy L. Harris

Baywood Publishing Company, Inc.
AMITYVILLE, NEW YORK

Baywood Publishing Company, Inc.
26 Austin Avenue
P.O. Box 337
Amityville, NY 11701
(800) 638-7819
E-mail: baywood@baywood.com
Web site: baywood.com

Library of Congress Catalog Number: 2013017867
ISBN: 978-0-89503-865-4 (cloth)
ISBN: 978-0-89503-866-1 (paper)
ISBN: 978-0-89503-867-8 (e-pub)
ISBN: 978-0-89503-868-5 (e-pdf)
http://dx.doi.org/10.2190/FAT

Library of Congress Cataloging-in-Publication Data

Final acts : the end of life, hospice and palliative care / edited by Gerry R. Cox, University of Wisconsin-La Crosse, Robert G. Stevenson, Mercy College.
    pages cm. -- (Death, value, and meaning series)
  Includes bibliographical references and index.
    ISBN 978-0-89503-865-4 (cloth : alk. paper) -- ISBN 978-0-89503-866-1, (pbk. : alk. paper) -- ISBN 978-0-89503-867-8 (e-pub) -- ISBN 978-0-89503-868-5 (e-pdf)
    1. Hospices (Terminal care). 2. Palliative treatment--Evaluation. 3. Terminally ill–Pastoral counseling of. 4. Terminal care--Psychological aspects. I. Cox, Gerry R., editor of compilation. II. Stevenson, Robert G., editor of compilation.
  R726.8.F552   2013
    362.17'56--dc23

                   2013017867

Dedication

John D. Morgan

Herman Feifel

Stan Hennen

William Lamers

Our colleagues in IWG

Table of Contents

SECTION 1
Professional Applications in End-of-Life Care . . 1

SECTION 2
Facing End-of-Life and Its Care 91

SECTION 3
Cultural Considerations 183

Foreword

On Monday, March 5, 1996, my mother suffered a massive stroke, and after being in a coma for 21 days, she slipped away. The chief of neurology informed me that the stroke was on her brain stem and that she would not recover and was essentially "brain dead." I found it hard to accept the futility of this diagnosis and tried everything possible to communicate with her. I read to her, told her stories, and shared memories, including recounting some humorous incidents that seemed to provoke some reactions and movement of her legs. I interpreted any movement as a sign or an attempt for her to communicate. I shared my newfound evidence and hopeful signs with the chief of neurology who quickly dashed my hope by explaining that all of my mother's movements were random reflexes.

My training and belief in psychology deepened my appreciation and respect for the power of the subconscious mind, even for someone in a coma. So I posted affirmations around her room and at her bedside. I also asked all nurses, doctors, and staff in the hospital's Intensive Care Unit, as well as all family members visiting, to step outside of her room when discussing her condition and related concerns. I forbid any negative talk in her presence. I felt a positive and hopeful atmosphere would help her fight to survive. In retrospect, my insistence might well have been more for my benefit than hers.

The ICU staff suspended the policy of allowing only three visitors in the ICU at a time and were very supportive, allowing approximately 20 family members to gather, encircling my mother's bed for a prayer vigil. The staff were culturally sensitive in allowing the family to create a meaningful ritual common in the African American experience.

My brother and I were in agreement, insisting that everything be done to save her life and give her the best care possible. I was at her bedside constantly to make sure that she got the best care possible. (My own research would later document a culturally distinct pattern for African Americans to insist on all lifesaving efforts and options be explored in spite of a terminal diagnosis.)

For 21 days my world was upside down, and I had no interest in anything else. Bargaining with God was in high gear. The loss of my mother posed a spiritual crisis for me because this was not supposed to happen. My unspoken prayer was to die before my mother. The thought of life without her was unfathomable. I felt God had let me down in not holding up his end of the bargain. Anger became a constant companion. I resented frivolity in others and could find little to laugh and be joyous about. I found myself wondering why God would take my mother as I became obsessed with identifying plenty of other more worthy candidates. Why her, why now? My assumptive world made no sense. Within a 2-week period, I lost 15 pounds in body weight. I had no appetite or interest in food. Very soon, the ICU nursing staff began caring for me as well, insisting I take more breaks, get more rest, and take better care of myself.

I had an upcoming speaking engagement in New Orleans that could not be cancelled or rescheduled. I was conflicted about the need to leave her bedside for a few days. The day before my departure, I brought my Walkman with headphones and began playing a Shirley Caesar gospel tape. Within a matter of minutes, while I stepped away to the nurse's station, when the nurse and I returned to her bedside, we witnessed tears streaming from my mother's eyes as she listened to the gospel music.

By the time I arrived in New Orleans, unpacked, and settled in my hotel room, my brother called to tell me that our mother had passed. (I would later learn and appreciate the numerous narratives and stories of loved ones who have had similar experiences in which a loved one slips away politely after a loved one leaves the room however briefly.) While in many instances people do die with loved ones at bedside, why some would choose to steal away in an unattended moment was confusing to me. Both my cultural and personal beliefs would lead me to choose to believe that the precise timing of my mother's departure or dying was not random, but rather strategic and intentional. I also believe that my mother, in her own infinite wisdom, knew that this was the best way to make her transition. Unceremoniously, she gently and quietly slipped away.

As I sat on the hotel bed, I stared into space for what seemed like an eternity, taking in my new reality. I recall that my eyes focused on two bright butterflies in a painting in my gaze. In the depth of my grief and despair, I knew my mother would want me to go on and give my scheduled talk the next day. The next morning, as I entered the New Orleans Convention Center for my keynote, I noticed a 10-foot sculpture of a beautiful butterfly.

The illness, end-of-life care, and death of my mother was one of the most traumatic and challenging experiences I have ever had to deal with. My personal experiences raised more questions for me about the experiences of end-of-life care and the dying process. I believe that we have merely scratched the surface in our insights and knowledge about the dying process. In our pursuit of truth, insight, and answers, the editor's have assembled an impressive diverse panel of contributing authors who share insights about end-of-life care, dying, death, and rituals.

This volume is dedicated to several iconic founders in the field of Thanatology, many of whom were also very instrumental in the organization of the International Work Group on Death, Dying and Bereavement (IWG). (IWG is an international professional organization of some international leaders in the field of Thanatology with 130 nominated members from approximately 25 nations from around the world.) These larger-than-life personalities were mere mortals who did some incredible work to serve and inspire others. Gerry Cox and Rob Stevenson have admirably continued the work and legacy of many of these giants in the field.

Jack Morgan's pioneering work at King's College started with organizing one of the first professional international conferences, attracting many impressive international researchers and scholars in the field of Thanatology. My first death and dying conference was at King's, and meeting Jack had a major influence on my passion and scholarship in cross-cultural Thanatology. Gerry and a group of dedicated organizers have continued Jack's legacy at the University of Wisconsin at La Crosse (UWLC) with its annual international death and dying conference. In addition to maintaining an eclectic mix of stimulating speakers and presenters, the UWLC conferences have maintained the balance in the programming that cares for the "whole person" (i.e., intellectually, emotionally, spiritually, and physically) with a setting, tempo, and organization to educate and enhance professional development and also promote self-care.

One of the things that I find exciting about cross-cultural research is the beauty and wonder of rituals from other cultures. In addition, Gerry and Rob have compiled an impressive volume of international scope, with leading scholars from around the world who provide an international perspective and lens for viewing end-of-life care, dying, and bereavement. At each annual meeting, typically in a different part of the world, IWG members give serious thought to best practices and the latest interdisciplinary perspectives from around the globe. Many of those perspectives and voices are reflected in this volume.

Ronald K. Barrett, PhD, FT

Preface

Gerry R. Cox and Robert G. Stevenson

As editors, we undertook this project to promote the International Conference on Death, Grief, and Bereavement in La Crosse, Wisconsin. The conference has a long history. The Center for Death Education & Bioethics held four conferences. The Center was moved to La Crosse, Wisconsin, where the conference has been held since 2002. It was hosted by Dr. John Morgan at King's College in London, Ontario, Canada, for 20 years ending in 2001. The conference has a history of having internationally known speakers. This book illustrates the quality of presenters at the conference.

After a half century or more of coping with the end of life, chiefly through avoidance or denial, people seem ready to finally address this period of life's story. In the mid-20th century, the topic of death was opened for discussion by Herman Feifel and Sir Colin Murray Parkes. It was popularized by Elisabeth Kübler-Ross. Then the quality of the end of life was finally given its due by Cecily Saunders and others through the Hospice Movement. It is this last topic that this book explores, along with the roles of Hospice and Palliative Care. The authors who have contributed here are very much a part of that time. They give quality to the end of life's story—its Final Acts.

As editors, we are honored to have our names associated with the quality people who have contributed chapters to this book. Section 1, Professional Applications in End-of-Life Care, begins with Currier, Hammer, and Neimeyer's chapter, Existential Empathy: Caregiver Understanding of Patients' Religious Beliefs at the End-of-Life, which examines the importance of the social network, including both religion and family, not just the individual, in working with those at the end of their lives. The authors analyze the impact of social support and its health implications. The second chapter, Attachments and Losses: Individual and Global Perspectives, by Sir Colin Murray Parkes, looks at the influence of child development on adult life and bereavement. Rather than simply showing how insecure child development impacts loss as adults, Parkes goes further to examine how insecure attachments in childhood can lead to extreme attachments to God, homes, territories, political leaders, and symbols. He then discusses interventions for these extreme attachments. Chapter 3, The Private Worlds of

Professionals, Teams, and Organizations in Palliative Care, by Danai Papadatou, develops a model for professionals and caregivers who work with the dying. She suggests that those who give care to the dying also have multiple needs and also face suffering. This chapter examines the private world of professionals and what is healthy and what is unavoidable. She also presents what are functional and dysfunctional coping patterns used by professionals. In chapter 4, Honoring Relationship in Pediatric Palliative Care, Kathie Kobler uses case studies to explain how to develop and maintain relationships with children and their families in pediatric palliative care. She offers strategies for using rituals and ways to initiate and maintain relationships with children and their families. Chapter 5, Meeting the Stress Challenge, by Neil Thompson and Denise Bevan, focuses upon the impact of working in situations involving high levels of emotion and the stress that may result. Thompson and Bevan make a strong case that such stress can do harm to individuals, groups, and whole organizations. They offer a model for a more holistic approach that incorporates social and organizational strategies and practical ways to prevent and manage stress. In chapter 6, When Birth and Death Collide: Best Practices in End-of-Life at the Beginning, Lori Ives-Baine and associates examine the application of pediatric and adult-based principles to the newborn. The authors discuss how to create the best situations for families in which life-sustaining medical therapy has been withdrawn, how to support the family, and the ethical challenges that perinatal palliative care presents. The authors offer models for care through the journey of palliative and bereavement care.

Section 2, Facing End-of-Life and Its Care, begins with chapter 7, To Be Is To Be, and the Do-ing Should Follow. In this chapter, Richard B. Gilbert presents a strong argument that caregivers need to honor the multiple tracks that come with dying while maintaining the focus on the wishes of the dying person. He offers ways for the team to better meet the needs of the dying person. Chapter 8, Stepping Through the Looking Glass Into "Cancer World," by Kent Koppelman, follows the journey of a friend who faced death. It is a powerful story that presents the journey from the point of view of the dying in a scholarly fashion. Chapter 9, The Psycho-Spiritual Side of Palliative Care: Two Stories and Ten Transformations Toward Healing, by Douglas C. Smith and Conley M. Potter, suggests that palliative care for the dying can be defined as offering "comfort care" for both the person who is dying *and* their loved ones. The authors present a model of the psycho-spiritual side of palliative care as a way of offering comfort to all those involved. Chapter 10, And the Sun Refused to Shine, by Susan Adams, examines different methods of working with patients and families complicated by factors of geographic distance, differences in reaction and treatment plan concepts, and meaning making, which become stumbling blocks to the prevention of positive support. Chapter 11, The Experience of Dying in Prison, by Nicole Pizzini, looks at the experience of dying in prison from the perspective of inmates who are terminally ill, the prison medical staff, and the prison security staff. She discusses how to maintain the dignity of the dying and a "good death" while still in prison. Chapter 12, The "Other" Kind of Pain: Understanding Suicide in the Context of End-of-Life Care, by Janet S. McCord, discusses suicide attempts by hospice patients and others diagnosed with terminal illnesses who wish to die either by their own hand or with physician assistance. She presents common risk factors, strategies to assess and postvention, and suicide in the context of hospice. Chapter 13, The End of Life: Two Perspectives, by Robert G. Stevenson examines children facing death.

Section 3, Cultural Considerations, begins with chapter 14, Stephen R. Connor's Palliative Care is a Human Right. Connor describes the need for hospice and palliative care around the world, the challenges of developing palliative care globally, and offers models that can be used around the world. Chapter 15, Spirituality in End-of-Life Care: A Roman Catholic Perspective, by Gerry R. Cox and Father Christopher W. Cox, suggests ways to offer end-of-life care to Roman Catholics who do not fit the traditional model of hospice care. An examination of the special needs, theology, and rituals is offered. Chapter 16, Grief and the American Indian, by Gerry W. Cox and Andrea R. Sullivan, offers suggestions for providing end-of-life care to American Indians by explaining cultural differences among American Indians and by giving suggestions of ways to improve care to a group that is generally neglected in hospice care. Chapter 17, "It Will Do When I am Dying": Navigating the Nuances of Fundamentalist Christianity's Understanding of Death and Dying, by Harold Ivan Smith, looks at the cultural differences and understandings of Fundamentalist Christian's view of a "good death" and the afterlife, ways to negotiate faith understandings that complicate end-of-life care, and developing ways to comfort individuals who may be marginalized in dying because they do not share the theological views of the dying individual or key family members.

Acknowledgments

This book is the result of the efforts of many people. The first to be acknowledged is John D. (Jack) Morgan, who began the International Death, Grief, and Bereavement Center at King's College in London, Ontario, and who served as Series Editor for the Death, Value, and Meaning Series for Baywood Publishing Company. Jack was kind enough to invite both of us to be speakers at his conference many times! He was a dear friend, mentor, and wonderful colleague! We would like to also thank Stuart Cohen, President of Baywood Publishing Company, and his excellent staff including Bobbi Olszewski, Julie Krempa, Astrid Loveless, and their staff for their aid in this project; and Darcy Harris for her support and help in this project. We would also like to thank each of the authors of chapters for their willingness to submit their work for inclusion in this book, for their timely completions of their chapters, revisions, and edits. We hope that each author will be pleased with the final product and that the product was worth the effort.

We are grateful for the support of our families. For me, my wife, Linda; our children, Christopher, Andrea, Kelly, Gregory, and Theresa; our sons-in-law, Dustin Motes, Jason Huggins, and James Sullivan; and for our grandchildren, Isaac Motes, John Sullivan, Elanor Sullivan, Olivia Motes, Finley Huggins, Alaina Motes, Declan Huggins, Eamon Sullivan, and Conor Sullivan.

We would also like to thank the people at the University of Wisconsin–La Crosse, who help support the conference and the production of the book: Penny Tiedt, Susan Niedzwiecki-Pham, Michael Brennen, Lori Pacourek, Andrew Vitale, Richard Gilbert, Rana Limbo, Jill Wilke, Carol Oldenburg, Kent Koppelman, Joe Gow, and Kim Vogt.

Gerry R. Cox

Like my fellow editor, Gerry, I want to acknowledge friends and colleagues. It becomes harder to do after so many years, but it is perhaps appropriate as I too approach my own end of life in the not-too-distant future. My thanks go to my colleagues in the graduate counseling program of Mercy College, especially Mary Ellen Hoffman and my *compadre* Fernando Cabrera, who gave me a third career. My family is always thanked for being my support throughout a lifetime, and I would not have been what I am without my wife, Eileen;

our sons, Robert Louis and Sean; the women in their lives, Eileen and Traci; and our beautiful granddaughter Kiera. The lives of many friends, leaders in this field who are now gone, are also in these pages in spirit, especially Jack Morgan and Austin "Bill" Kutscher. They lived life to the full, right to the end. May they rest in peace.

Robert G. Stevenson

http://dx.doi.org/10.2190/FATC1

SECTION 1

Professional Applications in End-of-Life Care

CHAPTER 1

Existential Empathy: Caregiver Understanding of Patients' Religious Beliefs at the End-of-Life*

Joseph M. Currier, Miyoung Yoon Hammer, and Robert A. Neimeyer

> The appreciation of [illness] meanings is bound within a relationship: it belongs to the sick person's spouse, child, friend, or caregiver, or to the patient himself. For this reason it is usually as much hedged in with ambiguities as are those relationships themselves. But in the long, oscillating course of chronic disorder, the sick, their relatives, and those who treat them become aware that the meanings communicated by illness can amplify or dampen symptoms, exaggerate or lessen disability, impede or facilitate treatment.
> —Arthur Kleinman (1988, pp. 8–9)

Religion has long provided a framework on which dying individuals and their loved ones construct meanings of illness and death (Park, 2005). In the above excerpt from *Illness Narratives* (1988), Kleinman highlights the importance of a

*The authors would like to express appreciation to the Fetzer Institute for funding this study and to Methodist Hospice in Memphis, Tennessee, for their partnership in conducting it.

1

systemic understanding in this regard—that the effects of irreversible health conditions can reverberate beyond the patient and touch those who are in direct relationship with him or her. Ironically, however, research on the impact of death and bereavement rarely adopts a systemic perspective, instead concentrating nearly exclusively on the adjustment of individuals without regard to relational or family factors (Hooghe & Neimeyer, 2012). Yet, particularly for persons at the end-of-life (EOL) who are increasingly dependent on their caregivers for the provision of basic needs, the meaning of their condition could be embedded in these relationships and reciprocally contribute to death anxiety and other existential concerns. Given the centrality of religion for many aging persons (Idler et al., 2003), mutual appreciation of the perceived role of religious faith in the dying person's life might affect his or her quality adjustment at the EOL. Focusing on a sample of hospice patients and their caregivers, this study explored whether such mutuality in the patient-caregiver relationship predicts patients' self-esteem and attitudes toward death.

There is evidence that having a reliable social support network in times of suffering generally carries positive health implications. Theoretically, a supportive caregiver relationship at the EOL can help the dying person maintain a sense of self-esteem, which along with companionship and instrumental aid, can buffer distress associated with facing one's death. However, caregivers do not always possess the resources to cope with the patient's illness and may hold opposing views regarding the dying process and religious (or secular) meanings of life and death. The term "support paradox" has been used to capture the burden that patients sometimes feel for a distressed caregiver who is unable to care for them due to negativity and potential opposition (Chan, Epstein, Reese, & Chan, 2009). In these instances, dissonance in the caregiving relationship about the patient's core beliefs can cause relational strain and emotional distress (Schumacher, Stewart, & Archbold, 2007; Skerrett, 2003). In contrast to many EOL contexts, when loved ones experience deep connection and healing (Sulmasy, 2002), such strains might eventuate in extreme isolation and guilt, thereby interfering with the patient's capacity to face death with a sense of integrity and acceptance.

Considering specific factors that might bear on patient adjustment at the EOL, the potential benefits of religion have been well documented (for review, see Koenig, McCullough, & Larson, 2001). For instance, studying a sample of over 800 older adults who were admitted to a general medical service, Koenig and colleagues (Koenig, George, & Titus, 2004; Koenig, George, Titus, & Meador, 2004) found that patients indicating greater spirituality had better social support, cognitive function, cooperation with medical staff, and less depression and need for long-term care across a 2-year span. In one of the few other studies with an EOL sample conducted to date, Ita (1995) found that hospice patients who reported greater spirituality had less death anxiety than those who rated themselves as being less spiritual. Results of a recent study by Neimeyer, Currier,

Coleman, Tomer, and Samuel (2011) from the current dataset similarly demonstrated that religiousness figured prominently in quality of life at the EOL. When controlling for a number of clinically relevant EOL factors (e.g., social support, past- and future-related regret), the degree to which hospice patients reported an internalized sense of religiousness was uniquely related to greater acceptance and less avoidance of death (Neimeyer et al., 2011).

These findings suggest that for individuals at the EOL, a sense of religiousness can aid in the adjustment process by evoking comforting emotions, offering strength, facilitating meaning making and acceptance of the illness, and reducing feelings of self-blame. Although many friends and loved ones can come and go across the life span, religious support—derived from a church or other religious community—might also provide a stable support network at the EOL (Ita, 1995). In addition to providing an interpretive framework for possible existential concerns in the face of irreversible illness (Park, 2005), dying persons and their families could be assured of help from like-minded individuals who will not abandon them in their time of need. Notwithstanding these possibilities, the lack of a reliable link between religion and death anxiety in the broader literature makes it clear that the former does not always positively influence attitudes toward dying. In addition, other research by Pargament and colleagues (2000) on negative religious coping has clarified ways in which religion may actually exacerbate death fears in some cases (e.g., by contributing to guilt and fear of punishment versus the hope of forgiveness).

From a systemic perspective, an integral aspect of religion at the EOL may entail the degree to which the religious orientation of the patient is empathically understood by his or her family caregiver. Generally, mutuality refers to the consonance, shared values, and affective intimacy that can exist in a relationship. As one may anticipate, research has documented that higher levels of mutuality between patients and their family caregivers frequently serve as a protective factor against depression and other negative outcomes (Ball et al., 2010; Schumacher, Stewart, & Archbold, 2007; Skerrett, 2003; Stricks, 1998). However, in some patient-caregiver relationships, the dyad may not share the same values but nevertheless be knowledgeable and mindful of one another's basic convictions and meaning systems. In such cases, the caregiver could still engender a sense of existential empathy in the relationship by respecting and honoring the patient's beliefs and values. In contrast, there could be dyads characterized by dissonance in which the caregiver is unable to appreciate the perceived role of religion in the patient's life. At worst, such empathic failure could subtly or unsubtly undermine the patient's attempt to draw on his or her beliefs during a vulnerable period or risk imposing religious convictions of the family caregiver that the patient does not share.

The present study attempts to address the possible role of caregiver empathic accuracy regarding the role of religion for the patient at the EOL. Extending prior work with this sample (Neimeyer et al., 2011), we hypothesized that hospice patients with high intrinsic religiousness (via both self and caregiver report) would indicate more adaptive attitudes toward death and greater self-esteem. However, when accounting for effects of demographic features (gender and ethnicity), religious affiliation, and a number of clinical factors at the EOL (social support, type of caregiver relationship, patient risk factors, caregiver risk factors), we hypothesized that high caregiver convergence in understanding patients' religious attitudes also would be associated with better EOL outcomes for the patients in the sample.

METHOD

Participants

Analyses were based on data from 108 patients receiving hospice care and their family caregivers. This dataset represents a subset of a larger sample of patients recruited to examine factors associated with psychosocial/spiritual adjustment at the EOL (Neimeyer et al., 2011). Participants selected for the present study included those who had a caregiver available to participate in an interview about their loved one's adjustment in the dying process. In contrast, the previous report concentrated exclusively on patient data.

Following institutional review and approval of the project, eligible participants were contacted about the study via telephone or in person by a clinical social worker on staff at a large hospice service located in the southern United States. Consenting patient-caregiver dyads were enrolled if the patient was at least 18 years of age, had a prognosis of at least 3 weeks but not more than 6 months to live, and both the patient and the caregiver had the cognitive ability and language skills to communicate in an interview and respond to objective assessment measures. Separate interviews were arranged with both the patient and primary caregiver in the patient's home. In an effort to reduce burden, only individual items were used from existing measures to assess study constructs rather than relying on the longer total scales.

In keeping with the predominantly bi-ethnic composition of the geographical region where the study was conducted, 69% of the patients were Caucasian and 28% were African American. The sample ranged in age from 39 to 99 years ($M = 76.12$, $SD = 11.57$) and had an almost equal proportion of men (45%) and women (55%). Just over half of the patients were married (56%) at the time of the study, with widowed (21%), never married (12%), and divorced (11%) individuals represented as well. The majority of the patients described themselves as Protestant in their religious involvement (73%), while smaller subsets affiliated with the Roman Catholic faith (7%) or professed no religious affiliation (21%). Caregivers' relationships to patients included spouses (40%), daughters (33%), sons (8%), siblings and other familial relatives (10%), personal friends (6%), and other types of nonfamily relationships (3%).

Measures

Intrinsic religiousness of the patients was assessed via two reporting methods based on Genia's (1993) revision of the Religious Orientation Scale. First, the patient rated him- or herself on the question, "My religious beliefs are what really lie behind my whole approach to life" on a 7-point scale (Strong Disagree = 1, Strongly Agree = 7). Second, in a separate interview without the patient present, the caregiver reported his or her perception of the patient's religiousness on the same scale for an adapted version of the question, "My loved one's religious beliefs are what really lie behind his or her whole approach to life."

The Death Attitude Profile-Revised (DAP-R; Wong, Reker, & Gesser, 1994) was used to assess the patients' attitudes toward death. Consistent with a contemporary emphasis on the multidimensionality of death attitudes (Neimeyer, Moser, & Wittkowski, 2003), the DAP-R consists of several subscales, including Fear of Death (e.g., "The prospect of my own death arouses anxiety in me") and Death Avoidance (e.g., "Whenever the thought of death enters my mind, I try to push it away"). Other subscales assess positive attitudes toward death, including Approach Acceptance (e.g., "I look forward to a reunion with my loved ones when I die") and Escape Acceptance (e.g., "I view death as a relief from earthly suffering"). Psychometric properties of the DAP-R have been shown to be favorable, with test-retest reliabilities in the range of .61 to .95 over a 1-month period and correlations with other assessments of death attitudes (Wong et al., 1994). Responses were scored on a 7-point scale for the patients (Strongly Disagree = 1, Strongly Agree = 7). Internal consistencies for the four subscales of the DAP-R ranged from .82 to .94 among the patients in the present sample.

Self-esteem of the patients was assessed with selected items from Rosenberg's Self-Esteem Scale (RSE; Rosenberg, 1965). The RSE is a widely used and well-established self-report instrument using a Likert-type scale. Items incorporated for this study included, "On the whole, I am satisfied with myself," "I feel that I have a number of good qualities," and "I feel that I am a person of worth." Internal consistency for RSE items was .93 in this sample.

So as to provide a fuller picture of the patient and caregiver, additional information was gathered from the patient's medical record. These measures included 16-item assessments of risk factors for both the caregiver (e.g., presence of physical/mental disability, substance abuse, conflicted relationship with patient, job demands, financial difficulties) and hospice patient (e.g., presence of family discord, caregiver competence, questionable spiritual issues, poor symptom control, other dependents in the home). In addition, this study included 5-item measures of the family's reaction to the EOL situation (e.g., presence of denial, anxiety, depression, anger, guilt) and degree of social/spiritual support for the patient (from family, friends, neighbors, church/synagogue, and other group). Each of these assessments had been completed using a checklist during the clinical social worker's initial psychosocial interview. For the purpose of the current study, items that were endorsed during the intake procedure were summed to provide a total score for each of the four clinical measures.

Plan of Analysis

In view of the significant overlap between patients and their caregivers on the intrinsic religiousness assessment, $r(108) = .36$, $p < .001$, two additional measures were created to capture the degree and nature of convergence within the dyads. First, the caregiver rating was subtracted from the patient's self-report, and the absolute difference score was computed for each dyad to reflect the degree of agreement between the two ratings.

Given the possibility for different types of convergence characterizing dyads in the sample, a second variable was also created using Latent Class Analysis (LCA) in MPlus, Version 6.1 (Muthén & Muthén, 1998-2010). Two variables were used in the LCA, namely patient religiousness (treated as an ordinal variable) and the convergence between patient's and caregiver's report of the patient's religiousness. We examined a 1-, 2-, 3-, and 4-class solution, and a variety of fit indices were considered when determining the best-fitting model. In particular, we considered the BIC and AIC (with lower values indicating better fit) as well as the Vuong-Lo-Mendell-Rubin (VLMR) Likelihood Ratio Test and the Parametric Bootstrapped Likelihood Ratio Test, both of which test the relative merits of a given model against a model with one fewer classes (e.g., a 3-class model vs. a 2-class model). We also report values for Entropy (with preferable values being closer to 1), which is a measure of classification uncertainty. Once a best-fitting model was established, probable class assignments were exported into SPSS for further analysis.

Associations between ratings of the patient's intrinsic religiousness and his or her death attitudes and self-esteem were tested with bivariate correlations. So as to minimize the threat of a type-1 error, we used multivariate analysis of covariance (MANCOVA) to assess whether patient-caregiver convergence accounted for unique variance in EOL outcomes (Fear of Death, Death Avoidance, Approach Acceptance, Escape Acceptance, and Self-Esteem). When again including patient demographics (gender and ethnicity), religious affiliation (yes or no), social support, patient and caregiver risk factors, type of caregiver relationship (spouse or other), and family reaction to EOL situation as covariates in the model, analyses of covariance (ANCOVA) were performed for each EOL outcome. For ANCOVAs that yielded a significant main effect for the patient-caregiver convergence factor, Fisher's least significant difference (LSD) test was then used to illuminate the specific differences across the three levels.

In a small number of cases, patients did not respond to one or two of the questions for the EOL outcome measures. Given the small number of omissions and strong internal consistency of the instruments in the current sample, numbers of missing cases were reduced by using the means of the completed items as the patients' overall scores in the analyses.

RESULTS

Bivariate Correlations between Patient Religiousness and EOL Outcomes

In keeping with results from our investigation focusing on the patient data (Neimeyer et al., 2011), self-reported religiousness on the part of patients included in this study was negatively related with both Fear of Death, $p = .054$, and Avoidance of Death, $p = .027$ (see Table 1). In contrast, patient's self-report of their religiousness was positively linked with the outcomes of Approach Acceptance, Escape Acceptance, and Self-Esteem, $ps < .001$.

Caregivers' perception of their loved one's religiousness was similarly negatively correlated with the patient's Fear of Death, $p = .034$, and positively linked with Approach Acceptance, $p = .001$. However, in contrast to patients' self-reports, ratings of the patients' religiousness among the caregivers failed to significantly associate with their loved one's Death Avoidance, Escape Acceptance, or Self-Esteem, $ps = .323$ to $.908$.

As presented in Table 1, the absolute amount of convergence within patient-caregiver dyads was positively correlated with patients' levels of Approach Acceptance, $p < .001$, and sense of Self-Esteem, $p = .011$. In addition, there was a nonsignificant trend for patients with greater divergence from their caregiver to also indicate more Death Avoidance, $p = .092$.

Convergence in Ratings of Patient Religiousness and EOL Adjustment

Indices of fit in the LCA generally supported a 3-class solution as the best-fitting model (see Table 2). Examination of participants based on their probable

Table 1. Correlations between Perceptions of Patient's Religiousness and EOL Outcomes

EOL outcomes	Patient self-report	Caregiver report	Absolute convergence[a]
Fear of death	−.19*	−.21*	−.10
Death avoidance	−.22*	−.10	−.17†
Approach acceptance	.80**	.31**	.38**
Escape acceptance	.30**	−.01	.08
Self-esteem	.37**	.06	.24*

[a]Absolute convergence = absolute score for the difference between patient self-report and caregiver report on intrinsic religiousness measure, with smaller values reflecting greater empathic accuracy or convergence of ratings.

†$p < .1$, *$p < .05$, **$p < .01$.

Table 2. Results of the Latent Class Analysis Examining Patients' Reports
of Religiosity and the Degree of Discrepancy between
Their Reports and Their Caregivers

	1-Class model	2-Class model	3-Class model	4-Class model
AIC	727.892	683.440	665.554	666.889
BIC	749.349	726.354	729.925	752.718
Entropy	—	.981	.966	.967
VLMR Likelihood Ratio Test p value	—	.006	.018	.353
Parametric Bootstrapped Likelihood Ratio Test p value	—	< .001	< .001	.040

Note: VLMR = Vuong-Lo-Mendell-Rubin; significant p values for the VLMR and Parametric Bootstrapped Likelihood Ratio Tests indicate significant improvement of the current model compared to the previous model with one less class.

class membership indicated that these three classes were made up of (a) patients with high self-reported religiousness and convergence in their report of religiousness and their caregiver's ($n = 87$), (b) patients with high self-reported religiousness and a low degree of concordance with their caregiver ($n = 10$), and (c) patients with low self-reported religiousness and a low degree of concordance ($n = 11$). Results of a MANCOVA with gender, ethnicity, religious affiliation, social support, patient and caregiver risk factors, type of caregiver relationships, and family reaction to EOL situation included as covariates indicated a statistically significant effect for the convergence factor produced from LCA, Wilks' $\lambda = 0.58$, $F(10, 154) = 5.63$, $p < .001$. Hence, we proceeded to explore the nature of the differences across the EOL outcomes assessed in this study.

A series of ANCOVAs revealed significant main effects for the convergence factor for Approach Acceptance, $F(3, 91) = 23.67$, $p < .001$, Escape Acceptance, $F(3, 91) = 4.10$, $p = .020$, and Self-Esteem, $F(3, 91) = 3.12$, $p = .050$. Patient-caregiver convergence was also marginally associated with Death Avoidance, $F(3, 91) = 2.74$, $p = .071$. Adjusted means and associated standard errors from these analyses are outlined in Table 3.

In terms of specific differences in patient-caregiver convergence, post hoc analyses revealed several significant results (see Table 3). Fisher's LSD test did not reveal significant differences in EOL outcomes between dyads with

Table 3. Adjusted Means and Standard Errors of EOL Outcomes for Patient-Caregiver Mutuality Groups

	High patient IR/ High convergence (n = 76)		High patient IR/ Low convergence (n = 9)		Low patient IR/ Low convergence (n = 7)	
	M	SE	M	SE	M	SE
Fear of death	2.32$_a$	0.16	2.53$_a$	0.49	2.52$_a$	0.57
Death avoidance†	2.76$_a$	0.21	3.29$_{ab}$	0.62	4.51$_b$	0.73
Approach acceptance**	6.52$_a$	0.12	6.93$_a$	0.37	3.54$_b$	0.37
Escape acceptance*	5.07$_a$	0.23	5.34$_a$	0.67	2.87$_b$	0.78
Self-esteem*	6.34$_a$	0.13	6.05$_{ab}$	0.39	5.16$_b$	0.45

Note: M = outcome mean adjusted for covariates, SE = standard error of adjusted mean, IR = intrinsic religiousness. $_a$ and $_b$ denote homogenous subsets or statistically equivalent groups of means.
$^†p < .1$, $^*p < .05$, $^{**}p < .01$.

high patient religiousness/high convergence and high patient religiousness/low convergence with their caregiver, $ps = .295$ to $.681$. However, when compared to dyads with high patient religiousness and high convergence, patients in dyads with low patient religiousness and low convergence indicated more Death Avoidance, $p = .025$, less Approach Acceptance, $p < .001$, less Escape Acceptance, $p = .009$, and less Self-Esteem, $p = .016$. In addition, this group also tended to have lower scores on the two types of death acceptance assessed in the study when compared to dyads with high patient religiousness/low concordance, $ps < .010$.

DISCUSSION

The possible helpfulness of religion in dealing with life's challenges has gained much attention over the past two decades (Idler et al., 2003; Koenig et al., 2001). However, there has been little empirical examination of systemic factors regarding how religion might contribute to the well-being of patients at the EOL. As such, this study examined how family caregivers' empathic understanding of patients' attitudes about the role of religion might predict patients' adjustment at the EOL.

As expected, results indicated a robust link between religion and the EOL outcomes assessed in this study, as in the larger dataset from which the current sample was derived. Bivariate analyses revealed that intrinsic religiousness was associated with positive attitudes toward death and self among the hospice patients. Whether on the basis of self-report or report of caregivers, patients with a greater internalized sense of religiousness had less death anxiety and engaged in greater Approach Acceptance, providing a methodological triangulation of findings that is rare in the EOL literature. In keeping with the results of Neimeyer et al.'s (2011) study, patients in the sample who reported higher religiousness also indicated less Death Avoidance and greater Escape Acceptance and Self-Esteem. However, reports from the caregivers about their loved one's religiousness were not significantly predictive of these latter outcomes.

Beyond these straightforward links between religion and EOL adjustment, other results indicated that the amount of convergence between the patient and caregiver was associated with multiple outcomes assessed in the study. Namely, dyads marked by greater empathic accuracy on the part of the family caregiver in grasping the patient's religious orientation also showed greater Approach Acceptance and Self-Esteem among the patients. Results similarly indicated a nonsignificant trend between convergence about the religiousness of the patient and less avoidance of the subject of death for the dying person. Consistent with systemic understandings of coping with illness and mortality (e.g., Kleinman, 1988), this pattern of results supports the possible importance of caregiver understanding of the patient's religious meanings in the closing months of life.

Nevertheless, the nature of family convergence might factor prominently in EOL adjustment, which called for more in-depth exploratory analyses. Results of the LCA procedure supported a 3-class model with respect to patients' self-report of religiousness and the degree of convergence with their caregiver. When considering the four possible constellations between patients' religiousness (high and low) and caregiver empathic accuracy in understanding patient's existential attitudes (high and low), we failed to identify a significant number of dyads in our sample in which the patient reported low religiousness and the caregiver converged with him or her. Instead, the LCA procedure indicated three distinct types of dyads in the sample: (a) highly religious patients with strong agreement with their caregiver, (b) highly religious patients with discordant responses from their caregiver, and (c) nonreligious patients with a discordant caregiver. Of the relative frequencies of the dyads in the sample, the majority of patients fit in the former group, reporting a highly internalized sense of being religious and having a caregiver who rated them similarly. When controlling for demographics and clinical factors, patients in these groups differed in Approach Acceptance, Escape Acceptance, and Self-Esteem. Other multivariate results demonstrated a marginal effect on death avoidance as well, above and beyond the effects of the other factors included in the analysis.

Results of the post hoc comparisons provided partial support for the impact of patient-caregiver convergence in this study. As anticipated, nonreligious patients with low convergence generally endorsed worse adjustment than highly religious patients with high convergence. However, the third group (low religiousness and low convergence) also reported less acceptance of death than their counterparts with high religiousness and discordance with their caregiver. In addition, other results indicated that the two highly religious groups failed to differ on any of the EOL outcomes. Hence, this overall pattern of results suggests that positive EOL adjustment tended to occur under conditions of high intrinsic religiousness, irrespective of the degree to which the patient shared a sense of mutuality with the caregiver. For less religious patients, however, misunderstanding of their existential attitudes by caregivers was predictive of a number of deleterious outcomes defined in terms of attitudes toward both death and self.

To our knowledge, this is the first study to examine the role of religion with persons at the EOL that included an assessment from the caregiver about their loved one's psychological and spiritual functioning. Despite this strength, there were several limitations to this study that hampered our ability to thoroughly test the impact of patient-caregiver convergence. We will briefly discuss three of these concerns with respect to the manner in which study constructs were assessed: (a) lack of assessment of the caregivers' own experiences, (b) incomplete assessment of religion, and (c) lack of a measure to directly assess relationship quality in the patient-caregiver dyads.

First, we were unable to incorporate information regarding the caregivers' own experiences in the analyses. For example, when considering the group of nonreligious patients with high discordance from their caregiver's assessment, the caregivers in this group may have been highly religious themselves and struggled to accept their loved one's differing spiritual orientation. Theoretically, mutual understanding about religion in the face of death would require that both members of the dyad contribute to an open dialogue based on their own beliefs and values. Although we might assume that this interplay took place among the dyads in this study, actual communication about matters of faith or philosophy was not assessed in the study. For example, it is possible that one or both members of the dyad tended to avoid discussion of existential or spiritual matters when they sensed or suspected that doing so could lead to conflict at a vulnerable moment. Research has demonstrated the importance of having a reliable caregiving relationship (Ball et al, 2010; Schumacher et al., 2007; Skerrett, 2003; Stricks, 1998), recourse to a spiritual belief system, and community support for dying persons (Ita, 1995; Neimeyer et al., 2011). At the same time, caregivers can also experience significant stress and strain, affecting their quality of life and placing them in need of social support (Bainbridge, Krueger, Lohfeld, & Brazil, 2009). For this reason, more understanding is needed about the role of religion in the psychological and spiritual adjustment of family caregivers as well as for the hospice patients they support.

In view of the complexity of measuring religion in general (see Hill & Pargament, 2003 for review), we are also cognizant of limitations in how we assessed this construct. Given the sensitivity of the sample, we restricted our assessment to the domain of intrinsic religiousness and utilized a single item from Genia's (1993) scale. As such, we lacked information on other important dimensions (e.g., religious coping, practices, organizational religiousness) that might have led to greater specificity in categorizing types of mutuality. For example, while the overrepresentation of highly religious patients enjoying convergence with caregivers could reflect features of the midsouthern region of the United States where the study was conducted, it is also possible that our manner of assessing religiousness failed to distinguish between the dyads in the sample. While the present approach prevented undue burden on both the participants and clinical staff who assisted with the study, future research on this topic would nonetheless do well to utilize more thorough and concrete assessments of religion and spirituality.

A final measurement concern pertains to the lack of assessment of the quality of the relationship between the patients and their caregivers. One might argue that understanding of the role of religion for patients at the EOL could in part be explained by the degree of cohesion or closeness within the caregiving dyad. We attempted to address this issue by controlling for a number of related factors in our analyses, including amount of social support, key risk factors for both the patient and caregiver, type of caregiver relationship, and family reaction to the patient being in hospice. However, even when accounting for these variables, the level of connection between patients and their caregivers may represent an important mechanism by which mutual understanding can develop in the first place, even in dyads in which the patient and caregiver do not share the same spiritual belief system. Conversely, it is possible that religious differences can loom large in the urgent context of the hospice care, exacerbating tensions in families. Future research on this topic therefore would do well to assess family closeness and cohesion in order to investigate both possibilities.

Study findings should also be interpreted in the context of the sample characteristics. For instance, the majority of the sample was affiliated with a Christian denomination and resided in an urban environment in the southern region of the United States. Given these sample characteristics, generalizations to more secular contexts or to those populations with different religious convictions should be considered with caution.

Notwithstanding these limitations, our findings highlight the need for further research and clinical consideration of the impact of systemic factors such as patient-caregiver understanding vis-à-vis religion at the EOL. In both research and clinical practice, it may serve professional caregivers well to view the dying patient as part of a larger family or community system. Ideally, this system can be an intimate source of support for the dying patient as well as for family members preparing for the death of their loved one. Fostering compassionate and respectful family discussions of the religious and existential perspectives of patients in cases of misunderstanding could further this goal.

REFERENCES

Allport, G. W., & Ross, M. (1967). Religious orientation and prejudice. *Journal of Personality and Social Psychology, 5*, 432-443.

Bainbridge, D., Krueger, P., Lohfeld, L., & Brazil, K. (2009). Stress processes in caring for an end-of-life family member: Application of a theoretical model. *Aging & Mental Health, 13*(4), 537-545. doi: 10.1080/13607860802607322

Ball, V., Snow, A. L., Steele, A. B., Morgan, R. O., Davila, J. A., Wilson, N., & Kunik, M. E. (2010). Quality of relationships as a predictor of psychosocial functioning in patients with dementia. *Journal of Geriatric Psychiatry and Neurology, 23*(2), 109-114. doi: 10.1177/0891988710363709

Chan, W. C. H., Epstein, I., Reese, D., & Chan, C. L. W. (2009). Family predictors of psychosocial outcomes among Hong Kong Chinese cancer patients in palliative care: Living and dying with the "support paradox." *Social Work in Health Care, 48*(5), 519-532. doi: 10.1080/00981380902765824

Fortner, B. V., & Neimeyer, R. A. (1999). Death anxiety in older adults: A quantitative review. *Death Studies, 23*, 387-412. doi: 10.1080/074811899200920

Genia, V. (1993). A psychometric evaluation of the Allport-Ross I/E scales in a religiously heterogeneous sample. *Journal for the Scientific Study of Religion, 32*, 284-290. doi: 10.2307/1386667

Hill, P. C., & Pargament, K. I. (2003). Advances in the conceptualization and measurement of religion and spirituality. *American Psychologist, 58*, 64-74. doi: 10.1037/1941-1022.S.1.3

Hooghe, A., & Neimeyer, R. A. (2012). Family resilience in the wake of loss: A meaning-oriented contribution. In D. Becvar (Ed.), *Handbook of family resilience*. New York, NY: Springer.

Ita, D. J. (1995). Testing of a causal model: Acceptance of death in hospice patients. *Omega: Journal of Death and Dying, 32*, 81-92. doi: 10.2190/3X1H-LPT2-JE6D-BVR6

Idler, E. L., Musick, M. A., Ellison, C. G., George, L. K., Krause, N., Ory, M. G., et al. (2003). Measuring multiple dimensions of religion and spirituality for health research: Conceptual background and findings from the 1998 General Social Survey. *Research on Aging, 25*, 327-365. doi: 10.1177/0164027503025004001

Kleinman, A. (1988). *The illness narratives: Suffering, healing, and the human condition*. New York, NY: Basic Books.

Koenig, H. G., George, L. K., & Titus, P. T. (2004). Religion, spirituality, and health in medically ill hospitalized older patients. *Journal of the American Geriatrics Society, 52*, 554-562. doi: 10.1111/j.1532-5415.2004.52161.x

Koenig, H. G., George, L. K., Titus, P., & Meador, K. G. (2004). Religion, spirituality, and acute care hospitalization and long-term care use by older patients. *Archives of Internal Medicine, 164*, 1579-1585. doi: 10.1111/j.1532-5415.2004.52161.x

Koenig, H. G., McCullough, M., & Larson, D. (2001). *Handbook of religion and health*. Oxford, UK: Oxford University Press.

Muthén, L. K., & Muthén, B. O. (1998-2010). *Mplus user's guide* (6th ed.). Los Angeles, CA: Muthén & Muthén.

Neimeyer, R. A., Currier, J. M., Coleman, R., Tomer, A., & Samuel, E. (2011). Confronting suffering and death at the end of life: The impact of religiosity, psychosocial factors, and life regret among hospice patients. *Death Studies, 35*, 777-800.

Neimeyer, R. A., Moser, R. P., & Wittkowski, J. (2003). Assessing attitudes toward dying and death: Psychometric considerations. *Omega: Journal of Death and Dying, 47*, 45-76. doi: 10.2190/EP4R-TULM-W52G-L3EX

Pargament, K. I., Koenig, H. G., & Perez, L. M. (2000). The many methods of religious coping: Development and initial validation of the RCOPE. *Journal of Clinical Psychology, 56*, 519-543. doi: 10.1002/(SICI)1097-4679(200004)56:4<519::AID-JCLP6>3.0.CO;2-1

Park, C. (2005). Religion and meaning. In R. F. Paloutzian & C. Park (Eds.), *Handbook of the psychology of religion and spirituality* (pp. 294-314). New York, NY: Guilford Press.

Prince, M. J., Harwood, R. H., Blizard, R. A., & Thomas, A. (1997). Social support deficits, loneliness, and life events as risk factors for depression in old age. The Gospel Oak Project VI. *Psychological Medicine: A Journal of Research in Psychiatry and the Allied Sciences, 27*(2), 323-332. doi: 10.1017/S0033291796004485

Rosenberg, M. (1965). *Society and the adolescent self image.* Princeton, NJ: Princeton University Press.

Schumacher, K. L., Stewart, B. J., & Archbold, P. G. (2007). Mutuality and preparedness moderate the effects of caregiving demand on cancer family caregiver outcomes. *Nursing Research, 56*(6), 425-433. doi: 10.1097/01.NNR.0000299852.75300.03

Siegel, K., & Schrimshaw, E. W. (2002). The perceived benefits of religious and spiritual coping among older adults living with AIDS/HIV. *Journal for the Scientific Study of Religion, 41*, 91-102. doi: 10.1111/1468-5906.00103

Skerrett, K. (2003). Couple dialogues with illness: Expanding the 'we.' *Families, Systems, & Health, 21*(1), 69-80. doi: 10.1037/h0089503

Stricks, L. S. (1998). *Mutuality in caregiving relationships: An examination of caregiver-care recipient dyads in patients with Alzheimer's disease* (Doctoral dissertation). Dissertation Abstracts International: Section B: The Sciences and Engineering (1998-95022-308)

Sulmasy, D. P. (2002). A biopsychosocial-spiritual model for the care of patients at the end of life. *The Gerontologist, 42*(Special Issue 3), 24-33.

Uchino, B. N. (2006). Social support and health: A review of physiological processes potentially underlying links to disease outcomes. *Journal of Behavioral Medicine, 29*(4), 377-387. doi: 10.1007/S10865-006-9056-5

Uchino, B. N., Cacioppo, J. T., & Kiecolt-Glaser, J. K. (1996). The relationship between social support and physiological processes: A review with emphasis on underlying mechanisms and implications for health. *Psychological Bulletin, 119*(3), 488-531. doi: 10.1037/0033-2909.119.3.488

Wong, P. T., Reker, G. T., & Gesser, G. (1994). Death Attitude Profile–Revised. In R. A. Neimeyer (Ed.), *Death anxiety handbook* (pp. 121-148). New York, NY: Taylor & Francis.

http://dx.doi.org/10.2190/FATC2

CHAPTER 2

Attachments and Losses: Individual and Global Perspectives

Colin Murray Parkes

The systematic study of the child's attachment to its mother in early childhood has revolutionised not only our understanding of mother-child relationships but the very nature of relationships and the problems to which they can give rise. In this chapter, I summarize some of the findings of what is now a large body of research and show how it has important implications for the care of the dying and bereaved and for a wider range of attachments, including attachments to God, homes, and nations.

How do we know we are in love? By the experience of distress when we are separated. Hence, love and grief are two sides of the same coin, you can't have one without the other. John Bowlby and his trainee, Mary Ainsworth, were the acknowledged parents of attachment theory. In the second of his three volumes on "Attachment and Loss," Bowlby focused on *Separation: Anxiety and Anger* (1973), both of them frequent consequences of bereavement. Separation anxiety is the distinguishing feature of both the threat and the actuality of loss. It distinguishes grief from all other emotions, and it reveals the primary function of all attachments, to keep us safe, for it creates the bond that is our most profound source of security and contentment. Sex may be the magnet that attracts adolescent and adults, but attachment is the glue that holds them together.

Bonds of attachment are more like elastic than glue, for they become stronger the further apart we are driven. Only in the relatively rare event of death, or other permanent separation, does attachment fail in its function. But even then, we are illogically driven to go on searching and fighting for the one we have lost, even when we know that the search is fruitless. Grief, it seems, is the price we pay for love.

But maybe the search is less illogical than it seems, for there is truth in the saying "He, or she, lives on in my memory." What does that mean? Each one of us, from early infancy, is building up, inside our heads, an internal model of the world, an assumptive world, which enables us to identify the objects and people

15

we meet and recognize the world around us. Everything we assume to be true is part of that assumptive world and, because each person's experience is unique, so is each person's assumptive world.

Small babies have no reason to believe that their mother continues to exist when she is not present. Hence their reaction when they realize she is absent is extreme and an effective way to bring her back. Only over time do they discover that they have no need to cry, that even if they remain silent she will return. It is this realization that enables children to tolerate short separations and to hold, within their memories, an image of a mother who continues to exist even when she is absent.

Out of this blueprint comes a new set of skills for surviving as the developing child consults the absent parents in its memory. "What would my mother or father do now?" provides many of the answers to the problem of keeping safe in the world and a measure of tolerance of separation that continues and, by adolescence, enables youngsters to leave home and start their own families. Even after bereavement, I recall a widow saying "Whenever I face a problem, I think, 'What would my husband have done about this?' And its almost as if I had him inside my head telling me what to do."

This reflects what Klass, Silverman, and Nickman (1996) call a "continuing bond," and it enables bereaved people, in the course of grieving, gradually to discover what are the habits of thought that only lead to a brick wall (e.g., "I must ask my husband about that") and what memories continue to enrich their lives (e.g., "I sometimes hear him inside my head saying 'Go on darling, you can do it.'"). Viewed in this way, grieving is a process of teasing out what are the chains of thought that we must let go and what we can carry forward with us. It is this experience that enables most bereaved people to come through their grief with a reasonable degree of resilience, not by forgetting the dead, but by finding a new place for them in their assumptive world.

But not always. Some untimely and horrific losses are so shattering in their impact that the brain protects itself by shutting out full realization of the loss. Such posttraumatic stress reactions interfere with the process of grieving and may impair entire families.

Other people may lack the resilience that would enable them to cope with more natural losses. Attachment research shows how it is that some people are more vulnerable to loss than others. This stems from the work of Mary Ainsworth, who developed a systematic way of studying how young children handle separation anxiety by exposing them to short periods of separation from their mother in a strange situation (e.g., an unfamiliar room with a few toys and a chair). To sum up a great deal of research (for a succinct account, see Parkes, 2006), she found that infants whose parent (usually mother) provided protection when needed but were also sensitively responsive to the child's need to play and explore, tolerated short periods of separation well. When, after leaving the room for a few minutes, the mother returned, they stopped playing and reached for a cuddle, but soon resumed their play. These babies Ainsworth termed "securely attached" and, in the years to come, they were found to have two major sources of security, trust in themselves and trust in others (see Table 1).

Three other patterns that, together, Ainsworth called "insecurely attached" arose from three different patterns of parenting. One group, termed "anxious/ ambivalent" had anxious mothers who provided protection but discouraged play and exploration. They disliked the strange situation and cried throughout the period of separation. When mother returned, their cries grew louder and more aggressive, as if they were punishing her for going away. In years to come, they lacked trust in themselves and tended to cling to others in a dependent way.

They contrasted with another group, whose parents were intolerant of closeness and who punished or ignored the infant's bids for attention. Already, by the end of the second year of life, these babies had learned to inhibit their impulses to cling and to cry. In the strange situation, they carried on playing and, when mother returned, they seemed uninterested. At first, Ainsworth thought that they were "detached," but subsequent research showed that when mother left the room, although they showed nothing, their heart rate went soaring up, and they showed other evidence of physiological response. In short, they had learned to avoid closeness and to stand on their own feet from an early age, but their apparent independence was a sham. In later years, they trusted themselves more than others. Ainsworth termed them "avoidant."

Finally, there was a small "disorganized" group who lacked trust in themselves *and* others. Their parents had problems of their own, which made it hard for them to provide consistent care. If the anxious/ambivalent infants coped by staying close to mother and the avoidant group by keeping their distance, this group developed no such strategies (see Figure 1). They suffered what Seligman calls "learned helplessness" (1975). In the strange situation, their behavior was disorganized, sometimes they ran back and forth toward and away from their mother, other times, they sat and rocked to and fro. In later life, they were the most disturbed group, with lasting vulnerability to anxiety and depression.

Table 1. Sources of Security Resulting from Each
Pattern of Attachment

Patterns of attachment	Self-trust	Trust in others
Secure attachment	+	+
Anxious/ambivalent attachment	–	+
Avoidant attachment	+	–
Disorganized attachment	–	–

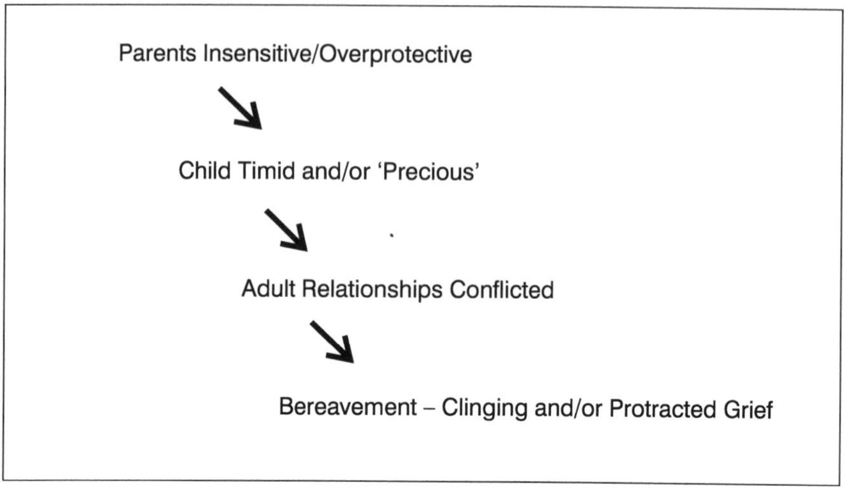

Parents Insensitive/Overprotective

↘

Child Timid and/or 'Precious'

↘

Adult Relationships Conflicted

↘

Bereavement – Clinging and/or Protracted Grief

Figure 1. Anxious/ambivalent attachment.

These tendencies tended to persist into adult life, and in my own studies of reactions to bereavement, I used a retrospective questionnaire to assess their childhood attachments (Parkes, 2006). Quantitative measures of insecurity of attachment were highly predictive of the level of distress after bereavement with those who reported parents who were sensitive and overprotective, rating themselves as timid or "precious" (Dresden Vase) children. In adult life, their relationships were often conflicted, either because of their continued dependence on their parents or because their partner could not stand their tendency to cling. After bereavement, they showed evidence of prolonged and persistent grief, with a tendency to cling to me as their parent/therapist.

Those who rated their parents as intolerant of closeness had grown up similarly inclined and distrustful of others (see Figure 2). As one might expect, their relationships were also conflicted, not least because of their difficulties in expressing affection. Following bereavement, they had similar difficulty in expressing the grief that they felt and blamed themselves for their emotional inhibition.

Finally, there was a group who reported rejection, violence, danger, or depression in the family (see Figure 3). They had been unhappy children, and as adults, they lacked trust in themselves and others. After bereavement, they showed high levels of anxiety, depression, and a tendency to abuse alcohol or other drugs.

These difficulties explained many of the psychiatric problems of my patients, and it was important to make use of that understanding in therapy. Many of them wanted to discuss the questionnaire because it had already helped them to understand the roots of their problems. I attempted to provide them all with a safe place and a relationship with me that would make them feel safe enough to think

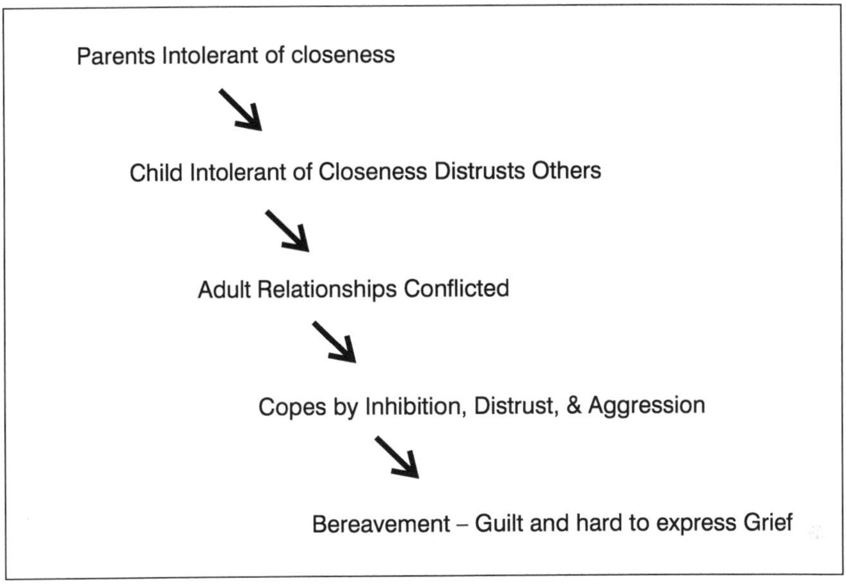

Parents Intolerant of closeness

Child Intolerant of Closeness Distrusts Others

Adult Relationships Conflicted

Copes by Inhibition, Distrust, & Aggression

Bereavement – Guilt and hard to express Grief

Figure 2. Avoidant attachment.

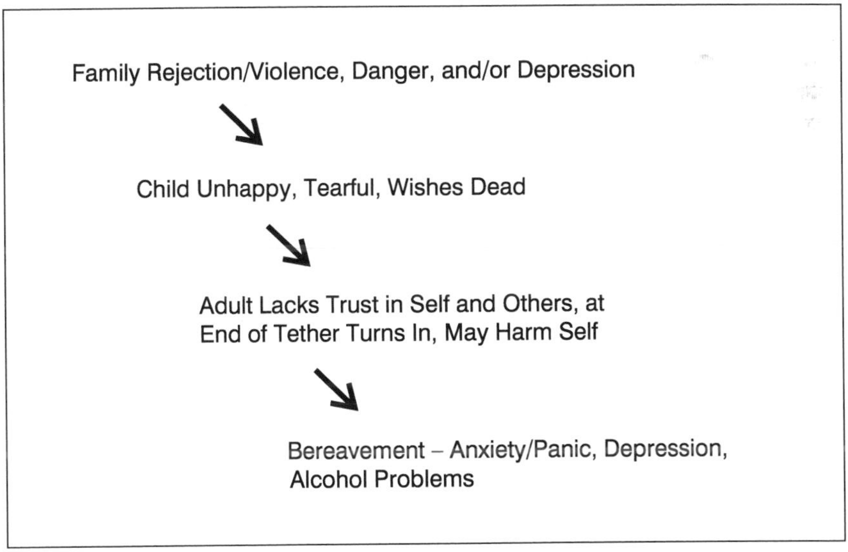

Family Rejection/Violence, Danger, and/or Depression

Child Unhappy, Tearful, Wishes Dead

Adult Lacks Trust in Self and Others, at
End of Tether Turns In, May Harm Self

Bereavement – Anxiety/Panic, Depression,
Alcohol Problems

Figure 3. Disorganized attachment.

about and to express the frightening emotions that threatened to erupt. Avoidants needed permission to grieve and reassurance that this was not a weakness. The most important thing I had to offer the anxious/ambivalent clingers was my respect for their true worth and value. They needed permission to stop grieving and reassurance that this was not a duty to the dead. The disorganized needed both permission to grieve and permission to stop grieving.

Attachment therapy is like parenting; indeed it may be the first time in their lives that clients with attachment problems have had an opportunity to meet someone who understands attachment. Of course, we all have an attachment history, and it is important for us to be aware of our own styles of attachment. Supervisors have roles to play in exploring these issues with us. Likewise, those of us who work as part of a team will find an understanding of attachments within the team most valuable.

Thus far we have been considering dyadic relationships between children and parents as well as clients and therapists. But most people have multiple attachments, mainly within their own families. Kissane and Bloch's (2002) studies have demonstrated the value of what they call Family-Focused Grief Therapy (FFGT). Working in the context of hospices, they have engaged with families before and after the death of patients with life-threatening illnesses. Their aim is to improve family functioning in families who avoid communicating thoughts and feelings, find themselves unable to resolve conflicts, or to share grief. These difficulties are typical of the avoidant/attachment pattern described above.

A random-allocation study (Kissane et al., 2006) has demonstrated that those whose families are cohesive and unconflicted or able to resolve their own conflicts, have no need of FFGT. Families who are hostile, unexpressive, *and* uncohesive are impossible to engage in therapy, but there is a substantial group with less hostility who can share enough to make therapy possible, and issues of low cohesiveness and communication can be tackled with significant benefit.

Kissane's studies link with similar studies of conflict resolution within groups and nations. Up to now we have focused on bereavement by death because this topic has been very fully studied, but there are many other types of attachment that deserve attention. People become attached to parts of their own bodies, to God, to homes, homelands, and much else. In fact, almost anything that I term "mine" is an object of some degree of attachment. Consequently, we suffer grief when these are amputated or lost (Parkes, 1972).

In my own study of the reaction to amputation of a limb, I interviewed 12 amputees who had previously lost a close family member by death. They all reported similar feelings of grief. Furthermore, many of the problems of rehabilitation bore a remarkable similarity to the problems of attachment described above, and readers who work in healthcare settings will be familiar with the forms that they took. Thus, there were anxious, dependent patients who clung to staff and remained crippled longer than (by any reasonable expectation) they should. They contrasted with the deniers, who refused to accept the extent of their disablement and blamed any persisting symptoms on their medication. And there were the helpless, withdrawn individuals who became depressed and gave up too easily on any attempt at rehabilitation.

Kirkpatrick points out that relationships with God have all of the characteristics of attachment relationships (1999; Kirkpatrick & Shaver, 1990). Most gods are father or mother figures from whom their followers expect protection from death in return for their devotion. Again, two types of problem arise. On the one hand, there are devotees whose extreme clinging to God and his priests is clear evidence of dependency, and there are avoidant individuals who see God as distant or nonexistent.

After attachments to parents, it is attachment to homes that provides the greatest source of security to most children. Most mammalian species and birds have homes, dens, or nests in which offspring are raised until they can look after themselves, when they find new homes elsewhere. Konrad Lorenz (1966, p. 186) says that homes have "mother valency," but mothers can also be said to have "home valency."

In Marc Fried's studies of the relocation of slum populations, he found that the intensity of grief experienced after relocation was directly correlated with the extent of the knowledge of the neighborhood. Thus, people who had invested most in the neighborhood had most to lose. Clingers show extreme homesickness, sometimes amounting to agoraphobia; avoiders, on the other hand, sometimes become homeless and rootless wanderers (Fried, 1962; Stroebe, van Vliet, Hewstone, & Willis, 2002).

Just as attachments to people often overflow to include favorite items, hats, pipes, tobacco smells, and even friends who are associated with them, so attachments to places include neighbors, neighborhoods, and even homelands. These can become encapsulated as myths of superior worth, idealized in much the same way that we idealize the people we love. Over 2000 years ago, Herodotus wrote, "Everyone, without exception, believes his own native customs, and the religion he was brought up in, to be the best, and that being so, it is unlikely that anyone but a madman would mock at such things" (Herodotus, 420 BC). It seems that his lesson has not yet been learned, for this naïve and biased assumption has a corollary: that other people's customs and religions are inferior.

Ariel Merari and his colleagues have carried out systematic studies of convicted Muslim terrorists in Israeli prisons (Merari, Diamant, Bibi, Broshi, & Zakin, 2010; Merari, Fighel et al., 2010). Comparing would-be suicidal terrorists with other terrorists, they found that the suicidal group was characterized by a dependent and avoidant style, while the majority of the nonsuicidal terrorists had an impulsive and unstable personality style. It seems that insecure attachment styles predispose terrorists to seek martyrdom. Terrorists expressed extreme attachments to Allah, their nation, or both.

It would be a mistake to conclude that all religious and nationalistic extremists are potential terrorists. It takes rigorous training and indoctrination to dehumanize our fellows and teach human beings to kill other human beings. But anyone who has served in armed forces knows how this is carried out, and it is no coincidence that terrorists, like other soldiers, are recruited from groups of young males at their most combative age. While terrorists are usually a small minority of the communities from which they come, their acts often initiate or perpetuate preexisting distrust. In fact, they are intended to do just that, for terrorism is a form of psychological warfare.

Deadly violence easily sets up cycles of further violence, and attachments play a significant part in this process. Figure 4 shows a modified version of a model of the cycle developed by members of the International Work Group on Death, Dying and Bereavement (IWG, 2005). They show how a terrorist or other attack is witnessed through the eyes of the media of communication, who have their own reasons for highlighting dramatic events. It regularly gives rise to fear and rage, which distorts our perception of the violence and too often causes us to overreact. The authorities, who are themselves overreacting, authorize further violence against the supposed attackers and may gain political support as a result. People rally to what they imagine is the defense of their families, homes, God, and nation. Polarization takes place, with everyone under pressure to take sides and demonize their supposed "enemy." Retaliation is the inevitable outcome, and another turn of the wheel leaves both sides trapped in a cycle of escalating warfare.

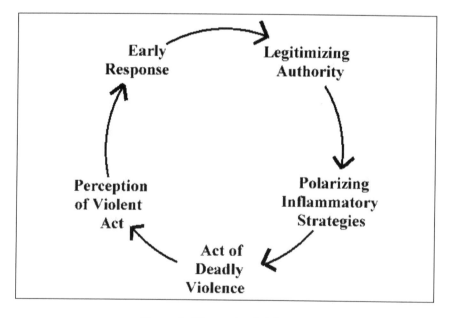

Figure 4. The cycle of violence.

But the IWG have also demonstrated that cycles of deadly violence can be prevented or broken (IWG, 2011). Indeed, there are many lessons to learn from members of the caring professions, whose ways of preparing patients and their families for the deaths that are to come and supporting bereaved families have much in common with the methods of education, support, and conflict resolution that are needed. Psychological studies and the careful analysis of peace processes in Northern Ireland, Rwanda, and South Africa show that both before violence erupts and afterwards, the cycle can be aborted or broken (Parkes, pending 2013). In this multicontributor book, we show how the psychological, social, and spiritual theories and methods that have been developed in recent years can be applied to education in schools and universities to empower youngsters to cope with and resist violence; how reassurance and psychological support of leaders at times of violence and threats thereof can be carried out; how communities benefit from being involved in the just treatment of terrorists; how the involvement and empowerment of women in parliament is reducing fears of masculine domination by a conquering army in Rwanda; how psychological care of the survivors of bereavement and other trauma in the wake of terrorist attacks and genocidal violence seems to be reducing the rage and desire for revenge.

Hospice has taught us that there is no such thing as a "hopeless case." People with life-threatening illnesses no longer have to be afraid. As one patient said to me, "You know, it's safe to die here." That security stemmed from trust in the care she would receive from her fellow human beings in the context of palliative care. It has been my privilege to have witnessed the spread of this philosophy of care across the world and to see the beginnings of an international network of care. Already that network is reaching out to people affected by traumatic bereavements and disasters as well as life-threatening illnesses. Is it time for us to tackle another "hopeless case?"

REFERENCES

Bowlby, J. (1973). *Attachment and loss. Vol. II. Separation: Anxiety and anger.* London, UK: Hogarth.

Fried, M. (1962). Grieving for a lost home. In L. J. Duhl (Ed.), *The environment of the metropolis* (pp. 152-153). New York, NY: Basic Books.

Herodotus. (420BC). *Histories* 3.38 cited in Lendering, J. (2013). Herodotus of Halicarnassus. Part 8. *Livius: Articles on Ancient History.* Retrieved March 24, 2013 from http://www.livius.org/

International Work Group on Death, Dying and Bereavement (IWG). (2005). Breaking cycles of violence. *Death Studies, 29*(7), 585-600

International Work Group on Death, Dying, and Bereavement (IWG). (2011). Can individuals who are specialists in death, dying, and bereavement contribute to the prevention and/or mitigation of armed conflicts and cycles of violence? *Death Studies, 35*(5), 455-466.

Kirkpatrick, L. A., & Shaver, P. R. (1990). Attachment theory and religion: Childhood attachments, religious beliefs and conversion. *Journal for the Scientific Study of Religions, 29,* 305-334.

Kirkpatrick, L. A. (1999). Attachment and religious representations and behavior. In J. Cassidy & P. R. Shaver (Eds.), *Handbook of attachment: Theory, research and clinical applications* (Ch. 35, pp. 803-822). New York and London, UK: Guilford.

Kissane, D., & Bloch, S. (2002). *Family focused grief therapy: A model of family-centred care during palliative care and bereavement.* Buckingham, UK and Philadelphia, PA: Open University Press.

Kissane, D. W., McKenzie, M., Bloch, S., Moskovitz, S., et al. (2006). Family focussed grief therapy: A randomized controlled trial in palliative care and bereavement. *The American Journal of Psychiatry, 163*(7), 1208-1219.

Klass, D., Silverman, P. R., & Nickman, S. (Eds.). (1996). *Continuing bonds: New understandings of grief.* Washington, DC and London, UK: Taylor & Francis.

Lorenz, K. (1966). *On aggression.* London, UK: Methuen.

Merari, A., Diamant, I., Bibi, A., Broshi, Y., & Zakin, G. (2010). Personality characteristics of "self martyrs"/"suicide bombers" and organizers of suicide attacks. *Terrorism and Political Violence, 22*(1), 87-101.

Merari, A., Fighel, J., Ganor, B., Lavie, E., Tzoreff, Y., & Livne, A. (2010). Making Palestinian "martyrdom operations"/"suicide attacks": Interviews with would-be perpetrators and organizers. *Terrorism and Political Violence, 22*(1), 102-119.

Parkes, C. M. (1972). Components of the reaction to loss of a limb, spouse or home. *Journal of Psychosomatic Research, 16,* 343-349.

Parkes, C. M. (2006). *Love and loss: The roots of grief and its complications.* London, UK and New York, NY: Routledge.

Parkes, C. M. (Ed.). (Pending 2013). *Responses to terrorism: Can the cycle be broken?* London, UK and New York, NY: Routledge.

Seligman, M. E. P. (1975). *Helplessness.* San Francisco, CA: Freeman.

Stroebe, M., van Vliet, T., Hewstone, M., & Willis, H. (2002). Homesickness among students in two cultures: Antecedents and consequences. *British Journal of Psychology* 93(2), 147-168.

http://dx.doi.org/10.2190/FATC3

CHAPTER 3

The Private Worlds of Professionals, Teams, and Organizations in Palliative Care*

Danai Papadatou

Thousands of years ago, Hippocrates supported in his teachings that every healer who offers services to the sick experiences "*a harvest of sorrows*" that results from being exposed to "the misfortunes of others" (Jones, 1923). This harvest of sorrows continues to be largely ignored. There is a widespread belief that suffering is experienced only by patients and families who are affected by the threat or reality of death. Professionals are expected to be strong, stoic, and immune to the suffering of others. This stoic approach was and continues to be espoused by the medical model of care which promotes a *disease-centered approach* that focuses on bodies and disease treatments rather than on people. With the advent of the *biopsychosocial model of care*, focus shifted from suffering bodies to suffering patients whose biopsychosocial and spiritual needs are being addressed. Thanks to the palliative care movement, this patient-centered approach has been enlarged to also include family members who are supported throughout the dying process and death of their loved one. Despite this holistic, family-centered approach to care, research evidence suggests that several families express dissatisfaction with end-of-life care. Their dissatisfaction is mostly associated with unsatisfactory *relationships* with care providers rather than to the medical and nursing aspects of care. They expect more understanding, more availability, more genuine concern, and compassion. In other words, they seek a different kind of relationship that professionals do not always provide.

The purpose of this chapter is to propose an alternative approach to care that focuses on *relationships* between those who receive and provide care in the face of death. More specifically, I wish to illuminate the private worlds of

*For in-depth elaboration on the concepts described in this chapter, refer to Papadatou (2009).

care providers, teams, and organizations that are affected by death in hope to better understand how they affect the people they serve at the end of life and through grief.

A RELATIONAL APPROACH TO CARE

A *relationship-centered approach to care* (or relational care) broadens our scope of understanding and highlights the reciprocal influence of a system of relationships through which care is offered and received (Beach, Inui, & Relationship Centered Research Network, 2006). In addition to understanding the subjective world of the person and family members who live with the uncertainty or reality of death, attention is also directed to professionals involved in the person and family's care, to the team that practitioners belong to, and to the organization they represent. *Intersubjective* is the space in which interactions and partnerships develop throughout the caregiving and care-receiving process. This space belongs neither to the dying or grieving person, nor to the professional(s), but to their unique relationship that unfolds in the context of a wider network of family, team, and organizational relations. These in turn are affected by the sociocultural and political context that determines the priorities, policies, and practices with regard to the care of the dying and the bereaved in a given society (Figure 1).

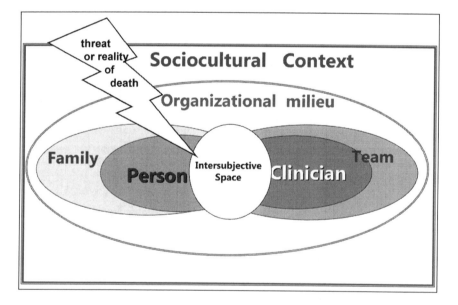

Figure 1. Relationship centered care.

In this intersubjective space, relationships are always affected by the *objective reality of death*. Exposure to death—both direct and indirect—evokes intense responses and renders the caregiving relationship distinct from other helping relationships. Unlike professionals in other fields of care who are expected to relieve people from their suffering, we assist people in bearing a suffering that cannot, and should not, be totally eradicated. Our relationships often become the recipient of a *violence* evoked by the finality of human life and the irreversible break of valued bonds and also of a *vitality,* manifested in a striving for life affirmation and in transformations that lead to personal growth and enriching encounters. We witness the vitality in the joy of a dying person who admits that the time since diagnosis was the best of his life; or in the excitement of a bereaved spouse, who confides that the pain over the loss of her partner has awakened her to a life with renewed purpose and meaning; or in the review of our personal life goals and choices that lead to actions that render our life more meaningful.

When we deny or dismiss death from the caregiving relationship and enact prescribed roles or become absorbed by the treatment of symptoms and diseases, and by the implementation of psychosocial interventions, then we limit and restrict the intersubjective space in which partnerships and collaborations can develop. Pseudo-mutuality and false familiarity with the patient and family members involve a subtle dehumanization and distancing that limits the inter-subjective space and opportunity for collaboration, change, and growth. By contrast, this space is enlarged when we remain open and aware of what tran-spires in each caregiving and care-receiving relationship. Growth occurs *between* people in the context of relations that become personal. Ehrenberg (2005) refers to the "intimate edge" in relatedness to describe the point of maximum and acknowledged contact at a given moment in a caregiving relationship. This contact does not result from fusion and does not violate the integrity and separatedness of each participant, but it requires a sensitivity to inner experiences and changes in oneself, in the other, and in the "between" of the interaction. It requires an understanding of what is verbally and nonverbally communicated by the person who seeks palliative or bereavement care services.

When people seek our services, they come with a request. Beyond the explicit request for pain relief, symptom management, advice giving, or practical assistance, almost invariably they express an *appeal for a relationship,* which contains a message such as "Take care of me," "Stand by me," "Help me bear my suffering," "Assure me that I will not go crazy," "Accompany me," "Tell me that I am unique, loved, appreciated," "Comfort and nurture me," and so on.

Responding to such an implicit appeal for a relationship in death situations involves a process of companioning. The word "companion" stems from the Latin roots *com,* which means "with," and *pan,* which means "bread." A com-panion "breaks bread with" a person while listening and facilitating the recon-struction of stories that have been disrupted by the illness and death.

COMPANIONS TO DYING AND
BEREAVED PEOPLE

Our role as companion is similar to the role of midwives who accompany a woman through labor and help the newborn to "pave" its way into life. In palliative and bereavement care, we help the dying person to pave a way out of life and assist the bereaved to pave a path into a life without their loved one. During these transitional periods, people are often vulnerable and display safety-seeking behaviors that involve a striving for safety, comfort, and nurturance that should not be perceived as childish or immature, but as an expression of healthy attachment behaviors in the face of separation and loss. These safety-seeking behaviors activate in us, the practitioners, a system of caregiving behaviors whose function is twofold: to provide a *safe haven* that promotes a sense of safety, stability, predictability, and continuity during a period that life is filled with ruptures, losses, or impending separations; and to create a *secure base* from which the person is encouraged to cope with the challenges of dying and bereavement.

To establish a safe haven, we need to possess an ability for *holding*. This involves the containment or the person's thoughts, feelings, and experiences no matter how extreme, powerful, explicit, or implicit they may be. We allow them to exist, and avoid the temptation to structure, interpret, or mitigate the person's thoughts or emotions through false reassurance or attempts to redefine the reality for him or her. We are "there," available as a holding presence of the individual's despair, fear, or resentment, but also "invisible" in order to create ample space for one's feelings, concerns, and experiences. To achieve this form of "invisible presence" demands that we *bracket our subjectivity* and withhold our own feelings, advice, comments, or interpretations that we avoid introducing in the relationship (Slochower, 2009). Quite often, the bracketing process is reinforced by the dying or grieving person who cannot tolerate our separate views, opinions, interpretations, or psychoeducational interventions and wants us to feel, think, and experience exactly as he or she does. For some professionals, this bracketing process is highly distressing because they feel constricted when they do not act, intervene, or make full use of their knowledge, skills, ideas, and responses. They cannot withstand being taken for granted, discarded, or insufficiently valued by the dying or bereaved who are totally absorbed by their experiences.

Being adequately held enables people to subsequently abandon the protection of the safe haven and engage in *explorative pursuits* in order to manage the practical challenges of dying and of grieving. To support theses pursuits, we must offer a *secure base* from which they can move forward and explore unknown territories, knowing they can always return to the safe haven when feeling vulnerable, distressed, or troubled. Our role then shifts from holding and containing to encouraging a process of coping with daily concerns and challenges. We facilitate the development of new skills and assist the person or family to meet the demands of a new reality, to work through unresolved issues, and to reconstruct a biographical story in the face of loss. During this process, our views, feelings, clinical interpretations, advice, or assistance are welcomed and taken into consideration by the person and family members.

Companioning people through the end of life offers opportunities for the development of intimacy. Intimacy, however is not a prerequisite for effective care; it occurs by surprise when we *truly connect* with another person as human beings who are transformed by their *relationship* and *confrontation with death* (Barnard, 1995).

ASPECTS OF PROFESSIONALS' SUFFERING

Companioning directly exposes us to the death or grief of a person. The sounds, smells, and physical touch of a dying patient, the despair of a bereaved child or adult, evoke powerful feelings and varied responses that have lasting effects. When we systematically suppress, neglect, or disguise our responses and avoid processing our experiences, they tend to become so overwhelming that our daily functioning is impaired. Suppression is further reinforced by the mistaken beliefs that we must "get used" to death, remain stoic and immune to the suffering of others, and control our emotions through the use of an approach of "detached concern." When our personal suffering is suppressed, it compromises our daily life and work and is manifested through symptoms or syndromes of *burnout, compassion fatigue* (i.e., post-traumatic stress disorder) and *vicarious traumatization*. Even though we refer casually to these conceptualizations to describe our distress, in reality they reflect serious mental health conditions that require professional help.

However, our suffering is not always associated with impairment. Some aspects are healthy, normal, unavoidable, and integral to the process of accompanying people through dying and bereavement. Manifestations of *compassion stress* result from being open and empathic with others, and manifestations of *existential distress* are often evoked when we are repeatedly exposed to human mortality. Concerns such as "Is my life fulfilling?" "Do I have regrets over the life I lead?" "Is there a life after death?" can sometimes trigger guilt feelings and regrets, but they invariably confront us with new choices in our pursuit of leading a meaningful life.

Grieving is another healthy aspect of a suffering that is unavoidable when caring for people who die. Our transcultural qualitative studies (Papadatou, 2000, 2001, 2009; Papadatou, Bellali, Papazoglou, & Petraki, 2002; Papadatou, Martinson, & Chung, 2001) led to the formulation of a model for understanding the grieving process of professionals who experience a wide array of losses when working with seriously ill and dying people. Characteristic of this process, which is largely disenfranchised, is an ongoing fluctuation between experiencing grief by focusing on the loss and avoiding or repressing grief by moving away from it. This fluctuation enables professionals to attribute meaning to the death of the person (why he died), to the dying conditions (how he died), and to their role throughout the caregiving process (How have I/we been helpful or unhelpful? How did I/we contribute to the quality of the family's life?). Grief complications occur when there is a persistent lack of fluctuation between experiencing and avoiding grief. Under those conditions, professionals become totally overwhelmed and consumed by grief or systematically suppress it and hide their vulnerability behind a stoic facade of invulnerability.

Professionals who do not address their suffering end up becoming *highly vulnerable*, unable to maintain boundaries and differentiate the person from their personal needs and responses. They "own" the suffering of others with whom they develop enmeshed and symbiotic relationships, which is never processed or elaborated. Highly vulnerable, however, are also professionals who persistently strive to *appear invulnerable* and project an image of control, omnipotence, power, and perfection. Some of them adopt a paternalistic approach and impose their views, interventions, and decisions, under the pretext of "benefiting" their patient or family. This approach cultivates avoidant relationships, since professionals are more concerned with control and power than with developing a true partnership with the people they serve. Other practitioners, who also strive to appear invulnerable, display what Speck (1994) refers to as "chronic niceness." They project an image of always being empathic, always understanding, unconditionally loving toward dying and bereaved people who are approached in exactly same way. In return for being so nice, they expect to be rewarded with a "good" or "perfect" death and "uncomplicated" grief process that will make them look competent.

It is only when we allow ourselves to be *vulnerable enough* that we can truly remain open, permeable, and available to others, willing to enter their private world. This openness to the other and to our self requires an ability for a *dual awareness* by recognizing what the dying or bereaved person is experiencing at the same time that we acknowledge what we experience within self (Weininger & Kearney, 2011). Without a dual awareness, we cannot fully understand the dynamics involved in partnerships that develop in the face of death.

TEAMS AND SUFFERING

According to the proposed relational approach to care, we cannot fully understand our experiences and responses without considering the context of the team we belong to and the organization we represent. Every team has its own psychology, which is often distinct from the psychology of its individual members. To understand its psychology, we need to explore three processes: (a) whether and how the team *integrates* the dying patient, the deceased body, and the bereaved family in its world and reality; (b) how the team *regulates the suffering* of its members and copes with the challenges of end of life care; and (c) what *meaning(s)* does the team attribute to dying, death, and bereavement.

Integration

In the early 1980s, when I first started working at a large pediatric hospital, I quickly realized that death was perceived as something negative, dirty, and bad. Whenever a child was dying, teams sent the patient to the most isolated room of the hospital or referred him or her to the ICU in order to avoid being exposed to death or to address the parents' desire for a relentless fight against death. After the child's death, grieving relatives were rushed out of the unit or ward, while the dead body was transferred to a morgue that was situated in the hospital's yard, next to a dump. There was no acceptable space in the life of any hospital team, for the dying, the deceased, and the grieving family.

With the international spread of the palliative care movement, teams that care for people with life-threatening diseases increasingly define goals that take into account the particular needs of dying patients and grieving families, validate their experiences, facilitate the passage from life to death, reserve a space for the dead body, create rituals, and offer supportive services to bereaved family members. As a result, acute care hospitals integrate palliative care units or offer consultation services by hospital-based palliative care teams, inviting professionals to broaden their goal of care and mode of operation in order to adapt to the needs of patients and grieving families.

Regulation of Suffering

Teams are organized in ways to help their members cope with death and regulate their suffering. More specifically, they establish rules that determine how professionals are expected to respond and cope with loss, death, and suffering. These rules affect the experience, expression, and coping with grief and suffering, and regulate the fluctuation process between experiencing and repressing it. Moreover, teams determine specific practices by which professionals are expected to manage patient dying, family grieving, and their own responses.

For example, a team that acknowledges and validates the healthy aspects of an unavoidable suffering associated with the care of the dying can provide support and supervision for its members and develop rituals that facilitate the sharing of feelings and co-construction of meanings. However, it may also adopt rules that regulate the intensity and expression of professionals' suffering, which are expected to be tempered and controlled so as to prevent emotional breakdown or become apparent to patients and relatives. By contrast, an another team may adopt rules that discourage the display of suffering, which "must be" suppressed. Professionals are expected to be strong and brave in the face of death and restrict team discussions to scientific debates about medical and nursing interventions. To avoid being affected by patients and families, they engage in procedures that limit visiting hours for relatives and extend the duration of a patient's sedation. The workload is broken down into small tasks in order to avoid intimate and personal relationships, and frequent transfers of staff members is encouraged.

Some teams overregulate the healthy aspects of an inevitable suffering, while other teams impose rules that underregulate it by expecting members to show certain emotions in order to avoid being labeled indifferent, cold, and distant. Problems occur when the team remains silent in the face of death, goes on with its usual business as if nothing happened, and is unable to create a meaningful account of the care that is provided in the face of death.

Meaning Attribution

Team members attribute various meanings to the dying process and death of their patients, which affect their relationships with them. When death is perceived as unacceptable and interpreted as the team's failure to save a person's life, professionals tend to transfer the patient to another unit or homecare service on the basis of "We have nothing else to offer," or they subject him or her to extreme lifesaving measures that prolong unnecessarily suffering in an attempt to compensate for their own feelings of guilt, anger, frustration, and/or resentment and justify their actions by supporting an "At least we tried our best" attitude.

By contrast, teams that perceive death as inevitable or unavoidable and natural strive to create appropriate conditions for the dying person and the grieving family members with whom professionals maintain relationships that are supportive, fulfilling, and meaningful.

Collective meanings become apparent during staff meetings, when team members exchange information about specific patients who are dying or died. In some teams, accounts focus on task achievement, disease issues, and medical or nursing interventions, while in others, discussions expand on relational issues with patients and families and the sharing of personal responses to loss. When the team remains silent in the face of death and goes on with its usual business as if nothing happened, its members are deprived of opportunities to create a meaningful account of dying, death, and of the caregiving process.

TEAM COPING IN DEATH SITUATIONS

Affected by death integration, suffering regulation, and meaning attribution, teams develop and perpetuate a set of coping patterns in the face of death. Some of these patterns are more functional than others. Usually, teams adopt dysfunctional patterns when they strive to avoid rather than confront and manage the suffering of their members. Following are described some of the most common patterns:

Fragmentation of Care

Fragmentation of care allows a team to divide an anxiety-provoking experience into small manageable aspects and diffuse responsibility among several professionals in order to control it and avoid its distressing effects. In this way, intimate and personal relationships are systematically avoided.

Violent and Aggressive Patterns

Instead of channeling the violence introduced by death into constructive behaviors and socially acceptable goals (e.g., fighting for conditions that ensure an "appropriate" and dignified death), some teams channel it into destructive behaviors and aggressive acts against dying and bereaved people who evoke suffering in professionals. These patients and their families are often forgotten, depersonalized, or treated as nonpersons, clinical cases, diagnostic classifications, or room numbers. Sometimes the violence manifests itself in enduring forms of bullying among colleagues, co-workers, and/or administrators who condone, through a laissez-faire approach, nonintervention tactics.

Scapegoating

When a team cannot tolerate the suffering of its members, it projects feelings and thoughts that are too threatening to acknowledge, to a "difficult and rebellious" patient, to an "ungrateful" family, to an "insensitive" colleague, or to an "incompetent" leader who is accused, blamed, rejected, or marginalized. Through scapegoating, the team displaces its suffering instead of addressing it.

Splitting

Instead of acknowledging and owning their experiences, team members divide and project them upon each other and engage in endless fights between the "nice ones" vs. "mean ones," the "sensitive" vs. "insensitive," the "conservatives" vs. "open-minded," and so on. What causes subgrouping to be dysfunctional is the rigidity and impermeability of each subgroup's boundaries as well as a private code of values and communication rules that exclude other team members.

Collective Somatization

Several team members manifest the same symptoms and diseases, thus unconsciously communicating an empathy for each other's suffering that cannot be articulated. Underlying the team's somatization of suffering are often enmeshed and undifferentiated relationships among team members, which aim to counteract the anxiety that death creates.

Systematic Avoidance of Elaboration of Distressing Experiences

Team members cooperate with one another to avoid processing their experiences. They tolerate colleagues who systematically monopolize discussions, who stigmatize emotional expression, or who systematically divert attention through interruptions, jokes, simultaneous talking, or the creation of chaotic situations, all of which aim to prevent reflection on distressing events and relations.

Systematic Avoidance of Change

Without the elaboration of experiences, no change can take place. Change involves an openness to the unknown that is too threatening to team members who choose to cling to a stereotypical and standardized practice. New projects or ideas are resented and systematically sabotaged.

Idealization of Team Operation

Professionals perpetuate an illusion of excellence. Practices are never questioned or reviewed, alternative courses of action are not considered, while team vulnerabilities and limitations are hidden and suffering is disenfranchised.

Dysfunctional coping patterns that are adopted in order to avoid suffering paradoxically increase it and perpetuate a cycle of discouragement and discontent among team members. The systematic use of dysfunctional patterns renders a team vulnerable to various forms of disorganization. Two extreme forms of "organized disorganization" are *team chaos* and *team immobilization* (see Figure 2). These have been also observed by Ausloos (2003) in families that present major dysfunctions.

Chaos prevails when professionals engage in an ongoing overactivity and overagitation as they move frantically from one situation or crisis episode to another. This overagitation *is not* the response to increased job demands but reflects a permanent striving to avoid a reflective process over the team's experiences and suffering. In a chaotic mode of operation, time is perceived and experienced as *event-full* and is determined by a sequence of events and crisis episodes. To slow down and develop personal relationships or reflect upon the team's experiences risks uncovering the professionals' anxiety and pain.

Immobilization occurs in teams characterized by a pervasive passivity and inertia. Suffering is often hidden behind a facade of normality (e.g., "Everything is fine") or under chronic disputes among professionals who become more absorbed in their conflicts than in those whom they serve. There is no investment in tasks that are stereotypically performed and no investment in relationships with patients that become formal and distant. Team members hide behind the closed doors of an office and spend endless hours in staff meetings that are boring, repetitive, and stagnant. In these teams, time is perceived as "frozen."

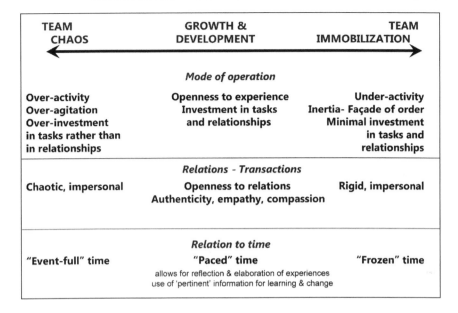

TEAM CHAOS	GROWTH & DEVELOPMENT	TEAM IMMOBILIZATION
	Mode of operation	
Over-activity Over-agitation Over-investment in tasks rather than in relationships	Openness to experience Investment in tasks and relationships	Under-activity Inertia- Façade of order Minimal investment in tasks and relationships
	Relations - Transactions	
Chaotic, impersonal	Openness to relations Authenticity, empathy, compassion	Rigid, impersonal
	Relation to time	
"Event-full" time	"Paced" time allows for reflection & elaboration of experiences use of 'pertinent' information for learning & change	"Frozen" time

Figure 2. Team disorganization and team growth.
Source: Adapted from figures in D. Papadatou (2009, pp. 232, 270).

There is no innovation, no creativity, no forward movement since there is no anticipation, no hopes or dreams (e.g., "What's the point of trying, nothing will change."). Moving forward would require energy that the team does not possess.

Intervention by an experienced consultant or supervisor can help a team that is organized around chaos to slow down, take the time to process painful experiences, and move out of chaos. It can also assist a team that is organized around immobilization to introduce a change or crisis in order to facilitate the exchange of information that can be useful and contribute to the team's development and growth.

RESILIENT TEAMS IN THE FACE OF DEATH

There are no functional or dysfunctional teams. All teams are active systems that choose (most often unconsciously) functional and dysfunctional coping patterns to manage the anxiety, distress, and suffering that the care of dying and bereaved people evoke. They are likely to develop functional patterns and grow if and when they foster the following three conditions (see Figure 3).

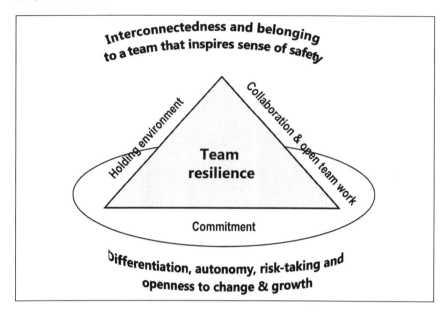

Figure 3. Team resilience.

Commitment

Commitment has two components: commitment to goals that are clearly defined, realistic, open to review from time to time, and meaningful to team members; and commitment to collaboration and mutual support. The latter involves (a) the exchange of information, (b) instrumental and practical assistance, (c) the sharing of personal experiences, and (d) collective attempts to make sense of death-related events and experiences (Papadatou, Papazoglou, Petraki, & Bellali, 1999).

Holding Environment

A holding environment provides a "safe haven" in which professionals feel free to express feelings, thoughts, frustrations, and concerns without the fear of being judged or criticized. They can be "safely overwhelmed" by their suffering, which is contained and validated by colleagues and superiors. In addition, a holding environment provides a "secure base" for the elaboration of distressing experiences, which are understood, reframed, and managed creatively. In so many words, a holding environment provides team members with "roots" (safety, belonging, and solidarity) and "wings" (opportunities to explore) that enable them to move forward, assume new initiatives, take risks, and grow (Kahn, 2002, 2005).

Conditions that undermine the team's capacity to develop a holding environment include the professionals' inability to trust others, the fear of being perceived as weak, resistance against sharing painful experiences out of fear that the exchange may open Pandora's Box and let loose emotions that will not be controlled, the unavailability of time, and conditions that do not ensure a safe enough space for holding (e.g., discussions in the corridor, over lunch breaks).

Interdisciplinary Collaboration and Open Teamwork

To understand the nature of team collaboration in palliative care, we must adopt a *developmental approach* that perceives teams as dynamic systems that evolve and have the potential to function with increasing degrees of competence. Their development is not linear. It is characterized by cycles of forward and regressive movement as well as by periods of stability, disorganization, and growth. What determines their level of development is their ability to establish and maintain collaborations among their members. This ability is reflected in three distinct modes of collaboration that correspond to three distinct levels of development and maturity (Papadatou, 2009; Papadatou, Bluebond-Langner, & Goldman, 2010):

- A mode of *co-existence* among professionals with different expertise, who simply tolerate the existence of one another. Care is divided and assigned to different professionals. Communication is fragmented and limited to referrals.
- A mode of *parallel collaboration* involves the acknowledgement of each other's knowledge and skills, and parallel collaboration toward the pursuit of shared goals and tasks. Although transactions are richer, communication remains superficial. Teamwork is *multidisciplinary*, with medical, nursing, psychosocial, and pastoral services being juxtaposed rather than integrated into a meaningful and comprehensive framework.
- A mode of *collaborative alliance* characterizes care providers who work interdependently, plan interventions together, and evaluate their services as a group. Teamwork becomes *interdisciplinary* when they share the same philosophy of care and work interdependently; it becomes *transdisciplinary* when they seek to educate one another in their respective fields of expertise and acquire new knowledge and skills that are subsequently used in clinical practice without being duplicated.

Both inter- and transdisciplinary collaboration facilitate *open teamwork,* which extends collaborations and forms alliances with other teams, agencies, or services in the community (Payne, 2000). This openness prevents professionals from being secluded and isolated in the cocoon world of their team, which, although safe and protective, limits their development, enrichment, and growth. Open teamwork involves a process of "going out-drawing in" information, which is critical to the care of the dying and bereaved people but is also beneficial to professionals who value their work by realizing what society gains from their services.

Teams that ensure the above basic conditions for their members are more likely to use functional coping patterns, which foster *resilience* under adversity. While resilience has been traditionally associated with the capacity of individuals to endure and "bounce back" from highly distressing situations, team resilience goes beyond endurance and return to a precrisis level of functioning. Resilient teams have the capacity to bear painful and distressing experiences, which is far greater than the capacity of their individual members. As a result, they are likely to take risks, move forward, and come out of a crisis or distressing situation stronger and more resourceful. Characteristic of resilient teams is the manifestation of *team growth*, which comprises positive changes in (a) the communication among patients, families, co-workers, and superiors; (b) the collaboration among team members, who also develop meaningful partnerships with other teams and organizations; and (c) the collective perception of the team's competence and resourcefulness.

Professionals who work in resilient teams value interconnectedness and belonging to the team but also function autonomously and promote differentiation. They use functional patterns to cope with their suffering and develop relationships with patients, families, and colleagues that are personal, authentic, empathic, and characterized by openness (see Figure 2.). Time is not perceived as event-full or frozen, but is *paced*, allowing for reflection, the exchange of different point of views, and the use of "pertinent" information that helps team members to understand how they operate as a team, how they manifest and manage suffering, how they use or misuse their resources, and how they benefit, personally and collectively, from working with dying and bereaved people.

ORGANIZATIONAL CULTURE IN PALLIATIVE CARE ORGANIZATIONS

As has already been suggested, a relational approach to care involves the study of multiple subjectivities and an understanding of the reciprocal influence of a system of relationships through which care is offered and received. Such an approach focuses also on the *organizational culture* of each work context, which represents "how things are done around here." Being socially construed, the organizational culture results from the shared experiences of a group of people belonging to the same organization and provides a framework for understanding and making sense of their work environment and experiences (Braithwaite, Hyde, & Pope, 2010). Schein (2004) defines organizational culture as a collection of traditions, values, policies, beliefs, and attitudes that constitute a pervasive context for everything that employees do and think in a given organization. He analyzes the organizational culture with regard to its (a) *basic assumptions* (often unconscious), which reflect how the organization and its members relate to environment, time, space, reality and each other, what actions they consider proper to take and when, and how solutions are to be applied to recurrent problems; (b) *values and beliefs*, which are articulated in ideologies, philosophies, and attitudes of what "ought to be" the work of the organization; and (c) *artifacts*, which involve the visible aspects of the organizational culture, such as the displayed symbols, language used, stories told, ceremonies and rituals performed, rewards given, and leaders remembered, all of which represent the organization's values, beliefs, and assumptions.

Each organization or service that provides palliative care is distinct with regard to its organizational culture, even though all may promote or advertise the same philosophy, values, and principles of end-of-life care. Given that there is not one singular culture per organization but several subcultures, it is worth exploring those subcultures that may contribute to the resilience of an organization that provides services to the dying and the bereaved.

A Culture of Care

An organization that promotes a culture of care values both the quality of care provided to individuals and families who are served as well as the care of employees whose professional, educational, and developmental needs are recognized and addressed. It operates under the assumption that the extent to which professionals are emotionally held by their organization affects their ability to hold dying and bereaved people in similar ways. Self-care and staff support occur both at an individual and organizational level.

Irene Renzenbrink (2004) uses the concept of "relentless self-care" in palliative care to emphasize the importance of engaging with persistence, determination, commitment, and discipline, in activities that are helpful to relieve job distress and suffering. Some of these measures can help professionals to disconnect from their daily stresses (e.g., time off, vacation, exercise, social, cultural, or other play activities), replenish their batteries, and feel good about self. These activities, however, are never enough if their only goal is to distance self from work and avoid distressing experiences. Self-care should always involve self-reflection and meaning attribution to job-related experiences; this can be facilitated through journaling, meditation, mindful practice, and activities that increase self-awareness and address personal unresolved losses or relational issues (Kearney, Weininger, Vachon, Harrison, & Mount, 2009; Liben & Papadatou, 2010).

An organization that fosters a culture of care provides time and space for employees to acknowledge their distress, grieve their losses, find the "right" balance between their professional and personal life, and confront their mortality. The latter can awaken them to an appreciation of the extraordinariness of being in the presence of death through the ordinariness of their daily encounters.

Staff-support measures are not imposed by superiors but codesigned with employees in order to meet their individual and team needs. They are not limited to stress management courses, staff rotations for burnt-out employees, or referrals to an Assistance Employee Program, which have often limited value because they tend to pathologize and discriminate against employees. Effective supportive services presuppose the identification of both the stressors and appropriate measures to prevent, mitigate, and cope with distress. What is appropriate for one team is not necessarily appropriate for another.

With limited available funds, organizations must carefully plan and develop a *comprehensive support program for employees* that is structured, formalized, and sufficiently diverse to meet the needs of individuals and teams in a safe and caring environment. An example of such a support program, led by a support coordinator who collaborates closely with an interdisciplinary committee of professionals, is implemented at Victoria Hospice in British Columbia (Wainwright & Breiddal, 2011).

A Culture of Collaboration

Even though interdisciplinary collaboration is highly valued by palliative care organizations, daily practice often suggests that such a collaboration is not always achieved (Wittenberg-Lyles et al., 2009). A culture of collaboration flourishes in organizations that have permeable boundaries to allow the circulation of information within and beyond the organization. Members respect and value different views and approaches, and seek ways to integrate and learn from them in their daily practice. Time is devoted to reflect, process, and evaluate collaborations within and between teams as well as with other professionals, teams, agencies, or services in the community. Members do not operate under the "fallacy of harmony" nor perceive conflict as a breakdown in their ability to function effectively. Instead, they mobilize functional coping strategies to manage conflict and prevent its escalation. Rather than personalizing conflictual situations, they take into consideration the wider contextual factors that affect manifestations of anger, resentment, or aggression, which are inherent in death situations.

An example of the value placed on collaboration among members of an organization is described by a Merimna, a Greek nonprofit organization for the care of children and families facing illness and death, which runs an *open space group* (or "sensitivity group") for all members of the organization once a month. This group, which is facilitated by an external consultant, provides professionals, secretaries, the administrator, and chair of the board of directors with opportunities to discuss relational issues in their collaborations with each other and to share concerns, frustrations, disappointments, gratifications, and achievements that are integral to the pains and joys of growing and maturing as an organization (Papadatou, 2012).

A Culture of Learning and Development

A culture of learning goes beyond the provision of staff training. The organization considers learning a high priority and creates "protected time" for *learning together* from complex issues, from achievements and mistakes, and from regular reviews of employees' goals, values, and mode of operation. Shortcomings and mistakes are viewed as opportunities to expand the team and organization's knowledge and capacity to change, rather than being occasions to criticize or blame others.

A culture of learning in palliative care organizations values staff supervision and perceives it not as an option but a necessity. "Super-vision" enables professionals to develop an alternative view of reality, and an "out of the box" vision of their practice and lived experiences, and challenges their "comfort zone" of doing things (Hawkins & Sohet, 2006). It fosters reflective practice and facilitates new learning about self, relationships, collaborations, and about the culture of the work setting.

Furthermore, a culture of learning promotes the integration of research into clinical practice. Professionals are not only informed about the new advances in the field of palliative and bereavement care, but also strive to integrate them into their clinical work. Moreover, they are encouraged to design studies on topics that are relevant to their team and assess the effectiveness of their interventions.

Audits, evaluation surveys, and annual review meetings are additional procedures reflective of a culture of learning. They offer possibilities for changes and innovations in the delivery of care that lead to new ways of doing things. These are tailored to the work setting and flexibly adapt to the availability of organizational and team resources. New ideas or practices are regularly reviewed and evaluated, and the advantages of innovative practices are shared beyond the level of the organization, benefiting other colleagues, patients, families, and communities that are better served.

An organization that is learning and developing from the top to the bottom is far more likely to address the needs of dying and bereaved people because it enhances learning and development in its staff and administration in learning and developing themselves (Hawkins & Sohet, 2006).

Nowadays various reforms are being implemented in the healthcare system of many countries. These reforms promote a competitive market-directed culture that exerts extreme pressure on task achievement and measurable outcomes. The long-term effects of such reforms upon the organizational culture of healthcare institutions are still unclear, but a growing number of studies are currently underway (Braithwaite et al., 2010). Palliative care organizations are and will be inevitably affected by these reforms. Even though they may change in the way of doing things, at least at a superficial level of daily practice, their greatest challenge is to safeguard the deeper assumptions, values, and beliefs that promote a culture of care that is humane and relationship oriented.

CONCLUSION

We live in a world of major socioeconomic changes that affect both the personal and social life of people as well as their health and well-being. In this context, our top priority should be to foster resilience in both teams and organizations that promote a culture of care, of collaboration, of learning, and of development. Rather than "doing more with less," we are challenged to do things *differently* by sharing resources with other teams and organizations and by exchanging valuable information that can benefit both those who receive palliative and bereavement services as well as those who provide them.

REFERENCES

Ausloos, G. (2003). *La competence des familles: temps, chaos, processus.* Ramonville Saint-Agne: Editions Eres.

Barnard, D. (1995). The promise of intimacy and the fear of our own undoing. *Journal of Palliative Care, 11*(4), 22-26.

Beach, M. C., Inui, T. N., & Relationship-Centered Care Research Network. (2006). Relationship-centered care. A constructive reframing. *Journal of General Internal Medicine, 21*(Suppl 1), 53-58.

Braithwaite, J., Hyde, P., & Pope, C. (2010). *Culture and climate in health organizations.* Hampshire, UK: Palgrave Macmillan.

Ehrenberg, D. B. (1974). The intimate edge in therapeutic relatedness (originally published in 1974). In L. Aron & A. Harris (Eds.), *Relational psychoanalysis: Innovation and expansion* (Vol. 1, pp.3-28). Hillsdale, NJ: The Analytic Press.

Jones, W. H. S. (Trans.). (1923). *Hippocrates* (Vol. 2). Cambridge, MA: Loeb Classical Library.

Hawkins, P., & Sohet, R. (2006). *Supervision in the helping professions.* Buckingham, UK and Philadelphia, PA: Open University Press.

Kahn, W. A. (2002). Holding environments at work. *Journal of Applied Behavioral Science, 37*(3), 260-279.

Kahn, W. A. (2005). *Holding fast: The struggle to create resilient caregiving organizations.* New York, NY: Brunner-Routledge.

Kearney, M. K., Weininger, R. B., Vachon, M. L. S., Harrison, R. L., & Mount, M. M. (2009). Self-care of physicians caring for patients at the end of life: "Being connected . . . a key to my survival." *Journal of American Medical Association, 301*(11), 1155-1164.

Liben, S., & Papadatou, D. (2010). Self care: The foundation of caregiving. In J. Wolfe, P. Hinds, B. Sourkes (Eds.), *Textbook of interdisciplinary pediatric palliative care* (pp. 168-178). Philadelphia, PA: Elsevier.

Papadatou D. (2000). A proposed model on health professionals' grieving process. *Omega: Journal of Death and Dying, 41,* 59-77.

Papadatou, D. (2001). The grieving health care provider: Variables affecting the professional responses to a child's death. *Bereavement Care, 20*(2), 26-29.

Papadatou, D. (2009). *In the face of death: Professionals who care for the dying and the bereaved.* New York, NY: Springer.

Papadatou, D. (2012). Merimna: The society for the care of children and families facing illness and death. *Grief Matters, 15*(3), 64-68.

Papadatou, D., Bellali, T., Papazoglou, D., & Petraki, D. (2002). Greek physicians' and nurses' grief as a result of caring for children dying of cancer. *Pediatric Nursing, 28*(4), 345-353.

Papadatou, D., Martinson, I. M., & Chung, P. M. (2001). Caring for dying children: A comparative study of nurses' experiences in Greece and Hong Kong. *Cancer Nursing, 24*(5), 402-412.

Papadatou, D., Papazoglou, I., Petraki, D., & Bellali, T. (1999). Mutual support among nurses who provide care to dying children. *Illness, Crisis & Loss, 7*(1), 37-48.

Papadatou, D., Bluebond-Langner, M., & Goldman, A. (2010). The team. In J. Wolfe, P. Hinds, & B. Sourkes (Eds.), *Textbook of interdisciplinary pediatric palliative care* (pp. 55-63). Philadelphia, PA: Elsevier

Payne, M. (2000). *Teamwork in multiprofessional care.* New York, NY: Palgrave.

Renzenbrink, I. (2004). Relentless self-care. In P. Silverman & J. Berzoff (Eds.), *Living with dying: A handbook for health care practitioners in end-of-life care.* New York, NY: Columbia University Press.

Schein, E. (2004). *Organizational culture and leadership.* San Francisco, CA: Jossey-Bass.

Slochower, J. A. (1996). *Holding and psychoanalysis: A relational perspective.* New York, NY: Routledge.

Speck, P. (1994). Working with dying people: On being good enough. In A. Obholzer & V. Z. Roberts (Eds.), *The unconscious at work: Individual and organizational stress in the human services* (pp. 94-110). New York, NY: Brunner-Routledge.

Wainwright, W., & Breiddal, S. (2011). Staff support: A shared responsibility at Victoria Hospice Society, British Columbia, Canada. In I. Renzenbrink (Ed.), *Caregiver stress and staff support in illness, dying, and bereavement* (pp. 111-126). Oxford: Oxford University Press.

Weininger, R., & Kearney, M. (2011). Revisiting empathic engagement: Countering compassion fatigue with "exquisite empathy." In I. Renzenbrink (Ed.), *Caregiver stress and staff support in illness, dying, and bereavement* (pp. 49-61). Oxford: Oxford University Press.

Wittenberg-Lyles, E. M. et al. (2009). Exploring interpersonal communication in hospice interdisciplinary team meetings. *Journal of Gerontological Nursing, 35*(7), 38-45.

http://dx.doi.org/10.2190/FATC4

CHAPTER 4

Honoring Relationship in Pediatric Palliative Care

Kathie Kobler

INTRODUCTION

As medical technology advances, infants and children with serious medical conditions are living longer, requiring innovative approaches to their care. Pediatric palliative care addresses the physical, emotional, psychosocial, and spiritual needs of children and their families, striving to enhance their quality of life, minimize suffering, and optimize function while providing opportunities for personal and spiritual growth (Friebert, 2009; Wolfe, Hinds, & Sourkes, 2011). Ideally, pediatric palliative care is delivered in an integrated fashion from the time an infant or child is diagnosed with a life-threatening condition and during the entire trajectory of care, through death and bereavement (American Academy of Pediatrics, 2000). The provision of such seamless care requires the collaborative efforts of interdisciplinary team members working in partnership with the child and family to develop an individualized plan of care incorporating their goals, values, and preferences. Using a holistic approach, children may receive palliative care at the same time as disease-modifying therapies, with the mutual goal of maximizing quality of living while minimizing suffering.

Key to providing effective pediatric palliative care is establishing supportive and caring relationships between the child, the family, and the healthcare team. Parents report the importance of having their children known individually by a core group of caregivers who share expertise and knowledge while offering a consistent, compassionate presence (Heller & Solomon, 2005). Recognizing the unique gift inherent in each child, pediatric palliative caregivers meet families in the tender place where grief and hope intertwine. This chapter will discuss quality perinatal and pediatric palliative care provision with a focus on strategies to empower and honor relationship throughout the child's living, dying, and beyond.

45

BACKGROUND

The field of palliative care experienced tremendous growth in the 1990s, yet it was not until the early 21st century that the literature reflected extension of palliative care principles to the perinatal, neonatal, and pediatric populations (Field & Behrman, 2003). It is difficult to ascertain from existing data the exact number of infants and children with serious medical conditions who would benefit from palliative care (Friebert, 2009). Annual death statistics provide one vantage point. In 2009 there were over 48,000 deaths of children ages 0–19, with an infant mortality rate of 6.30 per 1,000 live births (Kochanek, Xu, Murphy, Miniño, & Kung, 2011). In addition, each year there are over one million fetal deaths, the majority before 20 weeks completed gestation, and approximately 26,000 fetal deaths at 20 weeks gestation or more (MacDorman, Kirmeyer, & Wilson, 2012). These impressive numbers signify opportunities to provide quality palliative care and compassionate support for children with life-threatening conditions and their families.

PEDIATRIC PALLIATIVE CARE
DELIVERY MODELS

Infants and children may receive palliative care in a variety of settings, including hospitals, community-based and free-standing pediatric hospices, and long-term care facilities (Carroll, Wright, & Frankel, 2011). At the time of this publication, the Center to Advance Palliative Care (www.capc.org) was in final analysis of national survey data to ascertain the number and types of pediatric palliative care programs in the United States. Currently, no worldwide central repository is available to track the evolution of pediatric palliative care programs, although a systematic review of the literature found the following program development data: 65.5% of countries had no findings of pediatric palliative care provision, 18.8% had capacity-building activities, 9.9% had localized provision, and only 5.7% of countries had pediatric palliative care programs reaching mainstream levels of care delivery (Knapp et al., 2011).

Hospital-Based Programs

The American Academy of Pediatrics has called for the establishment of pediatric palliative care services in tertiary medical centers and hospitals that care for children (American Academy of Pediatrics, 2000). In a groundbreaking cohort study, Feudtner and colleagues (2011) captured the current state of pediatric palliative care delivery at six major hospitals. Data was collected during a 3-month enrollment interval for all new and established patients receiving a palliative care referral. The cohort teams' top four reported goals for their patients were managing pain and symptoms, facilitating communication, supporting decision making, and assisting in coordination of care. After 12 months, over two thirds of the study's patients were still alive, validating the pediatric palliative care teams' role in maintaining relationship with children over extended periods of time.

Home Palliative Care Programs

For those receiving pediatric palliative services at home, coordination of services among all health team members is vital to achieving seamless care. Parents reported significant improvement in their child's symptoms and increased coordination of care as a result of their home palliative team's presence (Vollenbroich et al., 2012). In addition to improving children's quality of life, moving care from hospital to home with the support of community-based pediatric palliative programs may result in medical cost savings. Gans and colleagues (2012) reviewed cost data from California's Partners for Children (PFC) home pediatric palliative care program, finding the PFC saved an average $1,677 in healthcare costs per child per month. This amounted to an 11% decrease in spending as a result of coordinated in-home family-centered pediatric palliative care.

Hospice and Concurrent Care

Hospice care in the United States is both a philosophy and a model of care delivery, accessed when patients are expected to live less than 6 months. Pediatric hospice care is provided by interdisciplinary teams who continue to embrace palliative care principles of minimizing suffering, promoting comfort, and enhancing quality of living. Children may receive hospice care at home or in free-standing hospice facilities designated to meet their needs at the end of life.

The Patient Protection and Affordable Care Act includes Section 2302, titled "Concurrent Care for Children," which requires that State Medicaid or Children's Health Insurance programs must allow children access to hospice services while also receiving disease-directed therapies. Each state is now charged with the task of developing processes in order to apply the Concurrent Care Act principles (National Hospice and Palliative Care Organization, 2011). However, such implementation is expected to produce issues as caregivers expand existing services to meet the needs of medically complex children. Pediatric palliative care teams attempting to initiate concurrent care are already identifying complex barriers related to insurance reimbursement, durable home equipment access, and care coordination (Miller, LaRagione, Kang, & Feudtner, 2012). Readers are encouraged to access National Hospice and Palliative Care Organization's free *Concurrent Care for Children Implementation Toolkit* for further clarification on this relatively new healthcare initiative (National Hospice and Palliative Care Organization, 2011).

BARRIERS TO PEDIATRIC PALLIATIVE CARE

While evidence grows regarding the benefits of pediatric palliative service models, significant obstacles persist, hindering care. Pediatric caregivers acknowledge that multiple factors may impede their ability to implement timely palliative care, including uncertainty in prognostication with children, hesitancy for families to acknowledge a life-limiting condition, discrepancy in treatment goals and communication between staff and family members, and insufficiency of healthcare provider knowledge regarding end-of-life care for children (Davies et al., 2008). Although optimal palliative care begins when a life-threatening condition is diagnosed, many pediatric clinicians struggle with the misconception that palliative care is only for dying patients and may delay early referral to a pediatric palliative care service (Thompson, Knapp, Madden, & Shenkman, 2009). Barriers in hospital and community settings may vary, requiring creativity and flexibility as children transition between sites of care and interact with multiple healthcare team members. In addition, each family's personal, cultural, or religious perspectives on wellness, disease, or dying may result in their denial of pediatric palliative caregivers' full scope of service (Liben, Papadatou, & Wolfe, 2008).

CREATING A PEDIATRIC PALLIATIVE CARE SERVICE

Numerous standards, tools, and guidelines are available to caregivers interested in creating a pediatric palliative care service. Please refer to the Appendix for resources offered by national organizations committed to the growth of pediatric palliative care. The overall goal is to create a service that will provide seamless care to children with life-threatening conditions. Team availability should be organized in such a fashion that regardless of time of day or site of care, families have access to the expertise of an interdisciplinary pediatric palliative care team. The core team should include, at minimum, a physician, nurse, social worker, chaplain, and a child-life specialist who are proficient in palliative care principles (American Academy of Pediatrics, 2000). When asked about their wishes at the time of a palliative care referral, children and their families identified goals related to health maintenance, independence, and improved quality of life, including the wish to be free of symptoms and to experience minimal suffering (Tamburro, Shaffer, Hahnlen, Felker, & Ceneviva, 2011). As children often see multiple pediatric subspecialists during different stages of treatment, the palliative care team stands poised to offer invaluable continuity, conveying family care preferences to the entire team throughout the healthcare journey.

WHEN TO SEEK PEDIATRIC
PALLIATIVE CARE

Children diagnosed with life-threatening medical conditions affecting quality of life will benefit from receiving pediatric palliative care. The children referred to palliative care programs in the Feudtner et al. (2011) multicenter cohort study had a diversity of medical conditions. In order of prevalence, these included genetic or congenital, neuromuscular, cancer (leukemia, brain tumor, solid tumor), respiratory, gastrointestinal, cardiovascular, and immunologic. At the time of referral, over 47% of the study's patients had cognitive impairment, 30.9% were experiencing pain, and the majority of children were receiving substantial polypharmacy and medical interventions to treat their conditions (Feudtner et al., 2011). The Center to Advance Palliative Care offers an extensive listing of neonatal and pediatric diagnoses that should trigger a referral to a pediatric palliative care service (Friebert & Osenga, 2009).

Optimally, palliative care referrals occur at the time of diagnosis, allowing the team to support parents facing first steps in complex decision making about their child's care (Mack & Wolfe, 2004). Palliative care clinicians work in collaboration with a child's entire medical team, assisting in prioritizing and planning feasible treatment options and in identifying overall healthcare goals. Listening carefully to parents' hopes for their child while also acknowledging their grief over the diagnosis is essential to developing a compassionate presence. As a child's care trajectory unfolds, palliative care teams may meet the child in the hospital, in clinics, or at home, providing guidance as care needs shift over time. When a child approaches the end of life, pediatric palliative care clinicians join the family and healthcare team in exploring options of continuing, withholding or withdrawing aggressive medical treatments, and also in defining the extent of resuscitative measures to be used if the child's condition rapidly deteriorates.

Pediatric palliative care clinicians are also consulted to manage difficult-to-control, disease-related symptoms impacting the child's quality of living. This may include addressing all aspects of pain (physical, psychological, and spiritual), dyspnea (difficulty breathing), nausea, vomiting, constipation, excessive secretions, seizures, depression, and anxiety. A holistic approach is used to decrease a child's symptom burden, incorporating combined modalities aimed at promoting comfort. Interventions may include medications, cognitive-behavioral approaches (meditation, music, art, pet therapies), and complementary therapies (massage, aromatherapy, Reiki) (Friedrichsdorf & Kang, 2007).

Medications to relieve pain should be administered in accordance with the updated World Health Organization's (2012) two-step strategy, with dosing at regular intervals using the appropriate route of administration, while adapting treatment to the individual child's needs. A thorough discussion on expert pain and symptom management for infants and children is outside the scope of this chapter. Readers are encouraged to refer to the following resources for complete information on pain and symptom management for children: Carter, Levetown, and Friebert (2011); Foster, Bell, and Gilmer (2012); Friedrichsdorf and Kang (2007); Wolfe, Hinds, and Sourkes (2011); World Health Organization (2012).

Lastly, pediatric palliative teams are consulted when children transition to end-of-life care, focusing on alleviating the child's suffering by promoting comfort through titrating medications, adjusting treatments, and honoring special time with loved ones. Palliative caregivers strive to discuss parents' preferences regarding their child's end-of-life care before the moment of death approaches. Such conversations unfold over time, in a manner that respects families' cultural and religious preferences. Parents who engaged in discussions with their pediatric palliative care physician about their preferred location for the death reported feeling well prepared when the moment arrived, resulting in more home deaths and fewer hospitalizations (Dussel et al., 2009). No matter where or when the child's dying occurs, parents value caregivers who offer a supportive, compassionate presence; ensure meticulous symptom management; and provide bereavement support for siblings and parents (Vollenbroich et al., 2012).

PERINATAL PALLIATIVE CARE

As the field of palliative medicine grows, this care has extended into the perinatal and neonatal periods (Sumner, Kavanaugh, & Moro, 2006). Most parents begin their pregnancy in hopeful anticipation of their baby's healthy arrival. Advances in fetal diagnostics have resulted in prenatal detection of life-threatening conditions, often very early in the pregnancy. Parents are faced with the unanticipated and overwhelming task of taking in complex medical information in order to best make decisions for their unborn baby's medical care. Referral to a perinatal or neonatal palliative care service should occur when babies are (a) diagnosed with life-threatening conditions, including those considered incompatible with life; (b) born at the margin of viability; and (c) not responding to aggressive medical treatment or receiving treatment that may prolong suffering (Munson & Leuthner, 2007).

Perinatal palliative care is an interdisciplinary process, with potential provision at various points in the care continuum, from fetal diagnosis throughout the pregnancy, at the time of birth, and throughout the baby's living and dying (Boss, Kavanaugh, & Kobler, 2011). Parents receiving perinatal palliative care convey a desire for their baby's unique personhood to be recognized and value opportunities to treasure time with their baby after birth (Côté-Arsenault & Denney-Koelsch, 2011). Birth plans are created to capture the parents' preferences for care during labor and delivery. Neonatal advance plans of care are crafted to outline the baby's anticipated care needs and the extent of testing or treatments to be provided (Boss et al, 2011; Munson & Leuthner, 2007).

Perinatal palliative caregivers are often in the delivery room, ready to accommodate shifts in the baby's condition from the moment of birth. Treatment plans are modified to meet the baby's physical needs while reflecting parental preferences in care. As with older children, neonatal palliative care is focused on minimizing suffering during the baby's living and dying, while helping parents to connect with their newborn. For babies who have stabilized, surviving to the time when the mother is ready for discharge, collaboration with a community pediatric palliative care team is initiated to help the baby and family transition to home (Kobler & Limbo, 2011).

BEING IN RELATIONSHIP

Caregivers strive for integrity in relationship with patients, families, and others (Limbo & Kobler, 2010). However, maintaining relationship while engaging in complex medical decision making may conflict with a care provider's core values and beliefs. Staying connected with oneself and with others is integral to initiating, maintaining, and transitioning relationship. Being in relationship requires a sense of one's own expectations, intentions, and motivations while also attempting to understand the other's perception of the shared experience. This tandem pathway of understanding both self and other provides the fertile ground for relationship to grow. The remainder of this chapter will discuss strategies to establish, maintain, and transition relationship in pediatric palliative care.

ESTABLISHING RELATIONSHIP

Pediatric palliative caregivers meet children and families at critical points, such as the time of initial diagnosis, during episodes of pain escalation, or at the end of life. Both the parents and child may be overwhelmed with anxiety, uncertainty, and grief. As such, caregivers must have a strong sense of self-awareness prior to entering a relationship with those who hurt. Pausing to ask oneself, "What do I bring to each encounter with my patients and their families?" can be a helpful reflection. A personal inventory can be conducted prior to meeting a new patient by carefully considering one's expectations, beliefs, values, motivations, intentions, prejudices, past life experiences, and current feelings. Knowing oneself is a lifelong process, as is the ability to remain mindful of one's own limits of energy, comfort, and tolerance of difficult or painful situations (Rosenblatt, 2009). Such a reflective process also allows pediatric palliative caregivers to anticipate personal concerns or limitations that may arise due to the child's specific needs or circumstances. Through mindful self-awareness, clinicians ground themselves while entering into the tender place of establishing a meaningful relationship with the child and family in need.

MAINTAINING RELATIONSHIP

The pediatric palliative care team works in collaboration, drawing upon each member's strengths and expertise in order to establish trust with the child and family. Fostering secure attachments is an essential component of maintaining relationship with the pediatric palliative care family. Papadatou (2009) captures this concept well:

> When we develop secure attachments with the people we serve, we prevent isolation and hopelessness and integrate the dying and the bereaved into a world of meaningful connections that are affirmed. Secure attachments increase trust in ourselves, in others, and in the caregiving process. (p. 36)

Parents perceive continuity of relationship with trusted caregivers, and the coordinated provision of information, as key elements in quality of care and caring (Heller & Solomon, 2005). Parents also appreciate when the palliative team members work to establish relationship with each member of their family, learning who they are as individuals separate from the child's medical condition. (Widger, Steele, Oberle, & Davies, 2009)

Understanding Parents' Experiences

Figure 1 offers insight to the pediatric palliative care family's experience throughout the progression of a child's condition. This integrative model, created by Milstein (2005) and modified with permission by Kobler and Limbo (2011), illustrates that bereavement is part of a parent's experience from the moment of diagnosis. Trying to make sense of shifts in their child's healthcare needs, parents grieve losses and reconstruct hopes. This model of ongoing intertwined grief and hope should be held in mind as pediatric palliative caregivers come alongside families to provide support.

Caring for a medically complex child may leave parents feeling exhausted and alone. One mother described her 12-year experience of caring for her daughter, who was born with devastating neurological complications, with words that reflect both grief and hope:

> What does it feel like to have cared for her all these years? It feels like I am driving a giant SUV through a jungle. Inside the vehicle are my daughter and all of her medical equipment. No one else is with us. I'm trying to navigate the SUV through the dense jungle without a map. To make matters worse, the foliage is so thick that I can only drive a few feet at a time. Then I have to hop out to hack down more jungle leaves just so I can see a few a little bit farther ahead. My heart breaks with each passing day, yet I hope with my whole being that at some point, we will find our way. (A mother, personal communication, 2012)

Pediatric palliative caregivers should be continually assessing parents' perceptions of how the child's care needs are affecting the entire family's well-being. A

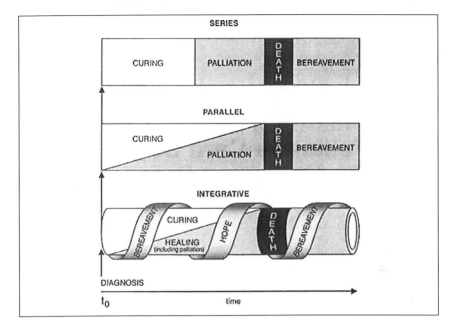

Figure 1. Integrative model of curing and healing (created by Milstein [2005] and modified with permission by Kobler and Limbo [2011]).

doctor or nurse may ask parents open-ended questions, beginning with, "I'm wondering about" or "Please tell me more" to learn about the family's experiences. The following assessment questions, recommended by Mazanec and Panke (2006) and Rosenblatt (2009), may be helpful in drawing out aspects of the parents' knowing impacted by cultural or spiritual beliefs and values:

- What is happening (has happened) to your child?
- What do you think caused this to happen?
- How have you and your family been affected by what has happened?
- What meaning does this experience have for you and your family?
- Tell me what else I would need to know to understand and help you.

Learning about the family's experience of living with the child's life-threatening condition can provide profound insight, as well reveal parents' values, expectations, and hopes, which can be used to guide future care planning discussions.

Understanding the Child's Perspective

Children's perception of their medical condition, treatments, and its impact on daily living is affected by their age, developmental stage, and cognitive function. Pediatric palliative caregivers strive to hear the child's voice, working collaboratively to understand the child's experiences, wishes, and preferences. To date, unless a child is over the age of 18 or declared an emancipated minor, the child is not allowed by law to give consent for their medical treatments. In addition, there is currently no legal advance care planning document applicable to children under 18 years of age. Instead, pediatric palliative caregivers facilitate a child's assent to the plan of care, using an interdisciplinary team modified to the child's developmental understanding of illness and death (Hurwitz, Duncan, & Wolfe, 2004).

A variety of integrative therapies, including art, music, play, pet, and bibliotherapy can be used to connect with children, helping them to work through their experiences and feelings at an individualized pace. As play is the language of children, play therapists trust the child's inner direction to lead play and conversation, thus allowing play to communicate fears, hopes, and perception of the situation (van Breeman, 2009). In addition to assessing understanding, integrative therapies may also be used to determine a child's level of spiritual distress or suffering. Individualized, concrete strategies, such as drawing a picture or writing a letter, may help a child address loneliness, express concerns about life after death, explore relationship with God, ask for forgiveness, or find meaning (Foster et al., 2012). For example, an 8-year-old boy became very withdrawn following a third relapse of cancer. After many months of trying to help him articulate his feelings without success, a breakthrough occurred as he was talking with this author about Lego Super Heroes. His wondering aloud, "I bet Superman can fly all the way to heaven!" led to opening a dialogue about heaven that prompted his sharing concerns about dying.

Communication

Effective communication is an essential component of providing quality pediatric palliative care. Parents report appreciating caregivers who convey information with compassion, concern, and honesty (Meert, Thursten, & Briller, 2005; Widger et al., 2009). It is especially important to use a collaborative approach when communicating bad news, doing so in a manner that both prepares and empowers the family for what is next (Feudtner, 2007). Davies, Contro, Larson, and Widger (2010) found that parental satisfaction increased when receiving comprehensive, sensitively delivered information, but trust in the healthcare team deteriorated when parents perceived they were being given insufficient information. The following three questions, when used on a daily basis, can serve as helpful tools to promote effective communication, while also acknowledging the parent or child's experience:

- What is your understanding of your child's condition/situation today?
- What is most important to you right now?
- How can I best help?

Language and cultural differences between families and caregivers may serve as barriers, so professional medical interpreters should be accessed to ensure effective communication. In addition, some parents have reported conveying a positive outward expression while inwardly experiencing deep hurt. Such masked communication may enhance the possibility of emotional miscues and consequent miscommunication with their child's healthcare team (Hexem, Miller, Carroll, Faerber, & Feudtner, 2012). Pediatric palliative clinicians must mindfully evaluate their effectiveness in communicating during each patient encounter, shifting as needed to assure they are meeting the family's needs.

There are times in working with dying children that the spoken word cannot begin to express a caregiver's thoughts while witnessing profound suffering or sorrow. During such special moments, silence can be used to convey caring in a gentle manner, honoring relationship. Compassionate silence stems from reflective practice and involves simply being present for another without expectations for conversation. Instead, the caregiver anchors silence by focusing on his or her own breathing (Back, Bauer-Wu, Rushton, & Halifax, 2009). Through the use of compassionate silence, the child or family can center on their innermost thoughts or feelings, which in time may find expression in words shared aloud with the caregiver.

Decision Making

Throughout the trajectory of care, pediatric palliative caregivers assist parents and healthcare teams in making decisions for the child regarding the extent of medical treatments and supportive therapies. As the illness progresses, such decisions may evoke strong preferences, values, and beliefs from both the family and clinicians. Information pertinent to the decision at hand must be provided in a manner that is relevant or consistent with the parents' preferred communication style so as not to confuse or distress (Haward et al., 2012).

A full discussion of neonatal and pediatric decision-making complexities and ethical dilemmas is outside the scope of this chapter. One issue, moral distress, warrants recognition here, as situations do arise when caregivers feel they are doing more *to* the child than *for* the child. Moral distress is physical or emotional suffering experienced when either internal or external constraints prevent one from following the course of action one believes is right (Rushton, 2011). When complex moral or ethical issues arise, the entire healthcare team must strive to maintain relationship with the family and with each other. Team meetings prior to family care conferences are a useful strategy to build group consensus prior to engaging in decision-making discussions with the family. If conflict persists, a medical ethicist may be extremely helpful in assisting the team to ascertain feasible care choices that promote dignity and comfort for the child.

When a child transitions to dying, parents experience critical turning points in their thoughts, feelings, and goals. Acknowledging the parents' love for their child is important during such end-of-life decision making as well as assuring the team's continuing commitment to providing compassionate care (Gillis, 2009). The entire healthcare team should work collaboratively to provide care choices that honor the precious relationship between parent and child as the dying process unfolds.

Connecting When Expectations Differ

Parents' expectations for care can strongly impact their decision making, often in ways difficult for the palliative care team to fully comprehend. Parents have described their role to be that of "bearers of hope," a responsibility taken seriously; parents are to hope the best for their child (Keene-Reder & Serwint, 2009). Families may also express belief that a miraculous healing will occur for their child, even up to the moment of death. The family's focus on the miracle may conflict with the healthcare team's medical understanding of the child's deterioration. Palliative caregivers may use open-ended questions, such as, "Help me to know more about what a miracle would mean to you," to better understand the family's perception (Delisser, 2009). Parents' answers may be useful to caregivers in framing a respectful response acknowledging the family's belief in the miracle, without challenging or offering false hope (Delisser, 2009; Keene-Reder & Serwint, 2009).

In addition, by drawing out the meaning of the miracle, caregivers may learn crucial information that will guide further care. For example, one family was praying over their child, who was dying from a malignant brain tumor progression. Their prayers reached an intensity and devotion that concerned the care team. The palliative care nurse gently asked, "Help me to know how you are hoping God will answer your prayers." The parents tearfully acknowledged their son was dying, but stated they were praying intently in hope that he would open his eyes. The parents shared their deepest desire to hear his voice one last time. This answer provided relief for the caregivers while also offering an opportunity to reassure the parents that their son could hear their voices and feel their love, even if he could no longer respond with words.

TRANSITIONING RELATIONSHIP

Transitions in relationship occur at differing points in time, depending upon the progression of the pediatric palliative care patient's condition. Some children reach a point of relative stability, which results in a decreased frequency of the pediatric palliative care team's visits. Some children, upon reaching a balance of quality of life and comfort, may actually be discharged from the palliative care service. Caregivers can help the child and family anticipate an upcoming transition from the palliative care team through proactive planning and a supportive presence during the change.

The most difficult transition occurs when a child dies. The pediatric palliative team takes special care in preparing the child and family for death. Choices are offered to honor cultural and religious values while allowing parents to connect with their child at a time and pace that is meaningful to them. Many hospitals provide opportunities for families to experience special moments together with relatives and friends or to create keepsakes such as photographs, plaster or ink prints of hands and feet, or locks of hair (Boss et al., 2011; Limbo & Kobler, 2010; Meert et al., 2005). Not every family will be open to all offered interactions during or after the child's death. Caregivers should be mindful that the parents are making the best decisions they can and should refrain from judgment or coercion (Limbo & Kobler, 2010). Respectfully meeting a family's needs around the time of their child's death may positively influence the parents' grief work and adjustment to the death (Meert et al., 2005). Many pediatric palliative care teams provide ongoing bereavement support to the family over the weeks and months following the child's death.

REINVESTING IN RELATIONSHIP

Caring for medically fragile children elicits strong emotions for the entire healthcare team as they faithfully support families through difficult situations. When a child's condition deteriorates or when death approaches, caregivers experience their own grief and heartache. Professional caregivers' grieving is marked with ongoing shifts between experiencing grief by focusing on the loss and avoiding grief by moving away from the situation (Papadatou, 2009). This continual fluctuation allows the caregiver to adapt to the loss in a healthy manner and to attribute meaning to their experience with the child and family (Papadatou, 2009). Pediatric palliative care teams may be called upon to provide bereavement support for staff, as often entire units collectively grieve the loss of a beloved infant or child.

Pediatric palliative caregivers are encouraged to identify and incorporate reflective practice into their daily routine. Caregivers are wonderful at reflecting *in* the moments of providing care, but often to not take time to reflect *on* the experience or accompanying feelings after a patient care situation has unfolded. Taking time to pause and contemplate helps one to modulate emotions, cultivate moral sensitivity, and reconnect to meaning (Rushton, 2006). Caregivers must also have a strong awareness of those self-care activities that provide release and renewal (Kearney, Weininger, Vachon, Harrison, & Mount, 2009). Engaging in self-care practices allows the caregiver to transition relationship and prepare for welcoming a new child and family in need of palliative care.

RITUAL AND LIFE TRANSITIONS

Ritual is common to all cultures throughout history, used to mark important life transitions such as birth, marriage, and death. The actions or words of a ritual help to express meaning, marking the significance of complex events. Ritual may incorporate both human and divine elements, balancing both earthly and sacred elements of life. In its purest form, ritual flows from relationship, and participants arise from the experience transformed (Limbo & Kobler, 2013).

Ritual plays an important role in supporting families and caregivers through a child's living and dying. When used in clinical settings, ritual has three beneficial dimensions: intention, participation, and meaning making (Kobler, Limbo, & Kavanaugh, 2007). Ideally, ritual should be co-created with the child and family to ensure their preferences or wishes for the ritual are honored (Limbo & Kobler, 2013). For example, a caregiver might invite parents to consider how they wish to experience the moment of holding their dying child. One couple responded to such an invitation by asking all of their daughter's caregivers to form a circle around the family. Once connected in the circle, the parents then asked all present to share special memories of time spent with their little girl. The words of thanksgiving, blessing, and love spoken as the ritual unfolded held special meaning to both the parents and caregivers alike.

The initiation and timing of ritual is critical; caregivers may notice moments ripe for ritual growing from subtle shifts or transitions. One beautiful ritual unfolded when a young woman let out a deep sigh at her boyfriend's bedside in the pediatric intensive care unit. He was on a ventilator and had just been declared brain dead, the victim of a drive-by shooting. Upon hearing such a significant sigh, this author asked, "Help me to know what you are thinking about right now." She answered, "When he hugged me, I always listened to his heartbeat. I'm wondering, can I hear his heartbeat one last time?" Together we lowered the bedrail so she could lean forward, placing her ear to his chest. This simple act of bending and listening helped this young woman connect with past memories, acknowledge her love, and begin to say goodbye.

Children are especially drawn to ritual, as they have a natural ability to co-create and give words to feelings and thoughts that honor relationship (Limbo & Kobler, 2013). Bereaved parents who participate in ritual find support, meaning, and facilitation of their grief (Macdonald et al., 2005; Meert et al., 2005). Ritual co-creation provides opportunities for caregivers to support bereaved families and also to facilitate their own grief work (Limbo & Kobler, 2013; Papadatou, 2009). Parents may use ritual to create meaningful connections with their child, even after death. One perinatal palliative care father confided to this author that he wished to sing to his daughter at birth so she would not be afraid. He continued to sing to her every night. Cradling her dying body, he invited her caregivers to join in singing to her one last time. He tearfully sang the same words at her graveside: *Hush little baby, don't say a word . . .*

CONCLUSION

Pediatric palliative caregivers are privileged to journey with children and families experiencing life-threatening conditions. Integral to this work is learning what is most important to the child and family and offering a compassionate presence promoting comfort and quality of living. Pediatric palliative caregivers honor relationship, emerging from shared experiences of the child's living and dying transformed.

APPENDIX
Standards, Guidelines, Tools, and Resources for Pediatric Palliative Care

American Academy of Hospice and Palliative Medicine: www.aahpm.org
- Training, education, and fellowship information
- Physician certification

American Academy of Pediatrics: www.aap.org

- Section on Hospice and Palliative Medicine
- Statements and guidelines related to hospice and palliative care:
  - *Palliative Care for Children* (2000)
  - *Forgoing Medically Provided Hydration and Nutrition in Children* (2009)
  - *Guidelines on Foregoing Life-Sustaining Medical Treatment* (1994)
  - *Honoring Do-Not-Attempt Resuscitation Attempts in Schools* (2010)
  - *Noninitiation or Withdrawal of Intensive Care for High-Risk Newborns* (2007)

Center to Advance Palliative Care: www.capc.org

- Extensive listing of tools and resources for building a hospital palliative care program
- Palliative Care Leadership Centers: Offering operational training and year-long mentoring; includes two pediatric sites recognized as centers of excellence, provide training
- CAPConnect Forum: Pediatric palliative care online forum

Hospice and Palliative Nurses Association: www.hpna.org

- Pediatric resources, education
- Pediatric online forum

The Joint Commission: http://www.jointcommission.org/certification/palliative_care.aspx

- Advance Certification in Hospice and Palliative Care (for hospital programs)

National Board for Certification of Hospice and Palliative Nurses: www. nbchpn.org

- Certification in Pediatric Hospice and Palliative Care Nursing

National Consensus Project: www.nationalconsensusproject.org

- *Clinical Practice Guidelines for Quality Palliative Care* (2013)

National Hospice and Palliative Care Organization: www.nhpco.org/pediatrics

- *Standards for Pediatric Palliative Care/Hospice* (2009)
- ChiPPS Pediatric Palliative Care E-Newsletter
- Online pediatric palliative care training modules
- *Concurrent Care for Children Implementation Toolkit* (2011)
- Pediatric State Leaders Forum

World Health Organization: www.who.int

- WHO Guidelines on the pharmacological treatment of persisting pain in children with medical illnesses (includes policymaker, physician/nurse and pharmacist highlights) (2012)

REFERENCES

American Academy of Pediatrics Committee on Bioethics and Committee on Hospital Care. (2000). Palliative care for children. *Pediatrics, 106,* 351-357.

Back, A. L., Bauer-Wu, S. M., Rushton, C. H., & Halifax, J. (2009). Compassionate silence in the patient-clinician encounter: A contemplative approach. *Journal of Palliative Medicine, 12*(12), 1113-1117.

Boss, R., Kavanaugh, K., & Kobler, K. (2011). Perinatal and neonatal palliative care. In J. Wolfe, P. S. Hinds, & B. M. Sourkes (Eds.), *Textbook of interdisciplinary pediatric palliative care* (pp. 387-401). Philadelphia, PA: Elsevier Saunders.

Carroll, J. M., Wright, J. L., & Frankel, L. R. (2011). Settings of care. In J. Wolfe, P. S. Hinds, & B. M. Sourkes (Eds.), *Textbook of interdisciplinary pediatric palliative care* (pp. 64-73). Philadelphia, PA: Elsevier Saunders.

Carter, B. S., Levetown, M., & Friebert, S. E. (2011). *Palliative care for infants, children, and adolescents: A practical handbook.* Baltimore, MD: The Johns Hopkins University Press.

Côté-Arsenault, D., & Denney-Koelsch, E. (2011). "My baby is a person": Parents' experiences with life-threatening fetal diagnosis. *Journal of Palliative Medicine, 14*(12), 1302-1308.

Davies, B., Sehring, S. A., Partridge, J. C., Cooper, B. A., Hughes, A., Philp, J. C., et al. (2008). Barriers to palliative care for children: Perceptions of pediatric health care providers. *Pediatrics, 121*(2), 282-288.

Davies, B., Contro, N., Larson, J., & Widger, K. (2010). Culturally-sensitive information sharing in pediatric palliative care. *Pediatrics, 125,* e859-e865.

Delisser, H. M. (2009). A practical approach to the family that expects a miracle. *Chest, 135*(6),1643-1647.

Dussel, V., Kriechbergs, U., Hilden, J. M., Watterson, J., Moore, C., Turner, B. G., et al. (2009). Looking beyond where children die: Determinants and effects of planning a child's location of death. *Journal of Pain and Symptom Management, 37*(1), 33-43.

Feudtner, C. (2007). Collaborative communication in pediatric palliative care: A foundation for problem-solving and decision making. *Pediatric Clinics of North America, 54,* 583-607.

Feudtner, C. et al. (2011). Pediatric palliative care patients: A prospective multicenter cohort study. *Pediatrics, 127,* 1094-1101.

Field, M. J., & Behrman R. E. (Eds.). (2003). Executive summary. In *When children die: Improving palliative and end-of-life care for children and their families.* Washington, DC: The National Academies Press. Retrieved from http://books.nap.edu/catalog.php?record_id=10845

Foster, T. L., Bell, C. J., & Gilmer, M. J. (2012). Symptom management of spiritual suffering in pediatric palliative care. *Journal of Hospice & Palliative Nursing, 14*(2), 109-115.

Friebert, S. (2009). NHPCO facts and figures: Pediatric palliative and hospice care in America. National Hospice and Palliative Care Organization. Retrieved from http://www.nhpco.org/files/public/quality/pediatric_facts-figures.pdf

Friebert, S., & Osenga, K. (2009). Pediatric palliative care referral criteria. *CAPC Clinical Tools.* Retrieved from http://www.capc.org/tools-for-palliative-care-programs/clinical-tools/consult-triggers/pediatric-palliative-care-referral-criteria.doc

Friedrichsdorf, S. J., & Kang, T. I. (2007). The management of pain in children with life-limiting illnesses. *Pediatric Clinics of North America, 54,* 645-672.

Gans, D., Kominski, G. F., Roby, D. H., Diamant, A. L., Chen, X., Lin, W., et al. (2012). Better outcomes, lower costs: Palliative care program reduces stress, costs of care for children with life-threatening conditions. *Health Policy Brief.* Los Angeles, CA: UCLA Center for Health Policy Research. Retrieved from http://www.healthpolicy.ucla.edu/NewsReleaseDetails.aspx?id=117

Gillis, J. (2009). "We want everything done." *Archives of Diseases in Childhood, 93*(3), 192-193.

Haward, M. F., John, L. K., Lorenz, J. M., & Fischhoff, B. (2012). Effects of description of options on parental perinatal decision-making. *Pediatrics, 129,* 891-902.

Heller, K. S., & Solomon, M. Z. for the IPPC Investigator Team. (2005). Continuity of care and caring: What matters to parents of children with life-threatening conditions. *Journal of Pediatric Nursing, 20*(5), 335-334.

Hexem, K. R., Miller, V. A., Carroll, B. S., Faerber, J. A., & Feudtner, C. (2012). Putting on a happy face: Emotional expression in parents of children with serious illness. *Journal of Pain & Symptom Management, in press,* 1-10. Retrieved from http://www.sciencedirect.com.proxy.cc.uic.edu/science/article/pii/S0885392412002941

Hurwitz, C. A., Duncan, J., & Wolfe, J. (2004). Caring for the child with cancer at the close of life: "There are people who make it, and I'm hoping I'm one of them." *Journal of the American Medical Association, 292*(17), 2141-2149.

Kearney, M. K., Weininger, R. B., Vachon, M. L., Harrison, R. L., & Mount, B. M. (2009). Self-care of physicians caring for patients at the end of life "Being connected . . . a key to my survival." *Journal of the American Medical Association, 301*(1), 1155-1164.

Keene-Reder, E. A., & Serwint, J. R. (2009). Until the last breath: Exploring the concept of hope for parents and health care professionals during a child's serious illness. *Pediatric and Adolescent Medicine, 163*(7), 633-657.

Knapp, C. et al. (2011). Pediatric palliative care provision around the world: A systematic review. *Pediatric Blood Cancer, 57,* 361-368.

Kobler, K., & Limbo, R. (2011). Making a case: Creating a perinatal palliative care service using a perinatal bereavement program model. *Jawa Pos National Network, 25*(1), 1-10.

Kobler, K., Limbo, R., & Kavanaugh, K. (2007). Meaningful moments: The use of ritual in perinatal and pediatric death. *MCN: The American Journal of Maternal Child Nursing, 32*(5), 288-297.

Kochanek, K. D., Xu, J., Murphy, S. L., Miniño, A. M., & Kung, H. (2011). Deaths: Final data for 2009. *National Vital Statistic Reports, 60*(3). Retrieved from http://www.cdc.gov/nchs/data/nvsr/nvsr60/nvsr60_03.pdf

Liben, S., Papadatou, D., & Wolfe, J. (2008). Paediatric palliative care: Challenges and emerging ideas. *Lancet, 371,* 852-864.

Limbo, R., & Kobler, K. (2010). The ties that bind: Relationship in perinatal bereavement. *MCN: The American Journal of Maternal Child Nursing, 35*(6), 316-321.

Limbo, R., & Kobler, K. (2013). Meaningful moments: Ritual and reflection when a child dies. La Crosse, WI: Gundersen Medical Foundation, Inc.

Mack, J. W., & Wolfe, J. (2004). Early integration of pediatric palliative care: For some children, palliative care starts at diagnosis. *Current Opinions in Pediatrics, 18,* 10-14.

Macdonald, M. E., Liben, S., Carnevale, F. A., Rennick, J. E., Wolf, S. L., Meloche, D., et al. (2005). Parental perspectives on hospital staff members' acts of kindness and commemoration after a child's death. *Pediatrics, 116*(4), 884-890.

MacDorman, M. F., Kirmeyer, S. E., & Wilson, E. C. (2012). Fetal & perinatal mortality, United States, 2006. *National Vital Statistics Reports, 60*(8). Retrieved from http://www.cdc.gov/nchs/data/nvsr/nvsr60/nvsr60_08.pdf

Mazanec, P., & Panke, J. T. (2006). Cultural considerations in end-of-life care. *AJN: The American Journal of Nursing, 103*(3), 50-58.

Meert, K. L., Thurston, C. S., & Briller, S. H. (2005). The spiritual needs of parents at the time of their child's death in the pediatric intensive care unit and during bereavement: A qualitative study. *Pediatric Critical Care Medicine, 6*(4), 420-427.

Miller, E. G., LaRagione, G., Kang, T. I., & Feudtner, C. (2012). Concurrent care for the medically complex child: Lessons of implementation. *Journal of Palliative Medicine,* online ahead of print. Retrieved from http://online.liebertpub.com/doi/pdfplus/10.1089/jpm.2011.0346

Milstein, J. (2005). A paradigm of integrative care: Healing with curing throughout life, "being with" and "doing to." *Journal of Perinatology, 25,* 563-568.

Munson, D., & Leuthner, S. R. (2007). Palliative care for the family carrying a fetus with a life-limiting diagnosis. *Pediatric Clinics of North America, 54,* 787-798.

National Hospice and Palliative Care Organization. (2011). *Concurrent care for children implementation toolkit.* Alexandria, VA: NHPCO. Retrieved from http://www.nhpco.org/i4a/pages/index.cfm?pageid=3689

Papadatou, D. (2009). *In the face of death: Professionals who care for the dying and the bereaved.* New York, NY: Springer.

Rosenblatt, P. C. (2009). The culturally competent practitioner. In K. J. Doka & A. S. Tucci (Eds.), *Diversity and end-of-life care*. Washington, DC: Hospice Foundation of America.

Rushton, C. (2011). Transforming moral distress in pediatric palliative care. In C. A. Corr, C. Torkildson, & M. Horgan (Eds.), *ChiPPS Pediatric Palliative Care Newsletter*, Issue 24. Retrieved from www.nhpco.org/pediatrics

Rushton, C. H., Reder, E., Hall, B., Comello, K., Sellers, D. E., & Hutton, N. (2006). Interdisciplinary interventions to improve pediatric palliative care and reduce health care professional suffering. *Journal of Palliative Medicine, 9*(4), 922-933.

Sumner, L. H., Kavanaugh, K., & Moro, T. (2006). Extending palliative care into pregnancy and the immediate newborn period: State of the practice of perinatal palliative care. *Journal of Perinatal and Neonatal Nursing, 20,* 113-116.

Tamburro, R. F., Shaffer, M. L., Hahnlen, N. C., Felker, P., & Ceneviva, G. D. (2011). Care goals and decisions for children referred to a pediatric palliative care program. *Journal of Palliative Medicine, 14*(5), 1-7.

Thompson, L. A., Knapp, C., Madden, V., & Shenkman, E. (2009). Pediatrician's perceptions of and preferred timing for pediatric palliative care. *Pediatrics, 123,* e777-e782.

van Breeman, C. (2009). Using play therapy in paediatric palliative care: Listening to the story and caring for the body. *International Journal of Palliative Nursing, 15*(10), 510-514.

Vollenbroich, R., Duroux, A., Grasser, M., Brandstatter, M., Borasio, G. D., & Fuhrer, M. (2012). Effectiveness of a pediatric palliative home care team as experienced by parents and health care professionals. *Journal of Palliative Medicine, 15*(3), 294-300.

Widger, K., Steele, R., Oberle, K., & Davies, B. (2009). Exploring the supportive care model as a framework for pediatric palliative care. *Journal of Hospice and Palliative Nursing, 11*(4), 209-216.

Wolfe, J., Hinds, P. S., & Sourkes, B. M. (2011). *Textbook of interdisciplinary pediatric palliative care*. Philadelphia, PA: Elsevier Saunders.

World Health Organization. (2012). WHO guidelines on the pharmacological treatment of persisting pain in children with medical illness. Geneva, Switzerland: WHO Press. Retrieved from http://whqlibdoc.who.int/publications/2012/9789241548120_Guidelines.pdf

http://dx.doi.org/10.2190/FATC5

CHAPTER 5

Meeting the Stress Challenge

Neil Thompson and Denise Bevan

INTRODUCTION

Stress is a topic that has received considerable attention in recent years, in large part due to the major changes that have taken in place in the modern workplace. The emphasis on downsizing, "flat" structures, the move toward fewer permanent posts, and more short-term contracts has made the world of work a much more insecure one. The tendency for technology to replace many work roles (and thus jobs) has been part of this, as have changes in philosophical approaches to work, such as business process reengineering in the private sector (Micklethwait & Wooldridge, 1997; Stewart, 2009) and managerialism in the public sector (Thompson, 2009a). The combination of these factors has produced the potential for much higher levels of workplace stress than was previously the case.

These factors are known as "extrinsic" factors, that is, they are not necessary features of the workplace; they exist as a result of historical development. They have arisen over time, and they can be changed over time. However, we should not neglect the significance of the other side of the coin, the "intrinsic" factors, that is, those aspects of the work that are part and parcel of the work itself: inevitable pressures of the particular job, setting, or type of work. For example, the risk of violence and the pressures associated with that constant risk are intrinsic to frontline police work. Providing palliative care brings with it certain intrinsic pressures (or stressors, to use the technical term). And of course, no palliative care setting will be free of its share of extrinsic pressures too.

This chapter therefore explores some of the key issues in relation to stress in end-of-life care. It begins with a discussion of why it is important to draw a distinction between pressure and stress. It then moves on to identify some common causes of stress, and this leads into a discussion of the impact of stress, the very damaging consequences that can arise if we are not able to avoid stress. Before bringing the chapter to a conclusion, we focus on the significance of stress, specifically within palliative care contexts, and use this as an opportunity to identify some important strategies for rising to the challenges involved.

PRESSURE AND STRESS

Many people use the words "pressure" and "stress" interchangeably. However, in the United Kingdom, the Health and Safety Executive (a statutory body with responsibility for regulating workplaces in relation to health and safety; www.hse.gov.uk) defines stress as "The adverse reaction people have to excessive pressures or other types of demand placed on them at work" (http://www.hse.gov.uk/stress/furtheradvice/whatisstress.htm). This builds on the earlier work of Arroba and James (1992), who argued that pressure can be understood to be either positive or negative: positive when it is rewarding, stimulating, motivating and energizing; and negative when it reaches levels that are harmful to the person concerned. The term "stress" is then reserved for the latter type of pressure: the pressure that causes harm (to health, well-being, relationships, quality of work, and so on).

This is a useful distinction, as it helps us to avoid confusion over such misleading ideas as "Stress is good for you." Sadly, we have come across many managers who have dismissed staff concerns about (harmful) stress by simply stating that stress is good for them, as if to suggest that stress is not something to be concerned about. Given the extreme harm that stress can do (see below), it is important that such a dismissive approach is challenged whenever it arises.

Pressure is something we should expect to encounter, and we should not see it as a problem in itself. Indeed, pressure (in manageable amounts) can bring great pleasure and satisfaction and can be an important part of who we are (e.g., in terms of our achievements and the pride we take from having dealt with the pressures involved). However, when it crosses that line and becomes stress (i.e., it starts to harm us in one or more ways), then we clearly have a problem that needs our attention.

One obstacle to dealing with such problems is a stoic or "macho" approach, which expects us to be able to cope with whatever pressures come our way, however excessive they may be. Sadly, this mentality is not uncommon, even in the caring profession, and can do a great deal of harm. In particular, it has a tendency to represent anyone who is experiencing stress as weak or inadequate, not "tough" enough to withstand the pressures. For this reason, such an approach can be described as a "pathologizing" one, in the sense that stress is assumed to arise from personal inadequacy or pathology. This is a form of "reductionism"— complex, multilevel phenomena are presented as if they were simple, single-level phenomena (Sibeon, 2004).

One very practical (and highly destructive) consequence of this reductionism is that it increases the chances of people who need support deciding not to seek any. In effect, asking for help becomes stigmatized (and thus discouraged) by this misguided stoicism. If asking for help equates to admitting one's own inadequacy, then it is going to take a lot of courage on an individual's part to admit that they need support. The fact that they are stressed is likely to make them less confident and thus to have less courage, and so they can easily become trapped in a situation characterized by harmful levels of pressure combined with a sense of feeling trapped, feeling that there is no way out without admitting to being a failure, and thus a problem for their colleagues.

From an organizational perspective, this is also bad news, in the sense that staff who could be relatively easily helped in the early stages of their problems developing may not only decide not to seek help, but may also actively conceal any possible signs that they are becoming stressed. By the time it becomes apparent that there is a problem, considerable damage may have been done, and efforts to rectify the situation may have to be much more extensive.

Recognizing that pressure can be positive much of the time, but also negative at times, resulting in harmful stress, is an important basis for acknowledging that stress is a very real danger in the modern workplace. Raising awareness of the fact that stress is a complex, multilevel phenomenon and not simply the sign of a weak individual is an important step forward (Thompson, 2009b).

THE CAUSES OF STRESS

In recognizing that stress is a multidimensional phenomenon, we also need to be aware that there are multiple causes (or contributory factors) that we need to take into consideration. These include (lack of) control; expectations; and our own response to the situation we find ourselves in. We shall consider each of these in turn.

Control

Having a sense of control can prevent pressure from overspilling into stress. This is recognized in the Health and Safety Executive (HSE) management standards, a set of guidelines that were developed to help organizations protect their employees from stress:

- *Demands*—this includes issues such as workload, work patterns and the work environment.
- *Control*—how much say the person has in the way they do their work.
- *Support*—this includes the encouragement, sponsorship and resources provided by the organisation, line management and colleagues.
- *Relationships*—this includes promoting positive working to avoid conflict and dealing with unacceptable behaviour.
- *Role*—whether people understand their role within the organisation and whether the organisation ensures that they do not have conflicting roles.

• *Change*—how organisational change (large or small) is managed and communicated in the organisation. (http://www.hse.gov.uk/stress/standards/index.htm)

Having a degree of control is likely to make pressures feel more manageable and therefore help to keep stress at bay. However, when people feel they have little or no control, they are likely to be more prone to stress as a result of the sense of helplessness a lack of control engenders.

Expectations

Expectations can be significant in the development of stress in at least three main ways:

• **Unrealistic expectations:** Individuals or even whole groups of staff feel that they cannot cope with the demands being made of them, likely resulting in stress. A common example of this is an excessive workload wherein employers expect too much of one or more employees. However, it is also important to recognize that individuals can create for themselves unrealistic expectations. For example, someone who expects to have a 100% success rate in their work may become quite stressed when they fail in some regard, even though a degree of failure is to be expected in any job or work setting.

• **Unclear expectations:** Not being clear what is expected of us can create additional tensions, and these in turn can lead to stress. For example, employers who are too vague in conveying what they expect of an employee can contribute to this problem. Alternatively, someone who is new in their role and has yet to grasp fully what is involved in it can experience a degree of stress. In addition, at times of significant change (for individuals and for staff groups or even whole organizations), the lack of clarity about what is expected in the new setup can generate additional pressures.

• **Conflicting expectations:** Tensions can arise because of conflicts relating to expectations. This can arise in a number of ways, not least the following: (a) conflict between what two managers seem to require of the staff; (b) conflict between what a manager seems to be expecting and what the formal policy seems to expect; (c) conflict between official expectations (through a manager, the written policy, or both) and what is expected within the culture of the team, staff group, division, or organization; (d) conflict between what the organization expects and what patients and their caregivers expect; (e) conflict between the expectations of patients and those of their caregivers; and (f) conflicts between what an organization expects and the professional values of people working within that organization. This is not an exhaustive list, but its length is indicative of just how easy it is for such conflicting expectations to arise, adding extra pressures to other aspects of the work.

It should be clear, then, that the topic of expectations is one that is worth exploring if we are to be serious about preventing stress and tackling it effectively when it does arise.

Our Own Response

There is a subjective dimension to stress, in the sense that it is not simply a matter of objective levels of pressure. How we respond to those pressures can be highly significant. This can apply in a variety of ways, but one important factor is confidence. There will, of course, be differences in levels of confidence across groups of staff and therefore differences in how confidently they deal with the pressures they face. There will also be differences in response according to preferred coping styles. For example, many people prefer active coping strategies (looking for solutions to problems, exploring strategies for reducing pressures and their impact, and so on), while others feel more comfortable with passive coping approaches (adapting to the situation, rather than trying to change it). Such methods would include listening to music, going for a walk, talking things over with friends—activities that do not change the pressures but can help us feel stronger in dealing with them. There is evidence to suggest that there are gender differences in terms of preferred coping styles, with men on average feeling more comfortable with active coping, while women tend to feel more comfortable with passive coping. For example, the work of Doka and Martin (2011) in relation to how men and women cope with loss raises awareness of the significance of gender in shaping people's reactions to trying circumstances.

It is important to note that including our own subjective response to pressure as a key factor in stress should not be equated with an assumption that people are responsible for their own stress. This tendency to "blame the victim" by pathologizing people who experience stress is a dangerous one, as it discourages people who need support from seeking it (for fear of being labeled as weak, inadequate, or a "poor coper"). It is an oversimplification of a complex set of issues. Stress needs to be understood as multidimensional and multifactorial (Thompson, 2009b). Our subjective response is one of those factors and therefore needs to be considered, but it would be a mistake to see it as the only one or even as the main one.

These, then, are three important sets of factors that can play a very significant role in the transformation of (manageable) pressure into (unmanageable) stress. However, we should also note that they are certainly not the only ones. Bullying and harassment are also significant sources of stress (Tehrani, 2004); as are loss, grief, and trauma (Thompson, 2009c); being exposed to aggression and/or violence (Balloch, Pahl, & McLean, 1997); conflict and/or organizational politics (Vigoda, 2003); and prolonged exposure to raw emotion (Papadatou, 2009) (we shall return to this final example below, as it is, of course, very relevant to end-of-life care situations). Our overall point should therefore be clear: there are very many ways in which pressure can be increased to the point at which it becomes harmful stress.

THE IMPACT OF STRESS

As we have already noted, stress arises when pressures reach levels wherein they are doing us harm in some way. In this section, we explore some of the ways in which harm can arise. We begin with the one that has received the most attention in the literature: health.

Stress is not an illness, but it can have a major detrimental effect on health. This applies in two ways. It can exacerbate existing health problems (asthma, heart disease, etc.) and can also lead to health concerns in their own right (headaches, gastric disturbances). Stress can also contribute to health issues indirectly, for example, by adversely affecting sleep patterns, diet, exercise, and other factors that can influence our health.

Stress can also affect our mental health or well-being. Stress tends to increase tensions and this can lead to anxiety-related problems, especially for people who tend to have a high level of anxiety to begin with. For some people, stress can result in depression. Feelings of hopelessness and helplessness can result in forms of depression ranging from mild to severe.

Other adverse consequences of stress include strain on relationships (people can take their work pressures home, resulting perhaps in a tense home life and thus additional pressures on family relationships and/or relationships with friends); lower confidence, quite possibly leading to a lower level of assertiveness; lower levels of concentration; reductions in quality and quantity of work (e.g., through a higher error rate); lower levels of learning; less creativity; and less job satisfaction. Clearly, then, stress can be detrimental not only to health but also to well-being more broadly—to our quality of life.

There are two aspects of the impact of stress that we feel are worth high-lighting, namely, the dangers of vicious circles developing and burnout. Sadly, vicious circles are not uncommon in circumstances involving stress. Imagine the following process developing:

> A combination of home and work pressures produces an unmanageable situation, and stress is experienced. Because the person concerned is stressed, the quality and quantity of their work go down (due to poor concentration, lower motivation, and a higher error rate). This results in further demands being made on them (e.g., rectifying mistakes and/or dealing with complaints), while they are less well equipped than usual to deal with these demands. They are not learning and are feeling stuck in tramlines because they do not feel energized enough to be creative or to explore different options. Job satisfaction goes down or disappears altogether. Perhaps tensions with colleagues or other key people emerge as a result of the negative feelings generated by the stressful circumstances. This then produces more pressure.

Other people sensing the tensions may back off because they feel uncomfortable, and so they become less communicative and less supportive. It may reach the stage where the person concerned takes sick leave because of the stress. This can then place additional pressures on the colleagues who remain while also making the person who is absent from work feel guilty and even ashamed for "letting the side down." In some circumstances, there can be a "domino effect" whereby the absence of one member of a team can place so much pressure on remaining staff that one or more of them also take sick leave. The pressures may get so great that some people start seeking alternative employment—and it is not unheard of, in extreme situations, for some people to resign their job even if they do not have another one to go to.

What tends to happen when such a destructive dynamic occurs is that pressures increase, while coping abilities and support decrease, producing a potentially very dangerous situation. It is therefore important to have a good awareness of the significance of vicious circles so that we can make all reasonable efforts to avoid them.

Burnout is also a highly significant phenomenon that we need to be aware of. Many people assume that burnout is a form of stress, whereas, in reality, it is a *response* to stress. Burnout can be understood as an extreme form of passive coping, a way of adapting to excessive pressures that is actually counterproductive, but the person concerned becomes locked into what have now become their characteristic responses to pressure.

Burnout is characterized by three main features:

- **Emotional exhaustion:** This refers to circumstances in which people become emotionally numb; it is as if they are protecting themselves from potentially painful or demanding experiences by not engaging at an emotional level. This tends to produce highly routinized approaches to work, a mechanical approach to just getting the work done without putting any heart into it. Burnt-out individuals therefore come across as unmotivated. They are likely to engage in minimalism, that is, to do just the bare minimum to get the job done, with no commitment whatsoever to doing the best they can.
- **Lack of individual achievement:** Burnt-out individuals are likely to be functioning at a level of competence far below their best. This can lead to a vicious circle in which lower levels of performance produce inferior outcomes and a reduced (or nonexistent) level of job satisfaction, which can then add to the sense of low achievement and fuel a sense of hopelessness and helplessness.
- **Depersonalization:** Someone who is burnt out is likely to relate to people in superficial ways, with no real human connection; clearly not acceptable in an end-of-life care context (see Maslach & Leiter, 1997).

These elements can also combine to produce negativity, defeatism, and cynicism. In extreme cases, burnout can become a team phenomenon in which morale is so low that little positive work is being done, and the team culture has come to be characterized by defensiveness and just mechanically getting the work done.

STRESS IN PALLIATIVE CARE

Working constantly with death, dying, and bereavement can be emotionally challenging and yet rewarding for those in a position to be able to care and to support people and their loved ones at the end of their lives. To bear witness to, and be with, the sorrow and distress of others demands that caregivers be emotionally and psychologically resilient.

Learning to be fully present for people facing death and to be able to tolerate life's uncertainty and the unknown is rooted in our own ability to be at ease with death, loss, and grief (Halifax, 2006). To be able to soothe the fear, stress, shame, and grief of those who are dying, practitioners need to be aware of their own death and loss history (Worden & Proctor, 1976). Attunement with our own losses—being aware of the way we respond to, and continue to live with, those losses—enables us to be aware of the need to manage our own processes while also attending to the suffering and grief of others.

Papadatou (2009) proposes that those working in palliative care are involved in their own existential journey, seeking to make sense of their own lived experience of life and death. In order to provide effective care that is sensitive and truly open to the pain of others, it is vital for the caregiver to attend to their own fears of death and dying.

There is little doubt that the intensity and complexity of palliative care work can have far-reaching effects on staff, both positive and negative. The opportunity to help another to prepare for their dying and death and then go on to support their loved ones in their grief can bring a sense of achievement and peace for professionals. As Papadatou (2009) acknowledges, the lessons we learn from being with those who are dying "opens up possibilities and offers new choices an incredible freedom to live differently" (p. 186).

The personal task of accommodating awareness of death and dying is an ongoing existential challenge. However, there are other challenges less in our control. The changing nature of care and advancements in treatments available for people who are living with advanced and progressive illnesses have resulted in a situation in which the goals of palliative care provision have become more medicalized. This means that services and practitioners have also had to adapt to these changes and will need to be prepared for ongoing future changes (Tookman, 2007). These significant developments in life-sustaining treatments have led to a need to maintain a watchful eye on the extent to which these approaches are consistent with the founding philosophy and practices that have promoted humanistic medicine in palliative care services since the work of Dame Cicely Saunders (Saunders, 2002). It will be important to ensure that such holistic care remains at the heart of what we do and that the changing demographics of people living with palliative care needs do not result in it being wholly lost. These changes are a challenge to the identity of those who work in this area, and Larkin (2011) asks whether this could be a factor contributing to the experience of stress and compassion fatigue for palliative care workers. Indeed, research suggests that it is not the intimate contact with the stories and sadness of dying, death, and bereavement that creates stress for the worker; rather, it is the organizational aspects of the work (Vachon, 1995).

Recent years have seen a worldwide recession that has inevitably affected both statutory and charitable sectors providing end-of-life care. Concerns about funding have meant that organizations are charged with measuring their worth in creating new working practices to provide evidence to commissioners of their value. A growing culture of managerialism in hospice and palliative care services may well be increasing staff anxiety and stress as they deal with the transition from the traditional values and philosophy of hospice and palliative care to more commercial values (and the disparity between the two sets of values).

Given the context of the changing nature of what palliative care means and the organizational pressures, the need for staff care is all the greater. Organizations can do much to safeguard staff by providing robust systems for staff support and supervision and by fostering a culture in which self-care is inherent in its ethos. Self-care recognizes that the use of empathy in helping others is essential, yet also a risk to the well-being of professionals who are exposed to working with trauma. Rothschild (2006), in her exploration of self-care strategies, argues that "the better we take care of ourselves and maintain a professional separation from our clients, the more we will be in a position to be truly empathic, compassionate, and useful to them" (p. 1). She argues that many practitioners are unaware of how they are being affected by their exposure to others' distress and the possibility of developing compassion fatigue, burnout, and vicarious trauma. Engaging with the emotions of dying people while developing intense therapeutic relationships can be emotionally exhausting (Hennezel, 1997). Ferro's (1999) study of oncology nurses found that these nurses experienced stress and emotional exhaustion because of the emotional work incurred during their interactions with patients and relatives. Similarly, Parkes (1985) also found significant levels of stress in nurses caring for dying people.

Given the evidence that there is a significant risk of palliative care workers experiencing grief, stress, or compassion fatigue, it is important to have an ongoing program of self-care to manage the cumulative effects of working with people who are dying and bereaved. Papatadou (2000) points out that to be an effective and compassionate worker coping with ongoing loss, professionals have to carefully balance their emotional responses between containing their grief (so that they can continue to function) and having the opportunity to experience grief. Similarly, Renzenbrink (2004) calls for professionals to be "relentless in self-care" and argues that the professional needs to continually practice caring for themselves and be committed to ongoing self-care and reflection (S. Thompson, 2012).

RESPONDING TO THE CHALLENGE

Stress, as we have seen, is a complex matter, and so it would be dangerous to attempt to come up with simple solutions (although there is a whole industry that has very strong tendencies in that direction). Any realistic strategy for responding to the challenge of stress therefore needs to be carefully thought out. It needs to be based on a sophisticated understanding of the issues involved. We would argue that it needs to be multidimensional, incorporating personal, organizational and social elements and their interaction (Thompson, 2011).

We would also contend that the precise context in which stress arises needs to be taken into consideration, as particular work environments will generate particular stressors. This is especially the case in relation to end-of-life care in which there will be specific demands, such as prolonged intensity of emotion, constant reminders of our own mortality, and the ever-present possibility of our own grief-related "wounds" opening up (N. Thompson, 2012), in addition to the range of demands that any workplace will evoke (and the home-based pressures that can be so difficult for us to leave behind when we enter the workplace).

CONCLUSION

Stress can be harmful in any context, given its potentially destructive consequences in terms of health, relationships, quality and quantity of work, job satisfaction, career development and learning, and other aspects of quality of life. However, in the emotionally demanding context of end-of-life care, the harm done can be of major proportions. There is therefore much to be gained from taking seriously the challenges involved in preventing, and responding constructively to, stress. It is to be hoped that this chapter has made a contribution to highlighting the need for a well-informed approach to stress that avoids the oversimplifications that have sadly come to characterize this aspect of working life.

REFERENCES

Arroba, T., & James, K. (1992). *Pressure at work: A survival guide for managers* (2nd ed.). London: McGraw-Hill.

Balloch, S., Pahl, J., & McLean, J. (1997). Working in the social services: Job satisfaction, stress and violence. *British Journal of Social Work, 28*(3), pp. 329-350.

Doka, K., & Martin, T. (2010). *Grieving beyond gender: Understanding the ways men and women mourn* (2nd ed.). London: Routledge.

Ferro, N. (1999). Evaluation of burnout in oncology nurses [Poster]. Hamburg, Germany: IPOS Congress.

Halifax, J. (2006). *Being with dying: Cultivating compassion and fearlessness in the presence of death.* Boston, MA: Shambhala.

Hennezel, M. (1997). *Intimate death: How the dying teach us how to live.* New York, NY: Knopf.

Larkin, P. (2011). Compassion: The essence of end-of-life care. In I. Renzenbrink (Ed.), *Caregiver stress and staff support in illness, dying, and bereavement*. Oxford: Oxford University Press.

Maslach, C., & Leiter, M. P. (1997). *The truth about burnout*. San Francisco, CA: Jossey-Bass.

Micklethwait, J., & Wooldridge, A. (1997). *The witch doctors: What the management gurus are saying, why it matters and how to make sense of it*. London: Mandarin.

Papadatou, D. (2000). A proposed model of health professionals "grieving process." *Omega: Journal of Death and Dying, 41*, 59-77.

Papadatou, D. (2009). *In the face of death: Professionals who care for the dying and the bereaved*. New York, NY: Springer.

Parkes, K. R. (1985). Stressful episodes reported by first-year student nurses: A descriptive account. *Social Science and Medicine, 20*(9), 945-953.

Renzenbrink, I. (2004). Relentless self-care. In E. P. Silverman & J. Berzoff (Eds.), *Living with dying: A handbook for health practitioners in end of life care*. New York, NY: Columbia University Press.

Rothschild, B. (2006). *Help for the helper: Self-care strategies for managing burnout and stress*. London: Norton.

Saunders, C. (2002). The philosophy of hospice. In N. Thompson (Ed.), *Loss and grief: A guide for human services practitioners*. Basingstoke: Palgrave Macmillan.

Sibeon, R. (2004). *Rethinking social theory*. London: Sage.

Stewart, M. (2009). *The management myth: Why the "experts" keep getting it wrong*. New York, NY: Norton & Co.

Tehrani, N. (2004). Bullying: A source of chronic post traumatic stress? *British Journal of Guidance and Counselling, 32*(3), 357-366.

Thompson, N. (2009a). *Practising social work: Meeting the professional challenge*. Basingstoke: Palgrave Macmillan.

Thompson, N. (2009b). Stress. In N. Thompson & J. Bates (Eds.), *Promoting workplace well-being*. Basingstoke: Palgrave Macmillan.

Thompson, N. (2009c). *Loss, grief and trauma in the workplace*. Amityville, NY: Baywood.

Thompson, N. (2011). Workplace Well-being: A Psychosocial Perspective. In I. Renzenbrink (Ed.), *Caregiver stress and staff support in illness, dying, and bereavement*. Oxford: Oxford University Press.

Thompson, N. (2012). *Grief and its challenges*. Basingstoke: Palgrave Macmillan.

Thompson, S. (2012). *Don't be your own worst enemy: Self-care for busy people* [e-book]. Available from Avenue Media Solutions: www.avenuemediasolutions.com

Tookman, A. (2007). Resilience and rehabilitation. In B. Monroe & D. Oliviere (Eds.), *Resilience in palliative care: Achievement in adversity*. Oxford: Oxford University Press.

Vachon, M. L. S. (1995). Staff stress in hospice/palliative care: A review. *Palliative Medicine, 9*, 91-122.

Vigoda, E. (2003). *Developments in organizational politics: How political dynamics affect employee performance in modern work sites*. Northampton, MA: Edward Elgar.

Worden, W., & Proctor, B. (1976). *Personal death awareness*. New York, NY: Prentice-Hall.

http://dx.doi.org/10.2190/FATC6

CHAPTER 6

When Birth and Death Collide: Best Practices in End-of-Life at the Beginning

Lori Ives-Baine, Jessica Faust, Jessica Drewry, Jatinder Kalra, Michael Marshall, Roop Johal, Alyson Mayne

Birth is traditionally thought of as a wonderful experience, filled with new hope, love, and short-term pain for long-term gain. In the world of the Neonatal Intensive Care Unit (NICU), this perfect birth story changes, because of a life-limiting or life-changing diagnosis that may lead to death as the final outcome. Our Neonatal Intensive Care Unit has been in existence for more than 50 years (1961) when a brave neonatologist (Dr. Paul Swyer, http://www. paeds.utoronto.ca/division/neon.htm) began the daunting work of developing and trialing ventilation with tiny newborns who were unable to breathe effectively due to their prematurity, birth trauma, or other medical and surgical conditions. In fact, our hospital (The Hospital for Sick Children, later called SickKids) is considered the birthplace of Neonatology in North America, a distinction that we are very proud of. Many of the babies cared for with this early technology died despite medical treatment, as technology was very primitive, but there were some survivors of these new technologies in those early years. As technology improved and our understanding of the clinical issues and treatments improved, so did our mortality rate. Currently, the mortality rate in this NICU is approximately 8/100 admissions, but this does not include the infants who died while in the care of our ACTS Transport Team or those who died after transition home for palliation (Simpson, Xiang, Hellmann, & Tomlinson, 2010).

With improvements in the technology to care for newborns, family involvement in that care and a reminder of the limits of medical intervention has emerged. A formal approach to helping families through end-of-life (EOL) care started in 1988, when a group of nurses began to meet to better help the families they were caring for. While palliative and bereavement care in the newborn population was

77

still a very new concept, these nurses recognized that each of them was doing what they "thought was best," but they felt that there was little consistency in what was offered families when a baby was dying or after he or she had died. As a result, our Clinical Nurse Specialist at the time, completed some of the first research into what families found helpful at the time of their baby's death. She identified in her work that families wanted options, including legacy creation, and they wanted support and guidance after their baby's death. As a result, the position of Bereavement Coordinator for the Neonatology program became a new role to this NICU. That initial work was 25 years ago!

The position of Clinical Nurse Specialist began in 1988 as a 1-day-a-week nursing role and has expanded to its current mandate, a full-time position with a resource team that is now interprofessional in composition. The role was intended to provide an initial follow-up with bereaved families, by telephone or letter, to ensure that any legacy creation was provided to the family and to send an anniversary card to them. The position was valued by families, and there were often voicemail messages left by parents when they received their communications or had questions. In 1999, the component of palliative care was added as a formal part of the role. The expansion of the Neonatology Program Palliative Care and Bereavement (NPCB) Coordinator's role led to a more formalized process in the program and created a role from which all staff could receive support, education, and mentoring. The present NPCB Coordinator has RTS Coordinator training and uses this model (Daley & Limbo, 2008) to support best practice. The role is supported by private donations and hospital funding to allow for full-time work in anticipatory grief guidance, family support, staff support, education (both internally and externally), and research. The current position is filled by a nurse who has been in the role for 18 years and who obtained her master's in Nursing with a pediatric and ethics focus to support this expanded position.

This role works closely with the interdisciplinary team, colleagues in the hospital's Palliative and Bereavement Care Service, and members of the NICU End-Of-Life (EOL) Resource Team, which was formed just over 2 years ago to increase knowledge and understanding for those interested in supporting optimal EOL care for families and healthcare providers on the NICU. The team is currently composed of nurses (in-charge nurse, transport, and bedside capacities), social workers, chaplaincy, a physician representative, and a respiratory therapist. Members of the NICU EOL Resource Team were drawn from those who expressed interest in helping families and their colleagues through the difficult experiences of care for a dying infant and family. Many of the team members are RTS Support trained (Daley & Limbo, 2008) and have been involved in the care of babies and families in this journey. When on shift, they may be assigned in the room to support their colleague who is caring for the baby or may be the primary caregiver to that baby. If not in the room, they are available to provide additional expertise to their colleagues and to families by lending support in legacy creation and advocating for appropriate pain and symptom management. Additional resources for families are available through the NPCB Coordinator's office, and these team members are able to access them.

As well, this group has been active in developing EOL guidelines that support the baby, parents, and all healthcare professionals (further information to follow). The group has been involved in the education of their colleagues, at various NICU Education Days, and in participating in the creation and dissemination of research on the experiences of nurses caring for dying infants on the NICU (Ives-Baine, 2011; Ives-Baine, Hannon, & Saini, 2011; Lindsay, Cross, & Ives-Baine, 2012).

While we have an expert group of clinicians to support best practice, it is important to acknowledge that much of the planning and facilitation of optimal EOL care is managed by the baby's nurse. She/he has to orchestrate final medical procedures; legacy building; meetings; rituals like baptism, naming ceremonies, blessings of the families; mobilization of the critically ill infant to a private room if possible; and negotiating the timing of all EOL care with the family and medical team. These tasks continue to grow as options for families are enhanced, including opportunities for families to go home for compassionate extubation (removal of the breathing tube), to be able to take their dying infant for a walk before death, and to facilitate enhanced social-media-based communication with extended family across the world (Pugh & Ives-Baine, 2012). The nurses will access the NPCB Coordinator when available, but the rest of the team also facilitates these many tasks.

The social workers in the NICU at the Hospital for Sick Children strive to meet each family upon a baby's admission to the unit. Social workers are responsible for orienting the family to the unit in terms of resources available as well as providing adjustment and supportive counseling. They are present throughout the different discussions and stages of treatment to support families. The relationship between the social worker and the family is usually well established prior to the medical recommendation to explore palliative/EOL care as alternate pathways other than aggressive treatment. Thus, given the strength of the relationship between the social worker and the family, social workers play an integral role in supporting parents as they navigate from an aggressive treatment EOL care. Support is typically provided through adjustment counseling as well as being present in medical discussions to advocate for the family's unique beliefs, values, and needs. Professional consultation with the interdisciplinary team (i.e., bedside nurses, clinical-support nurses, NPCB Coordinator, staff physician, occupational therapist, etc.) is also integral to successfully supporting a family in end-of-life care for their baby. Should the family choose or need to embark on a palliative pathway, and the baby dies, social workers will continue to support parents by providing counseling support immediately after the loss and resource information (e.g., funeral planning).

Our NICU has many respiratory therapists (RTs) who are an integral part of our team. They manage the respiratory (breathing) part of the patient's stay, which is often the main reason newborns are admitted to our unit. The role of the respiratory therapist in end-of-life care in the NICU is often undervalued. In many situations, RTs are expected to assist with transfer of dying babies to a private space to allow for final extubation when the family is ready. The RT may be the clinician completing the task of final extubation, with the knowledge that death might happen in hours or days after this action. These tasks are all happening while the rest of the unit is still very busy with the continuing changes to patient conditions. Unlike a nurse, an RT is expected to complete his/her tasks and turn around and manage another airway or ventilator issue, with little time to process and adjust to what has just happened. In our NICU, the RTs often have significant connections with our parents, which will have an impact on them as they perform these end-of-life tasks. It is important to recognize that this form of disenfranchised grief (Thompson, 2009) is underestimated and does need both recognition and support.

Our hospital has representation from a number of religious communities, including Buddhist as well as several Christian, Jewish, and Muslim chaplains. A chaplain is available in-house 24/7 for families in need of spiritual support. They also respond to crisis situations in our hospital and can be a calming presence in the chaos. We have one chaplain who supports our team and has been involved with the NICU for some years. He has facilitated discussions about spiritual issues and expression with many families and has helped the team and family to problem solve issues related to end-of-life care in our environment. He is an active part of our staff-support process, which will be discussed later in this chapter. The chaplains at our hospital offer similar supports to those at other centers, but as this is a pediatric hospital, much of the support is not only for the child, but for the whole family in crisis. They have presided over baptisms, blessings, prayer vigils, naming ceremonies, and other important rituals, and have provided spiritual counseling for families and for their colleagues in the clinical area. Chaplains have also helped families to connect with their own spiritual community, in their funeral planning, and resource support. When it comes to end-of-life care in our NICU, our chaplains maintain a presence for the families they work with. This is a very important role.

During this period of development in palliative care and bereavement in the NICU, chaplaincy's work has attempted to adapt to the changes of expression in religious and spiritual practice. A family's spiritual and religious needs require a response that best meets those needs in the difficult circumstances of an impending death. Once, the circumstances of this NICU experienced predominantly Christian and Jewish practices; now those practices in the context of end-of-life care are a broad spectrum that ranges from those who are atheist; pantheist; a devout member of one of the established religious practices like Hinduism, Buddhism, Christian, Muslim, or Judaism or those who have adopted or adapted some of the practices of these traditions; to those whose view of life and death expresses itself in self-created ritual and ceremony rooted in an inherent but undefined set of beliefs.

Spirituality has exploded the boundaries of ritual and ceremony and challenged the definition of religious care. Because of these changing circumstances, the team has had to learn to offer spiritual support in whatever way is meaningful to the individual and to the family.

APPLYING PALLIATIVE CARE PRINCIPLES TO THE NEWBORN POPULATION: GOING FROM "DO EVERYTHING" TO ALLOWING FOR DEATH

Before end-of-life or palliative care can occur, it is important to recognize that the decision making in the NICU is a difficult task. It is very appropriate to use the World Health Organization's (WHO) Tenets of Palliative Care (Munson & Leuthner, 2007) when considering what is in the best interest of this fragile population. However, this is challenged by the reality that many families do not consider death as a potential part of their child's birth, even when their baby has an antenatally diagnosed condition or is born extremely prematurely. It is often considered in ordinary life that we believe everything is fixable, when in fact not all conditions are associated with a "fix" or should be fixed. In Munson and Leuthner's paper on perinatal hospice (2007), they described these tenets as a way of focusing on quality of life and accepting that death is a part of this process (see Figure 1). Fulfilling these tenets presents both an opportunity and a challenge, depending on the circumstances.

In the NICU, families need time and support to process new medical information about their baby. When the conditions of the baby are life-limiting, many

1. Affirm life while accepting death as a normal process.
2. Intend to neither hasten nor postpone death.
3. Offer a support system to help families cope during a patient's illness and in their own bereavement.
4. Interventions are aimed at comfort and quality of life.
5. Consider values beyond the physical needs of a dying individual.
6. Apply palliative care early in the course of illness in conjunction with other therapies intended to prolong life.
7. Pediatric palliative care begins when illness is diagnosed and continues regardless of whether or not a child receives treatment directed at the disease.

Munson and Leuthner, 2007

Figure 1. Tenets of palliative care.

of the limitations are not easily visible for the parents. Newborn infants are expected to only eat and sleep and so appreciating the long-term impact of birth injury (lack of oxygen) or a metabolic condition that is not externally visible is challenging. The baby looks "perfectly normal" on the outside. Years of clinical knowledge and learning from previous cases puts the neonatologist in the "knowing" seat, but the family has a great deal of work to do to get to a similar place and keep pace. Although the decision to accept disability is an appropriate one (Farlow, 2008), some parents may come to a time when they believe their child will not be able to survive or their quality of life will be so impaired that it is time to stop providing aggressive interventions. When decisions are engaged to stop aggressive medical intervention and focus on quality of life and death, families often need to consult with their spiritual or religious leadership, extended family and friends, and others who may have varying degrees of influence about what to accept and what to decide. Agreeing to stop the interventions that are keeping the baby alive may seem impossible. Newborn care comes with a great deal of uncertainty in most cases, because we have often heard about the "miracle baby," and this may impact individual and community perceptions. Uncertainty will affect even the medical team, who may be unsure of whether or not to limit aggressive therapy.

On top of these challenges, our city is a very large cultural "melting pot," with more than 96 different languages spoken, so many times the primary language of the family is not the same as the caregiver. This leads to difficulties in communication, especially when issues that are difficult to translate are brought forward. Whether the interpreter (there should always be a translation professional) is at the table or on the telephone, we cannot always be certain that the family has fully grasped the complex nature of the concerns we have for their baby. The healthcare team needs to communicate in language that is appropriate to the family's level of understanding. It is important to ensure that mothers have the same understanding as their partners, as the circumstances of being postpartum and the sometimes protective perspective of some new dads and family members may prevent mothers from being given the full picture.

Distance is also a challenge for our families and their ability to connect with the medical and surgical teams. Families come from across our province and even across our nation, which can include distances of more than 7 hours from the hospital. As they may not be able to be close to the baby for the whole time of admission, parents may not have the same understanding of prognosis and outcome that the team sees. Parents may also have other responsibilities, like their other children and their jobs, and as a result may not be able to be present as much as they would like.

Consistency and Continuity

As a regional center, we also have the challenges of many different medical services providing consultation to the clinical care of our patients. As each clinical group looks at the baby from their area of expertise, they may not appreciate the "big picture" of the whole child and the likely long-term outcomes of multi-system issues. The role of our neonatologists is to keep this focus, and because their time on service is only for a few weeks at a time, consistency is often a huge challenge. However, consistency is attempted through other means. Our social workers and chaplain stay connected to the family throughout the stay in the NICU and when a baby is premature and anticipated to have a long stay, has a complicated clinical situation, or is palliative. A group of core or primary nurses will be established to care for the family whenever on shift. This allows for more continuity but is still not an ideal situation. In the palliative care situations, the NPCB Coordinator becomes another member of that continuity team, to support families through the time until death, and they continue to provide support to the families during the years after. We must also recognize that the family is the ultimate in continuity for that baby, and they learn how to interact with the team to ensure that their baby's needs as well as their own needs are met.

As Death Occurs

As a team, our role in helping families is multifocal. When we consider how we help families before death, much of our work is focused on the following activities: ascertaining parent/extended family understanding of what has happened and what will happen; clarifying misinformation or perspectives that are not accurate; transparent sharing of clinical findings; identifying options for and concerns about their child; and accessing the resources that families will need in the coming hours, days, and weeks. Each of these activities might be initiated or continued by a different member of the interdisciplinary team. These will include referrals to the "experts in the area," including chaplaincy, NPCB Coordinator, and our hospital-based Palliative and Care Service consult team. Together, we offer our "best knowledge" of the outcomes, consider the best interests of the baby, and help parents when they need time to process information.

Earlier, we mentioned the difficulties with making sense of the injuries (often brain injuries) that our patients may have as a result of birth hypoxia or peri-natal depression. Severe injury in this condition may lead to decisions to limit aggressive therapy or withdraw life-sustaining medical therapy when there are signs that the baby will not improve despite our best efforts. These decisions are made collaboratively with the family with the knowledge that timing of death is uncertain and that prognosis is based on the clinical findings of irreparable damage to the brain. If the baby does not die immediately after extubation (sometimes living for days), a new set of decisions needs to be considered. Some of the families have to consider some very challenging decisions, including whether or not to use artificial means to provide nutrition and hydration to their severely compromised baby when they are unable to feed themselves independently and are never expected to be able to do this simple task (Hellmann, Williams,

Ives-Baine, & Shah, 2012). While this is not a frequent occurrence in this NICU, some of our families have required additional support during this experience as they adjust to the loss of the baby they anticipated and also helping them as they await their impending but comfortable eventual death. This subpopulation is offered many supportive interventions (pain and symptom management, legacy creation and family support, transition to home and family counseling) to help them through this time of active palliation but minimal intervention.

We encourage ritual as an ongoing part of neonatal care, and it is especially important when families are looking at end of life as the next step. Spiritual rituals like baptisms, blessings, or naming ceremonies immediately come to mind, but there are other equally powerful rituals that happen every day: the chance to hold (often for the first time) their newborn who is dying, to bathe, to sing to, or to introduce their baby to their family, either in person or through video capabilities (Pugh & Ives-Baine, 2012). We continue those activities throughout the child's life, including the legacy work that helps remind that the experience was real and supports the memories that families can treasure of their child's too-short life (Ives-Baine, 2010). These include photos (both personal and professional), prints of hands and feet, 3-D molds (Jung, Milne, Wilcox, & Roof, 2003), chances for the family to have privacy to hold and grieve the child they will not get to take home, the opportunity to try to take their dying baby for a walk (even on a ventilator), or to take them back to a hospital closer to home and to just be a family. These opportunities include siblings, extended family, and friends. As was quoted by one of our colleagues, "I think that what we are trying to achieve is a lifetime of memories in a very short life. For parents, it's about ensuring their baby has a legacy and a meaning and that they existed" (Mayne, personal communication, August 12, 2012).

In addition to legacy creation, chaplaincy services, and information provided by the interdisciplinary team, a variety of reading material is available to families during these difficult times. A number of books and articles on many topics related to infant death have proven to be of use to parents and families as they journey through the dying process with their child. Much of the writing is aimed at assisting parents in making difficult decisions on behalf of their child and offers to support parents with their coping and grieving processes. A wide range of booklets are available, which cover many topics, including prematurity, twin loss, grandparent grief, and funeral arrangements. Additional resources include information on how to involve and educate siblings, how to safely and effectively reduce pumping (for mothers pumping breast milk), and practical information to help parents know their rights, after their baby's death, on maternal/paternal leave or absence from work. To support our multicultural patient and family population, several books and pamphlets are also available in different languages. Much of the content found in current literature is important, as it will support these families in making tough decisions and assist in their ability to cope and grieve effectively. The greatest benefit of providing reading material to families is that it allows the staff to pass on significant information in a noninvasive and time-appropriate manner. At a very overwhelming and difficult time in their lives, we are able to ease some of the burden that comes with "information overload" by allowing parents and families to take in this information at their own pace. Another benefit is that this information can be read by parents and their extended family and friends to help them make sense of the experience.

How do we care for families after their precious baby has died? There are many family activities that staff on the NICU have been involved with and supported. Sometimes, the simplest tasks can involve attendance at funerals/ memorials or other celebrations of the baby's life (Macdonald, Liben, Carnevale, Rennick, Wolf, Meloche, et al., 2005). Staff will often attend these events on their own time, as part of saying goodbye to that baby, and offer their presence and support to the family. If they have not been able to participate in the ritual of goodbye, staff will send cards or make phone calls or provide their work e-mail to families. This practice has been an important addition, as personal e-mails were sometimes misused. This was not the best practice, as it put the staff at a disadvantage when they needed to separate their home and work lives. Many staff will also attend our annual NICU Remembrance Gathering to reconnect with families who attend, which is perceived by those families as a very important part of their healing (Macdonald et al., 2005).

Families are offered ongoing support through the NPCB Coordinator via phone, e-mail, newsletters, and when families visit the hospital, whenever they are ready. The standard follow-up for our NICU families is at 4–6 weeks (though families can be in contact earlier as they often need additional support and guidance in the early days); at 3–4 months, when bereaved mothers are returning to their jobs; at 6 months; and at the anniversary. At each of these time frames, a sensitive newsletter is provided, which includes edited stories from other families as well as links to community information and resources that may be helpful. For each time frame, there are topics, which include grieving siblings, subsequent pregnancy, and an offer to come back to speak with the team about their experiences as well as information identifying differences in parental grief. These are currently available only in English, due to translation costs for so many different languages (currently greater than 96), but we have learned that parents will share them with others who can translate the information, and they too find it helpful.

Between 4 and 6 months after a baby's death, parents who had consented to a postmortem examination or autopsy are offered the opportunity to come back and discuss the results with the team. This is facilitated by the NPCB Coordinator and has been done in person, by teleconference through the hospital's system, and on the phone. At this time, parents will often ask us to share these results with their current clinical team so that they do not have to remember all of the details of the discussion. Parents want their family practitioner and other providers to know these results so that they can have optimal care in future pregnancies. Parents have identified that the longer it takes to obtain results, the harder it is to process their grief, but they do acknowledge that results are not processed as rapidly as seems possible in the world of television, where all answers are obtained in 50 minutes. It is important to note that if the case is reviewed by the Coroner's Office, issues of timing and understanding can be even more overwhelming for parents.

A significant act of formal support is our NICU Remembrance Gathering for the NICU families, held each year at the hospital in a semipublic space so as to make possible a "public" expression of the experiences or stories of these grieving families. They are not "out on display" but are in a section of the hospital where others can see the event, with parents facing away from the public eye. The event is now beginning its 16th year and has helped thousands of parents, siblings, friends, and families to express their love, grief, and gratitude for the babies they have mourned and the team who has cared for them. The Remembrance Gathering has changed over the years, from a formal service to its current state, which includes coffee and tea and the sharing of treats (both before and after the event), picking up of a personal crystal memento with their child's name on it, and obtaining the family's copy of the program. The formal gathering consists of a welcoming to the event; the reading of the names; the placing of the crystals on the Memory Tree by the parents, who then have the option to speak of their child after they have placed their crystal; the reading of poems by the caregiving team; and bubble blowing to recognize the fragility of these lives, along with the memories that live on. It closes with a legacy-creating opportunity for all family and friends present (memory stones—1 year after death, messages in a bottle—5 years after the death, bracelets or bookmarks—2 years after the death). Over the past 8 years, these legacy-creation opportunities have been found to be cathartic for parents and others, as they provide another chance to remember and recognize, and to connect with other families whose babies have died in our NICU. They feel less alone in their grief when they have shared this event and memory making with other families.

Parents are offered the opportunity to come to future Remembrance Gatherings, especially if they were unable to make the one at the culmination of their first year of grief, and this invitation is taken up by between 5 and 8 families a year, with some coming for several years in a row, and most recently, with a family coming on their son's 19th birthday, as they had heard about the event and wanted the opportunity to acknowledge this baby on such a momentous occasion after so many years.

As we have learned in our program, it is not always the first year that is the hardest for families; many of them will access the supports available at other times that are important to them. Subsequent pregnancies, pivotal birthdays, or when another child has health concerns are examples of times that take families back to their emotional grief responses; they need support through these experiences. These are not frequent in nature but certainly do occur, and the NPCB Coordinator is open to these families accessing the support they need and will refer them to other services for more complex situations.

As challenging as this work is, it is very rewarding to see families grow from the devastation of their loss to those who can support others, empathize with others who are bereaved, and value the new lives that they may get to experience. These families teach us so much in their journey of grief; their resilience and development of strength is a large part of this teaching.

How Do We Help Staff?

The work of supporting staff through caring for families at the end of life includes opportunities to be mentored by the NPCB Coordinator and members of the EOL Team. This includes formal orientation classes for nurses, education sessions for residents and fellows, and sharing of new research that allows the team to increase their own knowledge and critical-thinking skills at their own pace. These go out across the program and so are also available to unit clerks and administrative staff should they want to learn more. Students who are mentored in the NICU are given the opportunity to shadow the Coordinator for a day, identifying that this is a good learning opportunity. The Coordinator has provided RTS Training sessions (Daley & Limbo, 2008) to hospital staff and colleagues in the local community over the years.

Changes in practice are communicated to the team via e-mail and face-to-face opportunities at the NICU Education Updates. As well, the Coordinator is available to support staff 24/7. In recent years, the calls to the Coordinator's pager have reduced significantly, due to the availability of the EOL Resource Team and additional documents being available to support best practices. This includes the NICU EOL Guidelines, which are currently in a draft form, but are planned to go live in the near future.

The NICU End-of-Life Guidelines is an evolving document that has been in development for several years as of 2013. As an evolving document, it may never to carved in stone. The aim of these guidelines is to produce a user-friendly and accessible document for staff, which summarizes the best practices in end-of-life care within the NICU. Anyone with access to the guidelines can easily acquire the information they need, without time and resource restrictions. Moreover, we hope that these guidelines will serve as the basis for a hospitalwide resource on EOL care in the near future. This 34-page document includes, but is not limited to, information on palliative care prior to death, care of the family (including cultural-specific considerations), the details of postmortem tasks, case-specific requirements (e.g., coroners cases, organ and tissue donation, specific religious requirements, families from out of town/province), and funeral/ceremonial arrangements. While the guidelines have not yet been finalized and made available to all staff due to the physician and committee reviewing process, we hope to have them available as a formal policy to all NICU health care providers soon. In addition to the guidelines, a shorter, quick-reference algorithm containing similar information has been created for the immediate, interim use for staff at the bedside.

Another way we support staff is through formalized opportunities to meet and discuss the challenges of caring in such an intense environment. It has been recognized over the years, and through research in this NICU (Lindsay et al., 2012), that nurses and others on the healthcare team grieve and struggle through caring for dying infants and their families (Jonas-Simpson, 2011). While they identify how difficult this is, they have also articulated that these opportunities to make a difference are empowering and humbling at the same time (Lindsay et al., 2012). Through this research and the staff's response to the research findings, regular places and times to talk about their experiences was underscored as important. One of these opportunities, called Voicing Space, is available to all staff every other week and is a 1-hour drop-in opportunity to sit with their colleague facilitators (usually two of NPCB Coordinator, chaplain, social worker) and talk about what is challenging them or causing difficulty. Whether it is cases that are talked about, relationships with colleagues and/or families, or personal issues needing to be let out, the facilitators offer their presence and a chance for participants to be heard. Issues that are clinically significant are shared with management through a de-identified means. The offering of Voicing Space has led to some clinical initiatives that have helped staff. As well, the facilitators are also being sought out at other times for those conversations that need to be shared; the facilitators help the participant to process what they are experiencing as well as consider strategies that might be helpful to them. This model is also accessible in urgent situations, which happen a few times a year, and the focus at these times is on the particular case or experience.

There are three rules for Voicing Space:

- What happens in Voicing Space stays in Voicing Space.
- Respect your colleagues and take your turn.
- Share what is important to you, while respecting confidentiality.

Debriefings

The staff has access to the process of debriefings after a clinical incident or traumatic experience. These are more formal events with a focus on processing the event rather than the feelings associated. Many staff find this to be a useful experience, as it strengthens their clinical skills and judgment and allows members of each discipline to interact and share views. From our debriefings, it has been identified that staff would benefit from another place to talk about their experiences. This is why Voicing Space came into existence.

Staff support is pivotal to a healthy team (Papadatou, 2009), and these forms of support will require evaluation, but informal response has been positive. There are other ways that staff support could be enhanced, and we are constantly looking for new opportunities to empower the NICU environment in this way. These components are key to staff retention and engagement, and support a positive work-life balance that all environments should strive for.

CONCLUSIONS

This chapter reviewed how the NICU Palliative Care and Bereavement Program came into being and described the roles that exist on this team within the context of the unit and hospital. It described what is offered to families when medical treatments are not successful or diagnoses are not favorable and how we can support our families and members of our team through the experiences of end of life and bereavement in the NICU. This chapter provided an excellent opportunity for members of the team to recognize the enhancements that have occurred in this time and to do so with pride. The authors are grateful to the unit and the organization for supporting this important work and recognizing the impact that it can have on families and their futures.

ACKNOWLEDGMENTS

The authors wish to acknowledge the members of the NICU End-of-Life Resource Team for their hard work and advocacy to enable best practices on the NICU.

As well, the Ontario Teachers Insurance Plan (www.otip.com) and the hospital's Women's Auxiliary (www.sickkids.ca/WomensAuxiliary/index.html) for their ongoing support of the Palliative Care and Bereavement Program in the NICU at the hospital.

REFERENCES

Daley, M., & Limbo, R. (Eds.). (2008). *RTS bereavement training in early pregnancy loss, stillbirth & newborn death* (7th ed.). La Crosse, WI: Gundersen Lutheran Medical Foundation, Inc.

Farlow, B. (2008). Decision to accept disability: One family's perspective. *Paediatric and Child Health, 13*(5), 367.

Hellmann, J., Williams, C., Ives-Baine, L., & Shah, P. (2012, March 23). Withdrawal of artificial nutrition and hydration in the Neonatal Intensive Care Unit—Parental perspectives. *Archives of Disease in Childhood Fetal and Neonatal Edition*, F2-F5. doi: 10.1136/fetalneonatal-2012-301658

Ives-Baine, L. (2010). Creating a legacy: Do items that support family memories really make a difference? *CHIPPS Newsletter* (pp. 4-9), August 2010. Available at http://www.nhpco.org/files/public/ChiPPS/ChiPPS_newsletter_20_August_2010.pdf

Ives-Baine, L. (2011). NICU's top ten ways nurses take care of themselves. *CHIPPS Newsletter* (pp. 42-44), August 2011. Available at http://www.nhpco.org/files/public/ChiPPS/ChiPPS_Issue24_Aug-2011.pdf

Ives-Baine, L., Hannon, C., & Saini, J. (2011). Walking in our shoes: The experiences of caregivers and the challenges of differing goals. *CHIPPS Newsletter* (pp. 19-25), August 2011. Available at http://www.nhpco.org/files/public/ChiPPS/ChiPPS_Issue24_Aug-2011.pdf

Jonas-Simpson, C. (2011). *Nurses grieve too* [DVD]. Toronto, Canada: Health Leadership & Learning Network, Faculty of Health, York University.

Jung, A., Milne, P., Wilcox, J., & Roof, N. (2003). Neonatal hand casting method. *Journal of Perinatology, 23*, 519-520.

Lindsay, G., Cross, N., & Ives-Baine, L. (2102). Narratives of NICU nurses: Experience with end-of-life care. *Illness, Crisis & Loss, 23*(3), 239-253.

Macdonald, M. E., Liben, S., Carnevale, F. A., Rennick, J. E., Wolf, S. L., Meloche, D., et al. (2005). Parental perspectives on hospital staff members' acts of kindness and commemoration after a child's death. *Pediatrics, 116*(4), 884-890.

Munson, D., & Leuthner, S. R. (2007). Palliative care for the family carrying a fetus with a life-limiting diagnosis. *Pediatric Clinics of North America, 54*(5), 787-798.

Papadatou, D. (2009). *In the face of death—Professionals who care for the dying and the bereaved*. New York, NY: Springer.

Pugh, J., & Ives-Baine, L. (2012). Using technology to connect families—Should we? *International Journal of Childbirth Education, 27*(2), 83-85.

Simpson, C., Xiang, Y., Hellmann, J., & Tomlinson, C. (2010). Trends in cause-specific mortality at a Canadian outborn NICU. *Pediatrics 126*(6), e1538-1544.

Thompson, N. (2009). *Loss, grief and trauma in the workplace*. Amityville, NY: Baywood.

http://dx.doi.org/10.2190/FATC7

SECTION 2

Facing End-of-Life and Its Care

CHAPTER 7

To Be is To Be, and the
Do-ing Should Follow*

Richard B. Gilbert

TO BE AND TO DO:
TO BE A GUEST, NOT THE DIRECTOR

Ira Byock, M.D. (1997) moves us to a new way of thinking about life and death and how we might walk as "be-ing" people who then become "do-ing" people. "Roll over and play dead" is harsh and unkind, but it represents how many approach the death of someone else or their own death. Finality chokes out living because many think (often based on false information from others) that this is the way it is to be done. This is one of many side effects of living in denial of death. Is there a rule that we are to stop living just because Death is knocking at our door? Living and dying are, in many ways, the markers that define who we are, our self-appreciation, and how we are influenced by death's approach.

Who provides this "wisdom"? A parent? A spouse? A child? A relative? A pushy neighbor? A healthcare Dr. Phil? A good book? God? The question most asked by the dying is, "Will you *be* with me?" Oftentimes the patient understands the distinction between knowledge and wisdom, while we continue

---

*This chapter is based on the workshop presented by the author at the International Conference on Death, Dying and Bereaved, June 2012, held at the University of Wisconsin–La Crosse.

trying to do everything. Will you help me, guide and befriend me, without telling me what I ought to do? Will you understand when I cry, "Leave me alone," without leaving me? Will you come back tomorrow? Will you keep me safe without treating me like a child? "Will you *be* with me?"

A recent *National Geographic* special studied dying and death in ancient Egyptian cultures. The narrator suggested that a culture is defined by many factors or yardsticks, but a culture's values and attitudes are shaped by our living, our dying, and the rituals that shape them and lead us through.

Death education has evolved over recent decades, each step accompanied by the resources and inspiration of professionals in the field, people who provide direct care, caring volunteers, and friends who offer strokes of love and care along the way. Most of all, this is about whom the dying person wants nearby. These choices may be influenced by feelings, ill health, pain, medicine, emotional woundedness, or the pressures applied by people. But *be-ing* must trump *do-ing*! The feelings are unscripted and fluid, and so are the folks nearby. People can "come and go," while the staff still has work to do.

Because of the emotional trauma of witnessing the dying and death of someone who has been in our lives, we discover that there are no scripts. Whatever prompts us risks being redefined by old stories and old wounds while claiming some familiarity with this "new way of dying." Death doesn't refine or rescue the wounds, but often heightens them. It anoints the pain by anointing the person who is dying. It can be hard to distinguish behavior and feelings, where they begin and might lead us. It could be the sadness of darkened ICU waiting room at 3 a.m., those uncomfortable chairs and dark corners, cold coffee and imposed limits on sleep.

Volatile outbursts come for many reasons. *Do-ing* can push us to "keep the peace," keeping patients on task, as dying has been scripted to help you. Sometimes the best we can do is spare the patient from the worst excesses while engaging those who are willing to engage and be engaged. Who will bear that light?

Byock's literary contribution, *Dying Well: The Prospect for Growth at the End of Life* (1997), captures a key theme that is often easily overlooked, even by the patient, and should be a good fit within our cultures, values, and beliefs. It still may be more of a foreign object—a contradiction—for family, friends, providers, and the person who is dying. Some speak of death as "the end." Others see it as a process of transition from dying to living in whatever context our beliefs and values proscribe for us. Said another way, it is the reminder that we do *not* have to stop living, creating, celebrating, lamenting, sharing and, again, *living*! The prophet Jeremiah spoke of "making all things new" and the last book of the Christian Scriptures speaks this same theme.

We cannot control death nor can we trick it. Sometimes a person may appear to stall for more time. Bargaining. We believe we can negotiate most anything. This stalling becomes memorable and memory-making when we cease to direct and respect the individual's living and dying. By controlling (do-ing without be-ing), we often risk losing the patient's trust while neglecting what we bear for patients and others. Byock (1997) writes,

> In reflexively turning away from reminders of death, we have at times inadvertently isolated loved ones who needed our presence, and we have robbed ourselves of precious opportunities. Socially we have paid dearly, and culturally we are poorer for failing to explore the inherently human experience of dying. (p. xiii)

Much of the frustration, fear, and consternation that accompany dying and death focus on pain, sadness, remembrance, and grasping for hope. It also is the result of wounds and difficult memories that the dying would want to leave behind. Byock (1997) addresses this within the context of hospice:

> Through my years as a hospice doctor, I have learned that dying does not have to be agonizing. Physical suffering can *always* be alleviated. People need not die alone; many times the calm, caring presence of another can soothe a dying person's anguish. I think it is realistic to hope for a future in which nobody has to die alone and nobody has to die with their pain untreated. But comfort and companionship are not all there is. I have learned from my patients and their families a surprising truth about dying: this stage of life holds remarkable possibilities. Despite the arduous nature of the experience, when people are relatively comfortable and know that they are not going to be abandoned, they frequently find ways to strengthen bonds with people they love and to create moments of profound meaning their final passage. (p. xiv)

Byock sets the stage for the discussion of care of the dying by putting the focus on the patient (not, of course, at the expense of others struggling to share the stage). Momentarily, we will look at a diagram intended to draw our attention to family systems. It is an attempt to measure the agendas, movements, relationships, feelings, and other factors that dwell with the person who is dying, with loved ones, family, extended family, friends, and others. Within this also rests the needs and struggles that wrap around those who are providing this care and support. When we try to be "the professional," we tend to diminish the significance of our feelings, which can easily disturb the patient. He or she may be clueless about the nature of those feelings, but the patients sense that something isn't right. This often translates back to the patient that something is wrong, and somehow, the patient is responsible.

While it doesn't always work as intended, patient autonomy is the center for ethical discussion. It is often wrapped in the assessments by the various accrediting agencies, professional Codes of Ethics, and the protocols that outline how care is to be provided in that place and with these questions. There are myriad examples of patients who have been stripped of their autonomy by overzealous professionals who ram things right through the patient and others, often only because it is more convenient for the medical professionals. Families, friends, and others can be equally at fault. They can be fraught with feelings, rules, family traditions, and personal well-being. These feelings are about the dying of someone who is part of the stories of others, but it is driven by our own feelings, needs, beliefs, and attitudes. Here are some things we might see:

- Overly aggressive physicians (and others) pursuing their interpretation of facts and concepts of treatment often hidden behind the mask of "doing what is best for the patient." The doctor may be right about the possible treatment plan, but this does not make the doctor right for *this* patient. Medicine rests on trust, personal values and feelings, and the respect held and for the patient. As Byock (1997) suggested in the quotes cited, the patient is the best resource to first state and clarify any feelings, concerns, or confusion. It is an argument in favor of earlier hospice referrals. This often happens with pain management. We order standard medications and doses based on our training and our sense of the needs of the patient. We often consider the fear of "making the patient an addict," a myth that just won't go away.

- To-do lists can provide written documentation that each person has concerns and generally wants to be helpful. Even though we commit to the wishes of the patients, it really is a juggling act, maybe even a tug-of-war, trying to balance all of the players without sinking the entire shipload. Tracking the people and roles in any family can be a thorny process. It often is a new version of musical chairs. People move up and down the rows or keep shifting seats in the ICU waiting room, built on personal agenda, the need to be helpful, a sense of obligation, and the pressures and expectations of one's ethnic and familial culture. It also should be stated that "ethics"—the work that we do to interpret values and beliefs as they attend to a specific need or question—is not just something "medical."

Some time back, a Laotian family came to the hospital. Most were first-generation immigrants. The grandmother was frail, struggling to breathe, terminal. The family gathered around the bed. They sang, bathed and showered the woman with flower petals, and shared in the rituals of the family and the ethnic group. The grandfather was equally frail. He knew the wishes of the patient, but their lengthy discussions and choices were articulated through her husband of 65 years. He designated a cousin to interpret and otherwise speak on their behalf. Where does this stand with regard to decisional rights and families?

It framed their love, and the family respected it. It was the staff who struggled. It also can bring various pressures and judgments from religion, community values, and discerning the particular culture within the larger ethos. "The family keeps singing," complained the nursing supervisor. "It's almost midnight, and the other patients are trying to sleep." It seemed the better solution even when risking the derailment of centuries of culture and tradition. As death approaches, the patient's clothing is removed and, with great dignity and gentleness, the patient is bathed. It is the cleansing (purification) that prepares a person for the next life. A housekeeper noted the naked patient and rushed to cover her with a sheet. She then called the nurse. The issue at hand was trying to match the events with the way we feel things ought to be done. How do we "enforce" autonomy? Who takes precedent? Who defines it?

- Cultural values and ethnic rituals are important. They also are confusing to some, insisted upon by some members of the family, yet scorned by others. Even professionals muddy the waters with, "I don't believe this is the way these things are to be done." Families are often divided by religion. The language of the "religious right" is that a person must accept Christ as personal Lord and Savior. It is one of those religious foci that seems often to resemble religious rules and dictates, more the thorn than the treasure. Suddenly, one pathway, "*My* pathway," is said to be the right one for everyone. Nothing else is acceptable because it is not equal in value. Soon the beliefs of the patient are crushed by those who *know* they are right. Cultural issues and pressures also vary by generations, most notably when working with first-generation family members as well as the more tenured generations.
- Tensions often mount as death draws near. It seems common among adult siblings. For many reasons, one sibling may become the primary caregiver. Sometimes it is the natural outcome of family life and love. It may also be based on geography. Others simply feel too distant or busy to step in and help. Any wounds, including some new ones, become heightened as the distant ones step in and attempt to take over. They try to rearrange and discredit the efforts of the primary caregiver based on their own needs and prejudices. They maneuver from one place to another as the needs and advantages present themselves. Where is that autonomy now?

DO-ING IS MORE EFFECTIVE WHEN IT EMERGES FROM BE-ING

In *May I Walk You Home?: Courage and Comfort for Caregivers of the Very Ill* Joyce Hutchison and Joyce Rupp (1999) give us that needed working moral ideal and emotional shaping. This powerful book offers insights through story and prayer that, like Byock (1997), draw us to the centrality of each patient. Consider these quotes from the back cover:

> Walking a companion home is an old-fashioned custom, often lost in our modern era. But there was once a time when walks home from school, from church, or from a dance were commonplace. Walking someone home was a way of offering protection and guidance, an opportunity to reflect on life and what had just been experienced . . .

Joyce Hutchison provides a wonderful example of what it is like to simply be there with one who is seriously ill or dying—how to listen, when to speak, how to provide encouragement, and most of all, how one's simple presence can enable the dying person to let go and make the final step of the journey in peace.

A quick look at the stories through their titles gives us much to think about:

- Giving permission to die
- Why did God give you cancer?
- A long-kept secret
- Always a bit of hope
- The gate won't open
- Afraid to die
- Intimate love—intimate death

As professionals, we don't park in the breakroom drinking coffee, trying to stare the call button into silence. Invitations may come, though the best invitation is that you go about the work you are meant to do. No chore is a chore. They are tasks, gift bearers, the marks of being with that person in his or her living and dying. The smallest gestures often prove to be the biggest treasures for the patient and the family. A glass of water. A damp cloth on the forehead. A smile. A pillow fluff. A walk down the hall. A prayer. Even conveyed as chores, the patient may still appreciate the gift. Expressed within the embrace of a be-ing with a being that was built over time, it is a blessing, a treasure, a hug.

Even in its fragmentation, there is a junction; an intersection of values, beliefs, stories of all who are involved. Seldom are there guarantees—this isn't a Disney movie. Only the determination to wade through some deep and dirty water until we reach that distant, unknown shore.

Molly Fumia (1992) writes, "Go where you will be healed, but take someone along who loves you, who will listen along the way, and with whom you can share a quiet toast when you reach your destination" (p. 113). Elsewhere, she expresses this nugget of wisdom: "Come grieve with me, my faithful friend. This is my time for mourning. When it becomes your time, you also will not be one, but two. We will do it together" (p. 135).

Yet it is at this meeting point that story, relationships, trust, and hurt can finally merge or emerge. It is where meaning is to be found. Doka and Morgan (1993) say it so well: "Spirituality is experienced at the meeting point, or as some would say, the merging point, between our self and that which we usually feel is not our self (p. 52).

TO BE PRECEDES *TO DO* AND FULFILLS IT

Here is where the going gets tough. Of course, it need not be that way. We still can and ought to maintain *being* to *doing* as our standard, but some situations and people can crush even the best intentions. *Being* seems pointless when the door is slammed in your face. We don't fix people, and seldom repair family dynamics. If anything, dying and death take the way things are and inflames them.

There are things to be done: comforting the patient physically, emotionally, and otherwise. We tend to the family, often working around some dynamics in order to help those who are open to that relief. We respect the wishes of the patient, yet are on alert for disruptions, uncertainty, and disagreements from the family and within it. In my work as a chaplain, 3 × 5 cards were always in my pocket. Even with the best of memories, we need to grab hold of many details. It helped produce my "to do" list. Always in pencil! It was not a script, but a guide.

Working closely with colleagues, we sketched out a family operational plan that blended our observations and tasks with each person in the chart, noting their values and also any shifts in thoughts, behaviors, or feelings. Figure 1 represents the *linear model*, which is simpler to use, easier to change (there are many changes around caring for the dying), and engages us as we tend to the needs of all of the "players" in the scenario.

The triangle represents the primary person, the patient. You will see them as primary, a significant presence and influence on the patient. Always start with the legal views—those of spouse or partner (depending on the state). Adult child (some states lump all adult children into a group and a choice is made; other states specify a formula, usually by age or geography). Parent. Legal guardian. The Power of Attorney for Health Care is common to all states, but may be interpreted differently from state to state. This person is not automatically empowered for business matters. Others may act like they have this responsibility, and even if well-intended, it is not open for claiming. If no one is designated by the patient and the patient is still competent, that designation can still be facilitated and documented.

Extensive work has been done on multiculturalism and death. Several approach this through spiritual markers or religious affiliations. Several titles are of value here and are listed with the other references. Assuming there are no other factors or secrets to unravel it, we at least acknowledge the values and beliefs of each culture. Some variations arise among immigrants based on what generation they represent (first, second, third, etc.). Other families depend on specific family members or friends, including religious leaders, to clarify their viewpoints with

Figure 1.

regard to right to die, withholding or withdrawing treatment, rituals of dying, and other factors. Sometimes it is the one family member or friend who speaks enough English to communicate the patient and family wishes with reverence, respect, and accuracy.

The second person, the circle, is the one most closely linked to the patient. Usually it is the spouse/partner. The person may be the major vote when decisions are needed and would be expected to serve as an accurate reporter of patient wishes. This can be tricky when the spouse is from a second marriage, especially if the adult children are children of the first spouse. Many gay couples have support from family and a relationship that is respected. Even when approved by law, some families will work to destroy this relationship and its memory often because of their viewpoints and beliefs. In this situation, the person closest to the patient may be shoved to the end of the grid or even removed from it. These situations require at least our notice and may require an intervention. Our first commitment is to the patient, and then to the closest to the patient. We do owe care and courtesy to the others we have identified as part of the story, but sometimes we feel more like a referee than a healthcare professional.

The remaining blocks represent people who come and go, some who stay, and some who may not be warmly received. Track them. Observe how they move up and down the list. Be wary of those who arrive at the last minute, the "white knight," the self-appointed hero who wants to undo all that has been done because he or she knows a "better way." It often is a family member or friend who has self-isolated or otherwise been pushed aside and discarded. There may even be some voices determined to protect their financial or possession interest. All of this requires a common understanding and trust among the staff, and a lot of communication.

TO BE AND TO DO: TO BE A GUEST AND NOT THE DIRECTOR, II

Few positions in health care are as vigorous, emotionally challenging, and fulfilling as the care of the dying. Douglas C. Smith (1999) gives this road map:

> I do not believe we can even relate in any way to someone else's suffering until we first acknowledge our own. We cannot assist in the transformation of someone else's suffering until we first transform our own. We cannot heal someone else until we first know how to heal ourselves. The whole process of healing simply begins with recognizing that we all suffer, we are all wounded. Hinduism recognizes it. Buddhism recognizes it. The Jewish faith recognizes it. The Christian faith recognizes it. The Muslim faith recognizes it. Good psychotherapy recognizes it. Good medicine recognizes it. We start by acknowledging our own woundedness and work through it. By entering that woundedness and working through it, we learn how to heal ourselves and we learn how to assist in the healing of others: healing from and through and with our wounds. (pp. 23–24)

Some might look at this as a lot of extra paperwork when we are already choking under the load or a case management that may well rest squarely on the families and friends who preoccupy us and seem to require, as a minimum, oversight but are pushing their way to stronger management. At first, that may seem coarse, insensitive, and inappropriately judgmental. We are supposed to be guests, not directors of the entire performance. This observation can build a case from many memories of my own work with disjointed, disruptive, or dysfunctional families. Sometimes these dynamics become unreasonable, because we fail to communicate shift to shift. We get to know different members of the circle of family and friends based on how others relate to us, we to them, and because none of this is scripted. We only know that the group is now in a wilderness for which there is no real preparation, or at least not a step-by-step guide, so we fall back on past experiences, rekindle good friendships or old wounds, and are thrust into this tempestuous arena.

At this point, the to-do list may look something like this:

1. The patient has three brothers. One has been distant for years. Old wounds. Bruises abound. Some demand that he leave while others stand around the patient, walling him/her in. Who hears the patient cry, "Bring my brother to me?"
2. The patient, still relatively young, worries about his mother in a nursing home. Everyone promises to take care of her, but who will?
3. The patient and his/her family are active in the Roman Catholic Church. It has been a big part of their lives, defining and shaping their marriage and engaging their now-adult children in responsible living. Who is tending to their sacramental/ritual needs? Who guides them through prayer? A number of family members and friends have moved on from Catholicism to an evangelical thread that, at this point, may suggest a fired-up agenda, albeit well intended, to awaken the patient and family to the alarming news that he/she is not "saved." This is a most crucial time. This issue is more common than you might think, and how you react to it often reflects your own beliefs and rituals. Who manages that? Do you embrace the chaplain not just for the patient, family, and friends, but also for the staff?
4. While the patient is failing with some speed, he/she has things that need to be said. There were blessings and apologies. Scars were still there, and at least the patient wants that burden lifted. While any ritual is essentially for those who mourn, many also approach these decisions because it matters to the patient. Scripture readings matter. Hymns matter. Prayers matter.
5. When young children are part of the family, who asks, "Where are they?" "Who do they depend on?" "Who is listening to them?" At the same time, who is tending to the aged and infirmed, sometimes the closest person(s) to "family" for the patient? They can't be at the bedside. Who tends to them? What can be done to connect them to the patient?

It also needs to be said that, as urgent as these matters are, how much of it is overlooked because they are off our radar screen, we lack the time, or, with referrals coming in too late to address much of this, how do we feed the needs of the staff who feel so frustrated? "We could have done so much more if only we had the time!" Keep the needs of the staff, including the volunteers, on the list, too.

Molly Fumia (1992), speaking in *Safe Passage*, wrote,

> The embrace of we who grieve is desperate, yes, but also defiant. Because you dared to enter my desolation, what appeared to be meaningless has found meaning. Because you accompanied me in my vigil, what tempted us to remain separate has been overcome with solidarity. Whatever happens, from this moment on, will be grounded in a sacred partnership. (p. 270)

In a collection of pithy statements and clever phrases, H. Jackson Brown, Jr. (1991) gives us this piece of advice: "Never deprive someone of hope; it might be all they have." We need to keep this on the lists of those in our care, but the need to find it on our own lists may be more urgent.

REFERENCES

Brown, H. J., Jr. (1991). *Life's little instruction book: 511 suggestions, observations, and reminders on how to live a happy and rewarding life.* Nashville, TN: Rutledge Hill Press.

Byock, I. (1997). *Dying well: The prospect for growth at the end of life.* New York, NY: Riverhead.

Doka, K., & Morgan, J. (Eds.). (1993). *Death and spirituality.* Amityville, NY: Baywood.

Fumia, M. (1992). *Safe passage: Words to help the grieving hold fast and let go.* Berkeley, CA: Conari.

Hutchison, J., & Rupp, J. (1999). *May I walk you home? Courage and comfort for caregivers of the very ill.* Notre Dame, IN: Ave Maria Press.

Smith, D. (1997). *Caregiving: Hospice-proven techniques for healing body and soul.* New York, NY: Macmillan.

RESOURCES FOR FURTHER STUDY

Bushfield, S., & DeFord, B. (2010). *End-of-life care & addiction: A family systems approach.* New York, NY: Springer.

Cox, G. (2010). *Death and the American Indian.* Omaha, NE: Grief Illustrated Press.

Cox, G., Bendiksen, R., & Stevenson, R. (2003). *Making sense of death: Spiritual, pastoral, and personal aspects of death, dying and bereavement.* Amityville, NY: Baywood.

DeFord, B., & Gilbert, R. (Eds.). (2013). *Living, loving and loss: The interplay of intimacy, sexuality and grief.* Amityville, NY: Baywood.

Doka, K., & Martin, T. (2010). *Grieving beyond gender: Understanding the ways men and women mourn* (Rev. Ed.). New York, NY: Routledge.

Gilbert, R. (2003). Living, dying, and grieving in the margins. In G. Cox, R. Bendiksen, & R. Stevenson (Eds.), *Making sense of death: Spiritual, pastoral, and personal aspects of death, dying and bereavement* (Ch. 14). Amityville, NY: Baywood.

Gilbert, R. (2009). *Finding your way after your parent dies: Hope for grieving adults* (6th printing). Notre Dame, IN: Ave Maria Press.

Gilbert, R. (2012). *Heart peace: Healing help for grieving folks* (Rev. Ed.). Omaha, NE: Centering.

Goldman, L. (2000). *Life & loss: A guide to help grieving children* (2nd ed.). New York, NY: Routledge.

Grollman, E. (1981). *What helped me when my loved one died.* Boston, MA: Beacon. (There are later editions, and many other titles, all of which are available by contacting the author.)

Irish, D., Lundquist, K., & Nelsen, V. (Eds.). (1990). *Ethnic variations in dying, death, and grief: Diversity in universality.* New York, NY: Taylor & Francis.

Jeffreys, J. S. (2011). *Helping grieving people—When tears are not enough: A handbook for care providers* (Rev. Ed.). New York, NY: Routledge.

Martin, C. A. (2010). *Reflections of a loving partner: Caregiving at the end of life.* Naples, FL: Quality of Life Publishing.

McNish, J. (2004). *Transforming shame: A pastoral response.* New York, NY: Haworth (Routledge).

Minor, R. (2007). *When religion is an addiction.* St. Louis, MO: Humanity Works!

Neimeyer, R. (Ed.). (2012). *Techniques of grief therapy: Creative practices for counseling the bereaved.* New York, NY: Routledge.

Parkes, C. M. (2006). *Love and loss: The roots of grief and its complications.* New York, NY: Routledge.

Roukema, R. (2003). *Counseling for the soul in distress: What every religious counselor should know about emotional and mental illness.* New York, NY: Haworth (Routledge).

Sims, D., & Baugher, B. (2012). *In the midst of caregiving: Whether you come to caregiving by choice, chance, or circumstance.* Newcastle, WA: Caring People Press.

Smith, D. C. (1999). *Being a wounded healer.* San Francisco, CA: Psycho-Spiritual Publications.

Smith, H. I. (2002). *Finding your way to say goodbye: Comfort for the dying and those who care for them.* Notre Dame, IN: Ave Maria Press.

Thompson. N. (2012). *Grief and its challenges.* Hampshire, UK: Palgrave Macmillan.

Wilcock, P. (1996). *Spiritual care of dying and bereaved people.* London, UK: SPCK.

http://dx.doi.org/10.2190/FATC8

CHAPTER 8
Stepping Through the Looking Glass into "Cancer World"

Kent Koppelman

Before describing the palliative care and end-of-life experiences for my friend Craig Fiedler, I need to say a little about the kind of person Craig was. To begin by talking about his life after his cancer diagnosis (or, as he called it, AD) would be to give cancer a victory that Craig resisted until the day he died, which was not to allow cancer to become the primary factor in his identity. This was the point of the subtitle for his book, *Robbery and Redemption: Cancer as Identity Theft* (2012). In the book, he listed the specific ways that cancer had been already been successful in stealing and transforming his identity immediately following his lung cancer diagnosis:

> I took a medical leave of absence from my teaching position at the university.
> —I was no longer a professor.
>
> My plans for writing a new book on special education during my sabbatical the following year, were now completely up in the air.
> —I was no longer an author.
>
> I had to step down from my position as department chair.
> —I was no longer an administrator.
>
> I had always been healthy, never missing a class due to an illness.
> —I was now sick; a "patient" who was being examined, poked, and
> prodded by lots of medical personnel. (p. 6)

Despite cancer's early success, Craig refused to fly the flag of defeat but persisted in the struggle to maintain his identity in interactions with family, friends, medical caregivers, and others. His book records such efforts in descriptions of his palliative care and his end-of-life choices, but that's the story to come. For the moment, it is necessary to begin with a description of the unique identity he had created during the more than five decades of life in what he would come to call his BC (Before Cancer) period.

Craig grew up in a White, middle-class home in a town in the Midwest with a total population of more than 40,000 people, who were mostly White and middle class. He had a relatively unremarkable boyhood; in high school he loved sports, especially baseball, especially the Chicago White Sox. As an undergraduate, he went to the state university in his hometown and earned a degree in economics, then he went to law school at the University of Wisconsin. It was there that his adult personality began to emerge, with a major component being his passion for the underdog. In preparing for a career as a lawyer, he wanted to represent the most vulnerable people in our society, hoping to help them achieve some degree of justice. After graduation, he went with a friend (who had also just graduated from law school) to Appalachia to work for legal services, but was quickly frustrated by how little could be accomplished for the people being served by that office. Yet he would always acknowledge how much he learned from the people there and from this experience. Some of the learning was painful, including the discovery of how difficult it could be to overcome exploitation and injustice.

Craig returned to his hometown to work with a newly established legal services office and to determine how to serve others effectively, but the longer he engaged in legal work, the more he realized that he didn't enjoy being a lawyer, that engaging in legal work no longer seemed a satisfying career. Then life intervened (or luck or fate, take your choice), and he was offered a position as the coordinator of a new program designed to recruit and support advocates for people with a disability. In providing leadership for the Citizen Advocacy program over the next 3 years, the work was immensely satisfying because he was able to improve the quality of life for numerous individuals who were vulnerable. Through the program, he met Sheri, the mother of a severely disabled child named Jennifer, and fell in love with both mother and daughter. One of the people on the program's advisory committee was a university professor who had a PhD in Special Education as well as a law degree. In their discussions, Craig began to understand how a doctorate in Special Education combined with a law degree would enhance his ability to work more effectively as an advocate for people with a disability. He applied to several doctoral programs and was accepted at the University of Kansas. Upon graduation, he accepted a university position teaching Special Education. Over the next 23 years, he engaged in a career in higher education that felt both challenging and rewarding. If not for the cancer, it could have been longer. It should have been longer.

Another critical component for understanding Craig's personality may be surprising and even disturbing to some. From what you have read so far, you might be thinking that Craig was an optimist, perhaps even a Pollyanna, in his desire to confront and resolve injustices in the world. You would be wrong. Although Craig was an idealist with a genuine commitment to make a better world by promoting progressive policies and practices in our society, he was also misanthropic. He was never surprised by people's capacity for making bad decisions or engaging in hypocritical behavior if it served their self-interest, and yet his misanthropy did not provide immunity from the despair that often accompanies the recognition of such realities in the human condition. Friends jokingly referred to him as "Eeyore," the baleful donkey of Winnie-the-Pooh books. Like Eeyore, Craig tended to expect the worst outcomes from most situations, perhaps to avoid feeling disappointed in people, and yet he persistently engaged in efforts to right wrongs and to achieve a more just society. He was the embodiment of the myth of Sisyphus, approaching the top of the hill, straining with the weariness of his task; feeling victory slip from his grasp, he would simply trudge back down the hill, into the depths of his despair, and begin, once again, to make the effort that he knew would never end. Although knowing that a major victory would remain elusive, he derived satisfaction simply from doing the work, because it seemed like the right thing to do.

Craig's misanthropic side was most often expressed in humor. Although not really a joke teller, he was sensitive to the absurdities of everyday life and often amused people with mildly witty (but sometimes caustic) observations. Often the target of his own humor, his ability to laugh at himself and at others persisted even as he struggled with the cancer that would take his life. After the cancer diagnosis, Craig was quickly worked into a surgeon's schedule on the afternoon of the following day to see if his cancerous tumor could be removed. As he waited for the surgery, Craig wondered aloud if it was "better to have a surgeon operate on you right away in the morning when he or she is fresh or later in the day after they have 'warmed up'" (2012, p. 24). He concluded that it would probably depend on whether the surgeon was a "morning person" or an "afternoon person," and he emphatically hoped that his surgeon was an afternoon person!

Because it was such an important aspect of Craig's identity, it is important to offer a couple of additional examples of his humor. It is the part of him that most people who knew him remember best, and in the wake of his long absence, it cheers us to recall moments when his comments made us smile. After the surgery revealed that his lung cancer was inoperable, Craig's oncologist immediately scheduled him for chemotherapy and radiation. The radiation therapists made a plastic mold of the back of his head, because during treatments, it was important that patients not move their head or body. Each time Craig had a radiation treatment, the therapists would take his head mold from the shelf where they stored it and put it on the treatment table. Craig appreciated the irony: "Having my own personalized piece of apparatus felt like being a valued customer, like being a regular at a restaurant and having your own coffee mug" (2012, p. 33).

As the chemotherapy and radiation treatments continued, Craig had regular visits to the oncology clinic. When his name was called, he would go to an examination room, where the nurse would always weigh him, take his blood pressure, temperature, and pulse, followed by the question, had he ever smoked cigarettes? The first time he gave a slight smile when he said he had never smoked because he was proud of that. As months passed, the nurse continued to ask the same question, but although his weight, blood pressure, pulse, and even temperature might vary slightly, the answer to the smoking question never varied. Craig started to feel exasperated by this meaningless ritual, in part because it reminded him that even though he had never smoked tobacco, he still had lung cancer. Finally, he had had enough: "I complained to [the nurse] about being asked about my smoking habits every time I came . It was like asking for my height—that information was not going to change" (2012, p. 34). When the nurse explained that she was simply adhering to a routine she was expected to follow, Craig said he understood, but wondered if she would like him to smoke a cigarette occasionally so that she could write down a different answer on at least some of his visits. She assured him that this would not be necessary. Craig was not sure that she was amused by his comment.

These last two anecdotes have begun to address the topic of end-of-life care, and so I will continue. It was rough sailing at the start as Craig was given the worst news of his life by a surgeon who lacked the human sensitivity so essential for telling someone that they have a terminal disease. After the surgery, Craig felt mentally disoriented as he regained consciousness, and this was when the surgeon came into the room and bluntly stated that it was not possible to remove the tumor, so Craig would be scheduled for chemotherapy and radiation treatments. The surgeon concluded, "We will get you through this," but then left without even waiting to hear Craig's response, oblivious to the contradiction between his words and his behavior.

This incident was the impetus for Craig to think about what he wanted from the medical personnel who would be working with him. One of his highest priorities was that everyone should treat him as an individual and not as a generic "cancer patient." He wanted them to get to know him as a person and not contribute to cancer's dismantling of his personality, which he had already observed. He knew that cancer would ultimately eliminate him from the living as it had done to others in the past and would continue to do in the future, but he wanted to keep his identity for as long as he was alive. He would be Craig Fiedler, with all his shortcomings, but also with the qualities that shaped his life choices and his individuality. His wife, Sheri, and their daughter, Lindsay, supported him in this desire, and so did all of us who had come to know this amiable misanthrope, this jester in the court of despair, this idealist who lived under a cloud of skepticism and doubt. Friends and family members loved him for all of that and wanted to help him nourish this identity and maintain it in the bruising battle that was about to begin.

The blows came quickly and would persist throughout his battle with cancer. After listening to the oncologist describe the chemotherapy and radiation treatments being scheduled for the next 7 weeks, Craig asked the doctor about the chances for long-term survival for this type of cancer: "Without blinking an eye he said, 'Oh, about 22.6 percent.' I asked if we could round that number up to 23 percent" (2012, p. 29). The doctor smiled, and that reaction encouraged Craig to persist in expressing himself honestly as a way of reinforcing his identity and countering the perception of him as a "cancer patient." The ultimate goal was to create a sense of partnership with the doctors so that they could become a team that worked together on this difficult task. Anyone who loves team sports knows that when you're part of a team, you know the strengths and weaknesses of the other players, and you know how to encourage them to do their best. Craig would need all the support that was available to deal with this destructive force inside his body.

From the beginning, Craig was convinced that his pulmonologist was open to the idea of having a partnership. At their initial meeting, this doctor "entered the examination room with an animated and positive demeanor. I liked him immediately. He was easy to talk to, had a good sense of humor, and was very thorough" (2012, p. 17). Even when the pulmonologist had to deliver the bad news that Craig had Aden carcinoma and was probably at stage IIIA, he was still supportive and encouraging about the need for Craig to engage vigorously in the battle against this disease. Craig asked about survival statistics, but even though there was a lot of medical data available, the doctor refused to speculate because he insisted that such data could be misleading. Because there were so many variables from one cancer case to the next, the pulmonologist insisted that it made more sense to emphasize the factors that worked in Craig's favor, such as his age, his history of good health, and that he was a nonsmoker. This was exactly what Craig needed to hear, especially from his doctors—words of hope to lift his spirits and motivate him to confront his cancer with energy and determination.

Other doctors did not take such a positive approach but projected a more detached "professional" demeanor. After several months and numerous appointments with his oncologist, it suddenly occurred to Craig that during all of their conversations, this doctor had never referred to him by name, neither first nor last name: "He says hello upon entering the examination room and asks how I am doing. He is always pleasant in his interactions, but distant . . . it feels like I am just another 'cancer case' to him instead of a human being who is fighting for his life" (2012, p. 120). Craig was determined to find a way to break through this doctor's professional reserve and try to establish a more human connection with his oncologist.

An opportunity for a breakthrough occurred in the early summer when Craig and Sheri returned to Wisconsin from the Tucson area where they had purchased a home a few years earlier in anticipation of a long retirement. During his appointment with the oncologist, Craig talked about spring training games he had attended while in Arizona. The doctor acknowledged being a baseball fan and said he had been a pitcher while in college. He also mentioned that his son was a big fan of the Milwaukee Brewers. Craig had a Brewers bobblehead doll at home, and he brought it to his next appointment and handed it to the oncologist, telling him to give it to his son. The doctor graciously accepted this gift, and Craig hoped that this incident resulted in at least a minimal break in the doctor's professional armor. Perhaps it was, because Craig began to notice some difference in their subsequent interactions.

This change was also related to a strategy Craig employed quite consciously to build a partnership with his medical team; he talked openly about his academic background to make sure they all knew that he had a law degree in addition to his PhD, that he was not only a professor but an active scholar who had published five books and many articles in professional journals. The point was not to boost his ego, but to remind the medical staff that he was someone with the ability and skills to read research and learn everything that might assist him in his battle with cancer. During a meeting with his oncologist after their baseball discussion, Craig was struggling with almost overpowering feelings of despair; the doctor responded by reminding Craig of his strengths and emphasizing how important it was for Craig to use all the resources at his disposal, especially during the emotional downturns that were inevitable when a person was battling cancer. In making such comments, the oncologist demonstrated a more positive approach that bolstered Craig's fighting spirit. Moved by the doctor's sentiments, Craig returned home feeling better and with an even greater determination to resist his dark moods.

In addition to his medical caregivers, Craig was especially dependent on his wife and daughter to provide emotional support, and he gratefully acknowledged their efforts. He described Sheri as being more than a caregiver, that she was a "life-giver." He recognized how his cancer had increased her responsibilities such as "keeping track of all medical appointments . . . driving me to the hospital and oncology clinic, bolstering my spirits and much more . . . [and] she has managed to do them all with grace and a smile" (2012, p. 109). Yet Craig also recognized the need to pay attention to Sheri's state of mind and her health as well as his own. At his urging, she shared her frustrations—his one-word responses to her questions, his frequent failure to express appreciation for everything she was doing for him, his moods of dark despair that wasted what precious little time they had to be together and enjoy each other. Although such comments were painful for her to say and for him to hear, Sheri's honesty "was a much needed reality check" (p. 110). Even before the cancer diagnosis, Craig had a tendency to be self-absorbed and was often susceptible to dark moods that made him distant and uncommunicative. In the past, he had regretted such behaviors but always felt that he had time to atone for them, but time was no longer an ally. The minutes of each day were like grains of sand sifting to the bottom of an hour glass, and there was no way of knowing if the glass would be turned over at the end of each hour for one more hour, one more day, one more month. Time was precious now and not to be wasted.

His daughter consistently encouraged him and stoked his determination to live. Craig compared her to a boxing coach, an essential ally in the battle with cancer: "My body has been pricked and poked and prodded in every imaginable way. Sometimes I get tired and want to give up" (2012, p. 104). Lindsay gave him reasons to hope, words that revived his strength, or a vigorous rub for an aching muscle. Both Sheri and Lindsay were in his corner, assuring him that he could win this fight, getting him ready to go another round. They spoke of goals to live for—to attend someone's birthday party or a graduation ceremony or a wedding anniversary (including his own). Such events would require his survival for another year, or two, or five. Craig contributed to identifying such goals: "Since my two favorite baseball teams are from Chicago, my fantasy has always been to witness a Cubs-White Sox World Series. By making that my goal, I may achieve immortality!" (2012, p. 104).

Friends are always important in the battle with cancer, but it is often difficult for people to know what to say or how to say it. In the first month after the cancer diagnosis, Craig received cards from 129 friends and colleagues. Although he appreciated knowing that he was in their thoughts and prayers, he also noticed how few of the cards mentioned the word "cancer." The researcher in him could not resist the temptation to review the cards and take notes to determine the number of cards in which people had written the word "cancer." Of the 129 cards, only 17 (or 7.6%) of them included the word "cancer" in the written comments. The other cards included euphemisms that referred to his "health issue," "medical challenge," "difficult time," "obstacle," or simply lamented that he was "not feeling well." Such language reflects the enormous discomfort people feel in discussing a terminal illness, especially with the person who has been diagnosed with it. One friend who came to visit Craig was willing to talk about the cancer, but in an apparent effort to demonstrate empathy, the friend commented that since everyone is going to die, all of us are, in a sense, "terminal." The comment bothered Craig, but he could not determine the reason until he reflected on it later:

> I never assumed that my life would be spared from this universal fate, but given my general good health and family history of longevity, my assumption was that I had many more years of health and would enjoy a comfortable retirement. Learning that my life would probably end in the not-too-distant future was an existential thunderbolt of immense proportions. What was hurtful about my friend's well-intentioned comment was that it seemed to trivialize my fears and apprehension. (p. 100)

Despite such experiences, Craig always took genuine pleasure in visits from his friends, and he especially relished the opportunity to reconnect with old friends, in some cases going back to high school days. Although deeply enjoying the positive feelings that came from these reunions, he also regretted the disheartening silence from a number of other friends who seemed to have abandoned him. Yet he didn't blame them or view them critically. He understood that all Americans were part of a culture that attempts to deny death by not thinking or talking about it, and this was not possible if you were communicating with someone who has a terminal illness. So Craig focused on taking pleasure from the friends who did pay a visit, even if they occasionally said things that were inadvertently painful. He had read parts of a manuscript I was writing, and he said he liked this observation: "Remembering past experiences with family and friends can provide a sense of affirmation of our lives . . . [reminding] us that these relationships had deep roots that were watered with love" (Koppelman, 2010, p. 118).

What was far more painful to Craig was to have to endure the absence of friends that he wished he could see. Someone suggested that he should contact absent friends and tell them how much he wanted to hear from them or see them, but he couldn't do it. He felt the initiative had to come from them; otherwise, it would feel like a desperate person seeking sympathy, just as some people fish for a compliment. What was especially unfortunate about the friends who never came was that Craig did not insist on talking about cancer with visitors. In fact, some of the most enjoyable conversations were those focusing on baseball or politics or other issues that provided "a distraction from my 24/7 cancer obsession" (2012, p. 107). He also appreciated people talking about what was going on in their lives because that's what friendship is—sharing the most important parts of your lives with each other. Craig could not be sure how much longer his life would last, but he wanted to share it with as many friends as possible.

In addition to sharing his life with others, it is important for a terminally ill person to be as active as possible while it is still possible in order to enjoy whatever time remains. For that reason, Craig and Sheri made a "bucket list" of trips, primarily for the two of them, since Lindsay had only about a year of college left before graduation, and they did not want her to drop out of school at this point. They took a train to Seattle and boarded a cruise ship sailing through the Alaska inside passage. They also flew to New York and rented a car to drive to Cooperstown where Craig fulfilled a lifelong ambition of spending a couple of days at the Baseball Hall of Fame. As luck would have it, Craig happened to be there at the right time to witness a memorable rededication ceremony. Jackie Robinson had always insisted that if he were voted into the Hall of Fame, it should be for his achievements on the field and not for breaking the color barrier in baseball, therefore, his plaque simply listed his baseball statistics just like all the other plaques. But people at the Hall of Fame believed most baseball fans recognized that Robinson's career justified his inclusion in the Hall of Fame, and it was now time to acknowledge the important role he played in opening the door for players of color. The Robinson family agreed, and for that reason his widow, Rachel, and their daughter, Sharon, attended the rededication. While watching and listening to the moving ceremony, Craig had tears in his eyes, brought on by thoughts of the enormous courage that Jackie Robinson had demonstrated to achieve the goal of desegregating baseball. He hoped he could use this inspiration to achieve his own goal of overcoming cancer. When they were finished at Cooperstown, Sheri and Craig drove to Pennsylvania to visit the Civil War battlefield at Gettysburg. As a person who loved reading history, Craig had read much about this battle and peppered the tour guide with questions. Although the trip was tiring, it was also exhilarating, and Craig returned to Wisconsin feeling rejuvenated.

There would be other trips—to San Francisco, to a resort in the Dominican Republic, and two trips to their retirement home near Tucson. Every trip provided a respite and a distraction from the persistent drumbeat of bad news from the doctors that began from the earliest days of Craig's cancer treatment. Just before his regimen of chemotherapy and radiation was to begin, he was diagnosed with celiac disease, necessitating a gluten-free diet. During his cancer treatment, blood clots formed in both calves before moving up to his lungs, causing a pulmonary embolism that required hospitalization so the doctors could monitor him. By the start of summer, only 5 months since being diagnosed, his lung cancer metastasized, and his condition was downgraded from Stage IIIA to Stage IV. Through it all, Craig remained committed to the goal of being the "exceptional patient," one of the rare success stories of people who had survived with cancer for a long time. And he kept his sense of humor. Because he would frequently need to have blood drawn, his oncologist recommended that a port be inserted in his chest to provide a relatively painless way to take blood and infuse the chemotherapy drugs. After this surgery, the surgeon said that the port could be left in his chest for as long as 5 years. Craig smiled and asked the surgeon if that meant he could count on living another 5 years; the surgeon did not respond. Often these attempts at humor were met with silence, just as his attempts to be positive and optimistic about surviving the cancer were consistently thwarted along the way to becoming a cancer statistic.

Craig Fiedler did not want to die. If a strong will-to-live was all that was necessary to defeat cancer, he should still be alive. But it was not to be. Craig had stepped through the looking glass and into a world that was not a delight-fully curious "Wonderland," but a dystopian setting called "Cancer World." He described it as an amusement park that was not so terribly amusing "because the rides are really scary" and because his family did not get to choose what ride to take, but each and every day they were forced to ride the same "roller coaster" (2012, p. 132). At times, Cancer World seemed to lack any firm rules. At times, even the doctors could not agree on the interpretation of events. In early August, Craig had appointments with both of his doctors to discuss his computed tomography (CT) scan; yet the two meetings seemed to suggest that there were two different CT scans. His pulmonologist came into the examination room "full of enthusiasm with a big smile on his face and immediately said he wanted to share some good news" (2012, p. 115). Previously, four new tumors had appeared in Craig's right lung, and the doctors were concerned that the tumors were cancerous; the good news was that the CT scan clearly showed that they were not. Yet, in the subsequent meeting to discuss the CT scan, the oncologist spoke in subdued tones and did not seem to indicate that the scan had provided any good news until Craig finally asked if there was anything about the CT scan that should make him feel a bit more optimistic. The oncologist then made some comments that were consistent with the "good news" already expressed by the pulmonologist. In comparing the two meetings, Craig noted that "a patient should not have to plead for [positive] information; the doctor should provide it with an appropriate amount of hope and optimism" (2012, p. 115).

Craig read as much as he could about the success others have had in responding to cancer treatments, and he used all the tools at his disposal to implement strategies recommended in books or by friends. Sheri carefully monitored his diet; he frequently engaged in breathing exercises; he tried meditation; to promote a positive attitude, he read books and watched films that made him laugh, but nothing seemed to affect the inexorable progress of this disease. In the effort to maintain his hopes for survival, he continued to employ his sense of humor when interacting with others and was as active as his energy levels permitted. Even for an objective observer, it would be fair to say that for a person who was by nature misanthropic, he was making a superhuman effort to focus on the positive events that occurred each day. Even on those particularly exhausting days when he could barely get off the couch, the best moment might be when his Springer Spaniel came up and licked his face. Craig was comforted by such incidents and cherished such moments.

Throughout the ordeal, Craig desperately searched for reasons to have hope and optimism, but by the fall of 2008, he seemed to have become reconciled to his death. He still wanted his life to last as long as possible, but it was becoming much more difficult to believe that he had much longer to live. Part of his reconciliation stemmed from a change that had occurred during the fall in his conversations with his doctors. They were now talking about what they called "maintenance" strategies: "By maintenance, the medical goal is to slow the spread and growth of my cancerous tumors. It was an emotional blow when the focus of our medical discussions switched from cure to maintenance" (2012, p. 130). The doctors were describing treatment options in terms of the possibility of an option that might result in an additional 3 or 4 more months of life. For example, they discussed the option of preventive brain radiation therapy, and they called in another doctor who had used this therapy with some of his patients. This doctor tried to assure Craig by saying that the patients who had taken this option had some loss of cognitive functioning but he emphasized that they were not reduced to "zombies" as a result of this therapy. Craig's was not reassured:

> There was little comfort to be taken from this "zombie standard" of quality of life as employed by this doctor. On the other hand, it did make me look forward to the possibility of appearing as an extra on the upcoming remake of the film classic, *Night of the Living Dead.* (2012, p. 130)

So Craig battled on, using all of the wit and hope and will-to-live that he could muster, but as he wrote in a journal, cancer is a "workaholic," putting in 24 hours a day, 7 days a week. I called him in mid-December of 2008, and during that phone conversation, he gave a muted chuckle and said, "Well Kent, it's no longer an abstraction." And I knew he was talking about death, but I could not quite believe it. Two weeks later, Sheri called from Arizona and said Craig was having trouble breathing and could only speak in a whisper. She put him on the phone, but his voice was so soft I couldn't hear what he was saying. My wife and I made plans to leave immediately for Arizona. When we arrived, Craig was lying in a hospital bed set up in the living room; he was so weak that it took all of his strength just to breathe. Hospice workers came and did what they could to make him more comfortable. There were five of us there—Sheri, and Lindsay, my wife and me, and Lindsay's fiancée, Colin. We sat around the bed at different times holding his hands, touching his bare arms, stroking his hair, caressing and kissing him, and talking to him, but he was never able to respond. We took turns reading books to him, even when his eyes were closed, because sometimes that only meant he was resting, not sleeping. At one point, I told the others they should take a break and go out for lunch while I stayed with Craig. They took my suggestion and for the next couple of hours I was alone with my friend. At one point, he opened his eyes, and they were not cloudy but clear and focused as if he were quite conscious, even though he still could not speak. I closed the book I had been reading and talked to him. I said I wished this wasn't happening, but in the same way that he had stepped through the looking glass into Cancer World, I believed he was going to step through another looking glass and find himself in a different world, a better world, a world without pain. I kept talking and he listened for a while, but then his eyes became cloudy and unfocused again, and he closed them. Two days later, he stepped through that other looking glass.

Craig Fiedler was not a perfect human being and never claimed to be. He was modest about his accomplishments even though they represented significant achievements. His commitment to students and the enjoyment he derived from teaching were obvious to both students and colleagues. He also spent an enormous amount of time to prepare and provide evening or weekend workshops to assist families with disabled children, while prolifically publishing his own research and editing a journal on disability research. For almost three decades he engaged in a multitude of advocacy efforts for people with a disability; his passion for assisting the underdogs of the world never wavered. Despite all the disappointments, Craig persisted in making efforts to satisfy his ongoing desire to contribute in some way to making a more just society. The loss of such a person is so painful that it cannot be adequately measured. I often think of all the good he would have done had he lived longer. In moments of despair, I have to remind myself of what Victor Hugo wrote in his novel *Les Miserables*: "It is nothing to die; it is frightful not to live" (1887, p. 276). Craig's life was a full life, and he lived it fully until the end. His life was not a tragedy but the story of a good man with a sorrowful ending; of course, most human stories end in sorrow. The ache I feel is shared by all of us who knew him; it is the pain anyone feels for a loved one who leaves us too soon. I hope I was right in what I told him in that last conversation. I hope he has stepped through a looking glass and is in a different world, a better world. He deserves to be there.

REFERENCES

Fiedler, C. (2012). *Robbery and redemption: Cancer as identity theft*. Amityville, NY: Baywood.

Hugo, V. (1887). Jean Valjean, Part 5 of *Les Miserables*. In I. F. Hapgood (Trans.). Boston, MA: Thomas Y. Crowell & Company.

Koppelman, K. (2010). *Wrestling with the angel: Literary writings and reflections on death, dying and bereavement*. Amityville, NY: Baywood.

http://dx.doi.org/10.2190/FATC9

CHAPTER 9

The Psycho-Spiritual Side of Palliative Care: Two Stories and Ten Transformations Toward Healing

Douglas C. Smith and Conley M. Potter

INTRODUCTION

Palliative care for the dying can be defined as offering "comfort care"; comfort care for both the person who is dying *and* their loved ones. The psycho-spiritual side of palliative care involves offering psycho-spiritual comfort to all those involved. To achieve this psycho-spiritual comfort, we (Doug and Conley) suggest 5 steps a dying person can take and 5 steps the loved ones of the dying can take. A palliative care counselor can facilitate these 10 steps, or the 10 steps can be taken independent of a facilitator. We base these 10 steps on our experiences with terminally ill people as well as our review of palliative care literature. We will first present two personal stories of death: my (Doug) daughter's death and my (Conley) father's death, both of whom died quite young and both experienced great physical and emotional pain in their dying. We will then relate these two deaths to what we consider to be the 10 steps toward psycho-spiritual comfort, citing our personal experiences with each of the steps as we cite supporting palliative care literature.

Doug's Story of His Daughter Maren

My daughter Maren was born with a terrible disease called neurofibroma-tosis, sometimes referred to as the "Elephant Man" disease. It is a disease that is often characterized by huge tumors, multiple physical and mental handicaps, and frequent corrective surgeries as well as the additional social realities of shunning, isolation, and loneliness. Maren's life contained many of those characteristics from the very beginning—her first surgery to remove a tumor occurring when she was only 3 years old. Then, toward the end of her life, she experienced one

115

of the most painful transitions into death I had ever witnessed in my 25 years of working in hospice. She died June 11, 2004, at the age of 28.

I remember very clearly her first day of school. She came home from school crying, saying that the other children pointed at her and called her names because of a tumor she had on her right eyelid. She asked if I might walk with her to school the next morning, the school being just a couple blocks down the street. As we got closer, she said, "Dad, let go of my hand. Please walk behind me. Don't say anything." Then I saw the other children point, and I heard them call her names, and I watched my daughter walk through that gauntlet, head hanging down as she walked into the school.

After that day, I knew her life would be very difficult; she would have much pain and suffering ahead of her. But I also knew she would somehow face those difficulties with an immense amount of courage. I also felt she would not withhold her love from others even if they withheld their love from her.

Shortly after high school, Maren came to a decision. She had decided that if there was not anyone willing to be a receptive recipient of her love, she would create her own recipients. Maren decided that more than anything, she longed to be a mother. But she could find no one willing to be a husband, let alone a father. Yet she did get pregnant and gave birth to a boy, DeArzae, my first grandchild. DeArzae never did see his father, except for a few hours when he was 4 years old.

In becoming a mother, Maren had found the answer to her longings, and she had found her vocation. She also found love. She found love because a curious thing happens between mothers and children: children will love their mothers. Children will love their mothers even if their mothers have large tumors. Children will love their mothers even if their mothers do not have any friends. Children will love their mothers even if their mothers cannot run and have trouble walking.

Although Maren had found her vocation, she needed to also find an occupation, something to financially support her and DeArzae; and she found one. Maren made a phenomenal success in an occupation that is normally minimum wage—phenomenally successful; she became a telemarketer. The reason I believe she was so successful was because the people she interacted with did not see her terrible disease, they did not see she was a single mother, they did not see that she looked different from others, but they did "see" her. And when anyone "saw" Maren for who she really was, they would buy literally anything from her.

In her success, Maren was able to purchase a home across the street from a school. She bought groceries. She bought furniture. She purchased childcare for DeArzae during those times when she had to work.

Maren then decided to have a second child and gave birth to my second grandchild, Autry; he was also born with neurofibromatosis. Autry's father had a similar personality to DeArzae's father: abandoning Maren soon after the birth of the child. So Maren, handicapped though she was, began to raise two young boys with little assistance from anyone else.

Unfortunately, neurofibromatosis typically accelerates during times of hormonal changes. Consequently, Maren had been taking a great risk in becoming pregnant. And things became significantly more troublesome shortly after the birth of Autry: larger tumors, more operations, and more radical operations. With one operation, she lost a leg, with another, she lost a portion of her skull.

Much of the last couple months of Maren's life, she, along with Autry, lived with me in my home. With the help of some home health aides and some good friends, I was able to take care of my daughter. We talked and spent times of silence together; I tried to entertain her; I provided her with food and shelter; I tried to see that she did not lack in anything she wanted. I tried to be a father and a nurse to her: I cleansed her bedsores and many of the other things associated with caring for an ill person who is unable to do many things alone. During that time, I witnessed Maren's frustration, despair, and her anger; but I was much more aware of her phenomenal courage and fortitude as well as her unfailing love toward Autry and all those around her.

During Maren's final weeks, she willingly gave her children over to new parents, Steven and Jennifer, who had lovingly offered to raise DeArzae and Autry. Maren said goodbye to her mother. She said goodbye to me. She told Steven and Jennifer what she most wanted from them as parents. She told DeArzae and Autry what she most wanted from them as children.

Maren's very last days were spent in excruciating pain, those last days being spent in a hospice house in Mason City, Iowa. Maren was in terrible pain because as sophisticated as pharmacology has gotten in recent years, there is still one issue yet to be solved: when someone has a combination of nerve pain with tumor pain. The primary medication for the one can actually cancel out the primary medication for the other, and neurofibromatosis literally means tumors at the ends of nerves. A device was implanted in Maren's spine to send medication directly into her spinal fluid. She was confined to her side in a hospital bed, five pillows placed between her back and the bedrail. She would often scream out in pain if the fourth or fifth pillow had to be moved.

Maren requested that her brother, Joshua, my son, be with her during her last night of consciousness on this earth; Joshua recalled that night when he gave Maren's eulogy. He recalled, "I was blessed with the chance to spend the last night with Maren in which she was conscious. It was at around 7 in the morning in which I woke up to Maren saying to the hospice nurses, 'Let's sing a song.' One of the nurses responded, 'What song would you like to sing?' Maren said, 'Let's sing *Angels We Have Heard On High*.' So Maren and the two nurses sang the first verse of *Angels We Have Heard On High*. Maren then said, 'Let's sing another song,' Again the nurse replied, 'What song would you like to sing?' Maren replied this time, '*Lift High The Cross*.' Maren and the two nurses sang the first verse of *Lift High The Cross*. Afterwards Maren said, 'Let's sing *Angels We Have Heard On High* again.'" Joshua concluded, "All I could do was smile as tears came to my eyes. We knew Maren was right with her family and friends, right with her two sons, and at this point, I knew she was right with God."

Conley's Story of His Father, Tom

Throughout his entire life, my father, Thomas, was put through more suffering than any man should have to deal with, and, because of that, he also suffered from alcoholism. At the age of 15, my father lost his mother to what was declared a "heart attack." Family friends have said that if it hadn't been a heart attack, her death would have come very quickly because of the alcoholism that she suffered from as well. (My dad's parents were separated, and he lived with his mom at the time.) After her death, he went to live with his father. After 5 months of living with his father, his dad fell down the stairs in a drunken stupor and died. My dad was 15 years old and had lost both of his alcoholic parents. With no guidance, what is a young man to think? He was overcome with guilt, but the story doesn't end there.

My dad decided to live with a friend after the death of his parents. Things were not fine in this household either. His friend's brother was having problems with drugs. Not long after my father arrived at this friend's house, the brother died of a drug overdose. In the pandemonium, my dad was forced to leave. Because of the immense suffering that that family was going through at the time, my father was blamed for the death of the brother. This added onto my dad's guilt even more.

Now my dad had left three households where three people had died. Yet he still pushed forward in life and received his high school diploma at Packer Collegiate Institute in Brooklyn. He started looking for employment. He had periods of homelessness during this time. He was 18. He had no parents. He was kicked out of his friend's house. He was filled with guilt and didn't tell his extended family of his situation. He ultimately felt that he was at fault for the death of his parents. It was during this phase that his drinking began.

Despite some beliefs, drinking is uncontrollable for many—my dad included. He started drinking to cope with all that he was forced to go through. He didn't have any role model to tell him not to. In fact his parents had done the exact same thing to cope as he did. Although it was not until later in his life that his drinking became uncontrollable, my dad was not doing well.

After about a year of this, my dad's grandmother made him move to Madison, Wisconsin, where she lived. For a few years in Madison, my dad did fairly well. Despite everything that had happened, my father was a great man. He was the kind of guy everyone wanted to be around and everyone liked. He lit up a room, and he was said to be brilliantly intelligent and good at anything he did. He was outgoing, fun, and loved to dance.

A couple years after moving to Madison, my father met the woman who was to later become my mom. He was the manager of a restaurant in Madison, and my mom worked as a waitress. When my dad first saw my mom (so the story goes), he proclaimed to a friend, "I'm going to marry that woman." It just so happened that he did.

My parents started dating, and they fell in love. My mom and dad talked about their aspirations and goals. My dad wanted to open a restaurant. He loved people; he wanted to be in the hospitality business and make people happy. Together, my mom and dad talked about opening up a bed and breakfast featuring a gourmet restaurant. My mom loved decorating and homes, so it was a great idea for her as well.

What my dad wanted more than anything, however, was something that he had lacked since he was very young: a family. When my parents started getting serious, my dad met my mom's family. As it happens, they fell in love with him too. He was so grateful to have a normal family for the first time in his life.

When my parents got married, they knew they wanted to have children. In 1995, they had their first child, me. My brother Eann was born 3 years later. At this point, my family moved, and my dad got a great job. He was a very kind and caring father to us, but things were beginning to go amiss.

My mom didn't like the way that my dad drank; she didn't like for my dad to get drunk at home, around his children. His employers had similar concerns about his drinking at work. They were forced to lay him off, and they suggested that he seek help. This is when my dad started trying the rehab process.

My dad went through several different rehab centers. After the first time, he seemed to be doing well. He got a new job and started life in full stride all over again. He was becoming very successful at his new job, but the hours were extremely demanding. He began working 70-hour weeks. My dad relapsed, began drinking again, and walked out on his job. He once again went into a rehab center to try to stop drinking. We did not know that this was an exercise in futility. Alcoholism is a progressive disease; it cannot be controlled. After getting out of this rehab center, he began drinking again just as before.

My mom decided that she could no longer deal with what my father was doing or put my brother and me at risk, so she sold our home and left him. This was the hardest decision my mom ever had to make. She loved my dad with all her heart, and she wanted my brother and me to have a dad, but she knew that by staying with him, she was actually enabling him to drink. It was in the best interests of everyone to make the decision that she had to make.

For a time, my dad was able to see my brother and me on the weekends. These are the times I remember the most with my dad. He lived in Door County in the peninsula of Wisconsin. We would walk to the coast of Lake Michigan, explore Sturgeon Bay, and just spend quality time together. I did not know that I was making my last memories with my dad.

My dad could not control his terrible disease. He would drink around my brother and me when we were with him. My mom was worried for our safety, thinking that my dad could be drunk while driving, or neglect or hurt us in some way. It was becoming a problem for my dad to keep spending time with us. My mom would do breathalyzer tests with him every time he came to pick up my brother and me, and after several times of failing those tests, my mom had to make the decision to not allow him to see my brother and me.

I've stressed it several times, but I must take a minute to do it again. Alcoholism is an unpreventable disease. It is an unstoppable addiction. Although it reared its ugly head because of the sadness and guilt from his parents' death, my father was genetically predisposed to alcoholism. My dad loved my brother and me so much, but there was no way that he could stop the disease. The disease had a death grip on him.

My dad was not allowed to see or to talk to my brother and me; my mom lost all contact with him. She didn't want to hurt him; she wanted to help him. She would often think that maybe he would get better if he could see my brother and me, but she knew that that was not an option. She worried about him every day, thinking that she would get a call from the police department or a hospital about him. One day that call did come.

My dad had been in the hospital for quite some time with failing kidneys and liver. In testament to the guilt my father felt about his drinking and behavior, he did not want his family to be called when he was admitted to the hospital. It was the decision of a very kind nurse to finally call my family when she saw that my father was reaching his final days. We came in to visit my dad on his last night. There, on his deathbed, my mom talked to him. He had lost the ability to speak, but she told him that she loved him and held his hands. She apologized to him and communicated everything that she had wanted to communicate over the past several months before his death. Most importantly, she told him that she would tell my brother and me about the wonderful man that he was. (My father had a bad disease; he was not a bad person.) Many hugs and tears were exchanged and then we left. That night, my father passed away and left behind his legacy of love.

TEN TRANSFORMATIONS TOWARD HEALING

Smith (1999) portrayed a way of defining the difference between traditional medical care and palliative care by saying that traditional medical care focuses upon "curing," whereas palliative care focuses upon "healing." Medical care seeks to "eliminate" people's wounds by objectively/physically "curing" people: returning people to the condition they were before receiving their wounds. The "healing" of palliative care emphasizes more of a subjective/qualitative change in people; people's wounds are not "eliminated" in palliative care, but people are able to find some kind of "comfort" in their woundedness. In palliative care, people are not objectively/physically "reformed;" they are rather subjectively/qualitatively "transformed."

In palliative care, people can be subjectively/qualitatively transformed through palliative medications, medications that can provide bodily comfort through pain and symptom management. In addition to bodily comfort, there can be subjective/qualitative transformations that can provide comfort to people's minds, to their emotions, and to the spiritual side of their existence. In acknowledging this psycho-spiritual side of palliative care, we offer a prescription for healing that involves 10 steps in a transformational process: 5 steps for a dying person's loved one(s) and 5 parallel steps for the dying person. Each of the five steps follows a natural progression, even though there is often a need to revisit each of the steps.

Psycho-spiritual comfort can come after completing these 10 steps. Here follows our prescription for psycho-spiritual healing:

1. The loved one's acknowledgment of a sense of helplessness.

Doug: Throughout my daughter's illness, I had this sense of helplessness. I wished that I could somehow spare her all the pain and suffering she was going through (the physical, the psychological, the social, the spiritual), but I often found myself in what felt like a *quagmire* of helplessness. I wanted to help, but I had no idea what I, or *anyone*, could do. I felt immobilized. Yet I somehow knew that I needed to take a step beyond that sense of helplessness or I would just remain completely stuck in the quagmire.

Conley: During the time of my dad's disease, my mom certainly felt extremely helpless. She wanted to be with my dad and support him, but she also knew that she would only be enabling his drinking if she did. Yet she also saw that not allowing him to see his children was hurting him. She felt stuck, immobilized. There's also my own sense of helplessness that came later on in life when I looked back at me as an 8-year-old losing my father. I was helpless then, and now I cannot help him or bring him back. At times I have wished that I could have been older when he was struggling so that I could have said something or done something that would have made *some* kind of difference. More helplessness.

The literature: In describing this sense of helpless immobilization, Smith (1997) even speaks of the need and "the right" (p. 143) to cry and express anger—for we feel there is nothing else we can say or do. Longaker (1997) sees this helplessness as often taking the form of the feeling that "God has completely abandoned you" (p. 200), leaving you totally alone and powerless.

2. The loved one's sense of guilt.

Doug: I did much for Maren, but I always have haunting thoughts that I could have done more. I sometimes even wonder that if I hadn't divorced Maren's mother when Maren was in grade school, all of this might have been avoided. I sometimes look back and think that perhaps I should have cancelled all my scheduled work as Maren was in her final months, quit my job, and spent every minute with her, making all those minutes the best they could possibly be; maybe I could have even postponed her death had I done all of that. That's what I have sometimes thought or believed—not acknowledging how unrealistic, how impossible, that would have been.

Conley: Guilt was a key theme of the entire situation around my dad's death. My mom's helplessness went hand in hand with her guilt. She thought that if she had done something more for my dad or allowed him to see his children or stayed with him while he was drinking that maybe he could have gotten better. She wanted so badly to *save* him. For several years after his death, my mom felt full responsibility for the death. Even my dad's grandmother felt guilt that she could have done something more. Guilt has come to *me* as well, when I look back at my choice to not see my dad on his deathbed because I was just too scared. Yes, I know now that it would not have made any difference in the outcome, but I have still felt guilt nonetheless.

The literature: Smith (2001) says, "Every grief has within it some guilt" (p. 202). "Guilt can be a double-edged sword. It can call us back to do the right thing, or it can paralyze us" (Anderson, 2001, p. 57). More often than not it involves a little bit of both.

3. The loved one's need to express forgiveness— self-forgiveness and forgiveness of the dying.

Doug: No matter how logical/rational I've tried to be about my not being able to be the perfect father/savior for Maren, I have experienced moments of healing only when I have made the emotional/spiritual act of forgiving myself. Yes, I made some mistakes—more than a few—yet I genuinely *tried* to be the best I could be and I truly *loved* her, with all that entails. I was not a *terrible* father, and I have now come to *believe* that. I did well—maybe not the best—but I did well. And I forgive myself for not being the best. And, as strange as it sounds, I also now forgive Maren for leaving me: neither she nor I nor anyone can be anything other than human.

Conley: For years, my mom saw therapists to try and gain self-forgiveness; I have as well. My mom and I both have tried "talking to" my dad. This has been the biggest healing factor for my mom, along with her new profession working at a funeral home. Self-forgiveness obviously comes with time; it is a process that I am still going through today. I realize now that I did the best I could do as an 8-year-old. What helps me the most, however, is knowing that self-forgiveness is what my father would have wanted—he has "told" me that.

The literature: Byock (2004) and Goldberg (2009) emphasize the importance of our forgiveness in the ongoing healing process. Seeing this importance, Levine (1991, pp. 52–56) and Smith (2003, pp. 200–201) suggest tools for self-forgiveness and the forgiveness of the dying person.

4. The loved one's need to express love—
self-love and love of the dying one.

Doug: I expressed my love; I did that (maybe not to its full extent, but I did express it). It was sometimes expressed through a kind act, sometimes just through a simple exchange of looks, sometimes through a smile, sometimes simply through sharing some silence together. But I also sometimes did not express it when I truly had it: afraid of tears, afraid of any number of unidentifiable things. Yet I know she knew that I loved her, and she knew I knew she knew. I could have expressed it more (we always can), but I know I expressed it.

Conley: Because of our family's awareness of my dad's dying was quite short, a lot of our love has had to be expressed posthumously. However, my family was able to fit a lot of love into our last visit. We made that last visit specifically to express our feelings of forgiveness and love. To this day, we continue to express our love through visits to his gravesite and various acts of remembrance. I also personally express my love by striving to be what I know he would want me to be.

The literature: "A dying person needs to be shown as unconditional a love as possible, released from all expectations" (Rinpoche, 1992, p. 175). Notice the words "as possible." In outlining the role of the caregiver of the dying, Smith (1994, p. 125) says, "The caregiver reveals impartiality. She shows forgiveness. She announces compassion. She shouts love."

5. The loved one's placing of everything
within a spiritual context and understanding.

Doug: In my grieving over the loss of Maren, moments of peace have come when I have found a spiritual context to all that has happened and is happening. I experience moments of peace when I know that Maren was a sacred gift to me; she was a blessing to me and her children and her world. I have moments of peace when I know the gift of her and her gifts to us are now being extended from me to others as I tell her story to others in my work (and as I write this chapter). Because of my awareness of the profound spiritual effect Maren has had on me and others, I know she was a spiritual person and, as Joshua said, "She was right with God."

Conley: My dad is in a better place: he is out of agony and can finally rest in peace. My mom's anxiety and fears have now subsided, and so have mine. I know that my dad's death was not in vain; he taught me much and he gave me much. He has allowed me to live a safe life by all that he has given me financially, intellectually, emotionally. He is an integral part of my very being; his spirit and my spirit are fused together. And now he is at peace, which puts me at peace.

The literature: Longaker (1997) defines this task of discovering the spiritual context as "finding meaning in life" (p. 136), which means finding meaning in death. Smith (1994) writes, "What is sacred? It cannot be grasped; yet it can take hold. It cannot be pushed or pulled; yet it can move you. It cannot be taught; yet it can be learned. . . . In allowing yourself to receive another, the sacred is being revealed" (pp. 102–103). In acknowledging that we have received a true gift from and through another, we see what is spiritual, and we finally find peace.

6. The dying person's sense of helplessness.

Doug: Maren could not erase her illness. She often wished she could, and she certainly had hopes and dreams—though sometimes very unrealistic ones. Yet she could not avoid the inevitable waves of reality, the undeniable state of helplessness in the face of mortality. She could not wish or think her illness or mortality away; there was no diet, exercise, philosophy, pill, or operation that would do that. She was helpless within the throes of dying.

Conley: My dad's alcoholism was all about helplessness. He was totally helpless, at the mercy of its power. He finally gave in to the depths of its power when he could no longer see his family. He must have seen no other way of helping my brother and me except through his death.

The literature: Smith (1997, p. 2) outlines many of the contributing factors to this sense of helplessness: the loss of so many choices, the loss of medical options for undoing or reversing pain and suffering, the loss of employment, the loss of purposefulness, the loss of family roles, the loss of going where you want to go and doing what you want to do, the loss of dignity, even the loss of bodily functions—coupled with the realization that none of that will ever be able to be brought back.

7. The dying person's sense of guilt.

Doug: No matter how loving and caring Maren was, she was often plagued with feelings of guilt. She would often feel, and even say, things like, "Why did I deserve this?" "Why am I being punished?" "Why would God take me away from my children?" "Why me?" Just asking such questions (and we all ask similar questions when in distress) implies that people often associate guilt with their helplessness, with their pain and suffering.

Conley: My dad's guilt was the catalyst to his drinking. He felt somehow responsible for his mom's death, feeling that he had driven her to drink. He felt that he had driven his dad to drink, causing his death as well. And his guilt kept building.

The literature: Wilcox (1996) says, "Our response to our own helplessness is shame" (p. 4). Our "response" is often guilt, but that does not necessarily have anything to do with the "causes" of our helplessness.

8. The dying person's need to express forgiveness— self-forgiveness and forgiveness of family.

Doug: As with many people who are dying, Maren expressed self-forgiveness and forgiveness of her family by *transcending* all of the guilt. She accomplished that transcendence by passing her children onto Stephen and Jennifer. She also accomplished that transcendence by changing Joshua's priorities and ambitions. (Before Maren's death, Joshua was planning on going into sports business; after her death, he is working for Blue Cross and is a strong champion for victims of neurofibromatosis.) Through both of those accomplishments of Maren, she was proclaiming a type of *absolution* for both her and her family.

Conley: I will sometimes think that the saddest thing about my dad's life is that he never forgave himself. Yet in many ways, I feel he *exceeded* and *overcame* his guilt by letting my brother and me be with my mom, without his presence. In many ways, he *redeemed* himself by empowering my brother and me to want to become people who would make our dad proud. *How* he ever accomplished that I'm not too sure, but I *know* he accomplished it. And through that accomplishment, *redemption* occurred for him and us.

The literature: Forgiveness comes as a result of realizing that "death is neither evidence of personal failure nor a problem due to an unhealthy psyche" (Longaker, 1997, p. 25). The impermanence of our bodies is inevitable; but through forgiveness, all the failings of our bodies are transcended, absolved, redeemed.

9. The dying person's need to express love— self-love and love of family.

Doug: How amazing it is that people can muster up feelings of love in the midst of their own pain and suffering! I fondly remember Maren's multiple loving expressions toward all those around her, remembering most especially the times when she personally expressed love toward me. Many times she would even say, "I love you" when I was simply leaving to go to the grocery store. (She gave me a card, a card that I often carry with me in my travels, that says, "There will never be enough words to say or enough ways to show how much I love you and how proud I am to be able to call you my dad.")

Conley: I am amazed at the love my dad showed toward my mom, my brother, and me by disappearing for so long—as strange as that may sound. He had to have completely suppressed all his own desires and needs in order to do what he knew was the best for us. Although I did not understand this for many years, he was loving us and *blessing* us by *not* seeing us. He wanted to spare us from seeing what alcoholism had done to him. He wanted to protect us. He wanted us not to worry. He was completely sacrificing his self for our selves—distancing sometimes being one of the highest forms of love.

The literature: Byock (2004) sees this need as one of the most important needs of the dying: the need to communicate love, the need to, *in some way*, say, "I love you."

10. The dying person's placing of everything within a spiritual context and understanding.

The literature: With this subject, there is a prerequisite to realize that "a person can be spiritual without being engaged in organized religious practice" (Lord, Hook, Alkhateeb, & English, 2008, p. 16). The spiritual side of life can be considered "the glue" that holds our lives together, that which gives our lives "meaning" (Smith, Chapin, Vitale, & Potter, 2012, p. 12). Entering into the spiritual context of life is a "universal, sequential progression into deeper, subtler, and more enveloping dimensions of awareness, identity, and being" (Singh, 1998, p. 14)—"the glue" that keeps our personal lives together. Longaker (1997), once again, sees it as "finding meaning in life" (p. 136).

Doug: Maren discovered that "glue" through her children. Through them, she could hear "angels" singing "on high." Through them, she could "lift high" her own "cross." Through them, she was "finding meaning" in her "life" and in her death.

Conley: I believe my dad fought a very difficult fight until his very last hour; a fight for my mom, my brother and me. He literally gave of his life for us; we were his "glue" during the entire time he was fighting; whenever he might have been feeling meaninglessness, we were his "meaning." To this very day, my father lives on through my brother and me in our interests, our hobbies, our dreams, and our aspirations. I plan to live every second of my life for my dad, as I believe he lived for me. His "spirit" has given my "spirit" the power to have a great life.

Although we (Doug and Conley) have experienced wrenching deaths—deaths that have caused great personal suffering for both of us—we have also found palliation in that suffering. We believe that palliation, that psycho-spiritual comfort, could not have come without the occurrence of all 10 of the above steps. And so we have offered our stories in the hope that you, the reader, might find such comfort and/or perhaps facilitate comfort for others.

REFERENCES

Anderson, M. (2001). *Sacred dying: Creating rituals for embracing the end of life.* Roseville, CA: Prima Publishing.

Byock, I. (2004). *The four things that matter most: A book about living.* New York, NY: Free Press.

Goldberg, S. (2009). *Lessons for the living.* Boston, MA: Shambhala.

Levine, S. (1991). *Guided meditations, explorations and healings.* New York, NY: Anchor Books.

Longaker, C. (1997). *Facing death and finding hope: A guide to the emotional and spiritual care of the dying.* New York, NY: Doubleday.

Lord, J. H., Hook, M., Alkhateeb, S., & English, S. J. (2008). *Spiritually sensitive caregiving: A multi-faith handbook.* Burnsville, NC: Compassion Press.

Rinpoche, S. (1992). *The Tibetan book of living and dying.* New York, NY: HarperCollins.

Singh, K. D. (1998). *The grace in dying: How we are transformed spiritually as we die.* New York, NY: HarperCollins.

Smith, D. C. (1994). *The tao of dying.* Washington, DC: Caring Publishing.

Smith, D. C. (1997). *Caregiving: Hospice-proven techniques for healing body and soul.* New York, NY: Wiley.

Smith, D. C. (1999). *Being a wounded healer.* Madison, WI: Psycho-Spiritual Publications.

Smith, D. C. (2001). Spiritual perspective in end of life care. In B. Poor & G. P. Porrier (Eds.), *End of life nursing care* (pp. 201–209). Sudbury, MA: Jones and Bartlett.

Smith, D. C. (2003). *The complete book of counseling the dying and the grieving.* Madison, WI: Psycho-Spiritual Publications.

Smith, D. C., Chapin, T. J., Vitale, A. J., & Potter, C. M. (2012). *Spiritual growth and healing.* Madison, WI: Psycho-Spiritual Publications.

Wilcox, P. (1996). *Spiritual care of dying and bereaved people.* Harrisburg, PA: Morehouse Publishing.

http://dx.doi.org/10.2190/FATC10

CHAPTER 10
"And the Sun Refused to Shine"

Susan Adams

Death is the final stage in the lifespan development. No matter what age it occurs, it is the termination of human life. The process of emotionally, mentally, and physically preparing for our own death or the death of a significant family member is unique and influenced by a great number of factors such as age, relationship, and cultural influences (Adams, 2005; Dutro, 1994; Weiss, 1998). Culture is defined here in the broadest definition. Doka and Davidson (1998) identified cultural factors to include race, gender, geographic region, religion, socioeconomic, and sexual orientation. Dutro (1994) addressed a cultural group's beliefs, standards, attitudes, and mores as markers to be considered when looking at the reaction to death, while Neimeyer (2001) suggested that even within a specific cultural group, individuals make unique meaning out of a person's death. An attempt to address all these variables is beyond the scope of this chapter; however a brief journey into the world of two different client cases, and the factors that influenced the grieving process, will be examined from the perspective of the Transactional Analysis theoretical model (Berne, 1964; Gladding, 2000; Harris, 1969), Kübler-Ross' (1969) stages of dying, and Worden's (2009) tasks related to postdeath grieving in an attempt to understand family members' differences in coping with death.

TRANSACTIONAL ANALYSIS (TA)

According to Berne (1964) and Harris (1969) *transactions* are a series of interactive communications, both verbal and nonverbal, that occur between two people. Each line of the transaction includes a single stimulus and a single response. Over time, these individual transactions are strung together to establish a pattern that solidifies into what is known in Transactional Analysis (TA) terminology as a *script*. In fact, with family members who are a part of our routine living, we come to expect a specific script of interaction and are programmed to respond according to this script. "This 'programming' is a result of the composite of previous influences in our lives (social programming) and our reaction to them (individual programming)" (Powell, 1998, p. 14).

Family dynamics evolve as each family member plays individual prescribed parts within the context of the family to provide a shield for protection, get individual needs met, or as forms of recognition known as *strokes* (Berne, 1964; Harris, 1969). One common example of this is a universal script that occurs between a baby and a primary caregiver. The baby cries (transactional stimulus) and the adult caregiver responds (transactional response). This is an example of a single transaction. In a short period of time, babies learn to get their needs met by crying, so the pattern or script is established. Even though babies cry to get a variety of different needs met, experience teaches the primary caregiver to distinguish between the cries of being wet, hungry, tired, or afraid so that the appropriate response is forthcoming.

Transactions and scripts involve two or more of five ego states that are universal to all individuals. These five ego states are Critical Parent (CP), Nurturing Parent (NP), Adult (A), Free Child (FC), and Adapted Child (AC), and we carry them with us throughout life as an internal tape recorder (Berne, 1964; Gladding, 2000; Harris, 1969). A brief explanation of each of these ego states is required before proceeding to the case applications related to the pre- and postdeath of a family member.

CRITICAL PARENT (CP) AND NURTURING PARENT (NP)

Critical Parent and Nurturing Parent are the two ego states that store all of our childhood messages. They come from our parents and also from any primary caregivers who were directly and routinely involved in our growing up. These internal messages house both positive and negative messages and teach us how to interact with the world around us. These are the "rules" we learned about living in the world.

The Critical Parent is the negative ego state that taught us things like "Don't talk with food in your mouth" and "Don't interrupt adults when they are talking." The negative messages contain a lot of coulds, woulds, and shoulds. If our lives were filled with harsh criticism without balance, we grow up with low self-esteem and little resilience. However, negative messages are not all bad. Our Critical Parent is the ego state that indicates we should stop at stop signs, look both ways before crossing the street, and finish our work before leisure.

If our needs were met with loving interactions from our caregivers, then our internal Nurturing Parent ego state communicates that the world is safe and can be depended on. We learn that we deserve love, know how to get and give the love we need, and how to lovingly include others in our world. If we were indulged as children, we may have learned that the world is here only to meet our needs.

If we did not get love, or perceived we did not get it, for whatever reason, we grow up focused on ourselves and getting our own needs met; however we need to since no one else can or will meet them.

ADULT (A)

Think of the Adult ego state as a computer devoid of emotion, but logical in decision making. This is an entity whose responsibility is to make meaning of internal and external data. Mr. Spock of Star Trek fame is a superb example of this state. This ego state logically processes new information (external) and maintains balance or peace (internal) between the two parental and two child ego states. It also reprocesses old scripts or messages from any of the other four ego states (internal) to determine if the script is still valid or needs to be modified based on new information and experiences. Perhaps as a child, your mother was primarily a stay-at-home parent who had milk and cookies waiting every day when you returned from school. However, in today's world, you are a working mom, either by choice or necessity, and feel overwhelming guilt about not being a "good mom." The Adult reprocesses that childhood script and logically helps you find other ways to demonstrate your "good mom skills" to communicate that you care about your children.

FREE CHILD (FC) AND
ADAPTED CHILD (AC)

These two ego states are not to be confused with childishness. They are the repository for all our emotional responses and interactions of our past. All our hurts, joys, fears, angers, disappointments, happiness, and irresponsibility are housed here. The Free Child is that spontaneous, fun-loving part of us that often rises to the joy of the moment and surfaces during leisure activities. It also can be irresponsible in thought, judgment, or action; for example, when a person takes bill money to indulge in a leisure activity or partying late into the night instead of getting restful sleep to prepare for a major exam or work-related presentation.

Our Adapted Child contains the responses of our past from all of the other ego states and interactions with others. We have learned how to deal with life's situation from these responses and pull from this plethora of experiences and memories to determine how we will handle whatever situation we encounter next. From our example earlier, if we learned that we were loved and safe, then our Adapted Child will respond from this position. However, if we learned that it was a harsh and hurtful world, we will respond from this position.

While simplistic ·in definition, understanding the script interaction between two or more people is complex. All five ego states are necessary for healthy, well-balanced, age-appropriate living. "None of us remains permanently fixed in any of these ego states, but we may fluctuate from one to another, depending on the situation at hand and our needs of the moment" (Powell, 1998, p. 13). Throughout daily living, a combination of ego states surfaces; sometimes one at a time, but frequently there is a rapid, shotgun-type blend of them.

They are also fluid, and ego states can change over time. This change comes as a result of the Adult reprocessing old scripts and processing the intake of new cultural influences and daily interactions to create new meaning. This new meaning is stored in the Adapted Child until future necessity pulls it out.

This new meaning can be engaged because of life situations that cause us to encounter a unique situation that has never occurred before or because old scripting does not fit. One such challenge to a new encounter that clashes with old scripting is the death of a significant family member. Obviously, that person has never received a terminal diagnosis or died before, so there is no previous scripting to guide us through this foreign terrain. We are clueless in how to make meaning out of this, so we attempt to search our ego states for the closest possible solution. Sometimes our ego state that is used is culturally driven and intentional; sometimes the ego state used is driven by our own fears and insecurities. However, because we have been confronted with an unexpected life challenge, we may even be quite unaware of the ego state or states that are triggered. Transactional Analysis examples linked with the Kübler-Ross and Worden sections and applied to the case studies are provided to be illustrative, not definitive or comprehensive.

KÜBLER-ROSS' FIVE STAGES AND TRANSACTIONAL ANALYSIS (TA)

Becker (1973) purports that people have an innate fear of death, which leads to the fundamental denial of it or the dying process. Kübler-Ross' initial work was an attempt to understand human nature and family dynamics as she observed patients and their families during their final stage of living. Certainly there was clear evidence of denial, but there were also other patterns that seemed to surface as well. Rando (1984) found differences in thinking as well and stated "for all societies there seem to be three general patterns of response [to death]: death accepting, death defying, or death denying" (p. 51).

Kübler-Ross (1969) wrote her famous book to talk about dying and remove the stigma or fear that dying seems to elicit. Her model is not designed to be a linear model nor is it a counseling model. It is not a treatise to suggest that everyone must go through all five stages or the dying process is sequential, moving from will go from Stage 1 to Stage 2 and so on. She suggested that understanding of the dying stages provide psychological insights into the emotions of the dying patient (Kübler-Ross, 1975, p. 39). She wanted to teach families and caregivers how the dying person feels about the dying process and what they need.

Stage 1: Denial and Isolation

In Stage 1, Denial and Isolation, there is the typical "not me" or "this diagnosis is wrong" reaction. Kübler-Ross (1969) argues that "denial functions as a buffer after unexpected shocking news, allows the patient to collect himself or herself and, with time, mobilize other, less radical, defenses" (p. 35). The result may be isolation from people that would confirm this news, or it might be a frantic search for those who would refute the diagnosis.

Stage 2: Anger

The "Why me?" anger surfaces because people can no longer deny what is happening and lash out in rage, hostility, and resentment, as well as intense anger. While it is understandable that these reactions can be quite natural, Kübler-Ross suggested that it is a most difficult and painful stage for family members and caregivers alike because it is hard to not take the anger personally.

Stage 3: Bargaining

Bargaining is a cry for more time or another chance to do something. It is often a plea that arises from guilt over some unfinished business, amends that need to be made over some past experience, or more time for some future event.

Stage 4: Depression

Kübler-Ross (1969) identified two different kinds of depression in this stage: reactive depression and preparatory depression (p. 76). The first is a reaction to the terminal sentence, and the second is an inner emotional preparation for the finality of giving everything up. Attempts to cheer patients up will only interrupt this process.

Stage 5: Acceptance

Reaching acceptance brings the patient to a state of coherence, of becoming a more united self that comes from an authentic inner core. "The stage of acceptance, the final stage in the transcendence of the patient, is the time when the person's life becomes re-centered and more self-reliant and self-sufficient" (Kübler-Ross, p. 159). Patients begin to withdraw from outside events by choice. They may limit visitors and silent, nonverbal communication becomes more comforting than noisy words. "Acceptance varies but generally indicates some degree of emotional detachment and objectively: (Dennis, 2009, p. 66).

However, not all family members or medical staff reach this stage. Instead they encourage the patient to fight until the end and view acceptance as "giving up" or rejections of life or family connection. Kübler-Ross (1975) argued that hopefully caregivers and family members will at least gain insight that a dying patient wants to be treated with respect as a person and not just viewed as the changes in clinical test results or the outcome of some chemical experimentation. She also purported that those who share in the dying experience can reach their own level of acceptance, which will help them lead a more meaningful life after the person has died.

WORDEN'S FOUR TASKS OF MOURNING AND TRANSACTIONAL ANALYSIS

While Kübler-Ross' work has been linked to predeath experiences, Worden (2009) has identified tasks that the bereaved struggle with and ultimately become goals to work toward in processing grief. However, while those who are bereaved must work through these tasks, there is no prescribed timeline that must be followed, regardless of what society attempts to dictate. Since they are tasks of mourning, they apply to those who are grieving because the death of a significant person in their life has occurred.

Task 1: Accepting the Reality of the Loss

This first task occurs in the initial shock-and-numb period when one's denial defense mechanism surfaces. It is the buffer to prevent feeling overwhelmed as we grapple with the facts, meaning, or irreversibility of this specific death. This period typically does not last for an extended period of time, and people recognize that they can survive the loss that death has created. Therefore, they experience their pain and move toward expression of their grief.

Task 2: Experiencing the Pain of Grief

During Task 2, feelings associated with the death begin to surface. Death may uncover a magnitude of issues that have previously been unacknowledged or unrecognized, or it may overwhelm normal coping skills, leaving the person temporarily incapable of dealing with the resulting strong emotions. Grieving people may display gentle or stormy emotional expressions; however, if this exhibition of emotion persists for more than the "acceptable" cultural norm, people begin to send subtle or blatant messages that it is time to "suck it up and get over it." This veiled message is actually an attempt to cover others' own emotional discomfort or escape the reality that death is inevitable for us all.

Task 3: Adjusting to an Environment from which the Deceased is Missing

As we begin to adjust to our environment without the deceased person, we realize we must learn to cope on our own and adjust to living in our new environment. We also must recognize that we have changed; the degree of change depends on the relationship with the deceased and the void that this relationship created. As we examine this void, we discover the roles and demands that were and are no longer a part of our lives. However, the dawning of this realization can create the birth of new abilities and life opportunities to explore.

Task 4: Withdrawing Emotional Energy from the Deceased and Reinvesting It in Another Relationship

This is a time to acknowledge and grieve old memories while building new ones. This is not to suggest that the deceased will be erased. It is a realization that there are others to love and a new life to live that does not include the physical presence of the deceased. However, withdrawing the emotional energy that once was directed toward the person who died can ignite a strong sense of guilt and betrayal for some, but giving ourselves permission to slowly embrace this new life allows us to begin to heal from the sharp pain that the sad memories can trigger. Worden (2009) stated that this process is different for everyone and depends on so many factors, but a newfound stability in life will return in time if the work of the tasks is completed.

CASE APPLICATIONS

Case 1: Betty

Betty complained of balance issues when her doctor diagnosed the cancerous brain tumor. She had been divorced for over two decades. Her two adult sons, Roger and Bruce, were both married, without children, and lived within a 10-mile radius of her. She described her relationship with her sons and daughters-in-law as "very close, but each of us have our own lives."

Initially, Betty and her family all responded from Kübler-Ross' denial (Stage 1), and she sought aggressive medical treatment for the tumor. My initial contact with her was in my office when her initial goal was for support for dealing with the diagnosis "without being a burden to my family." Her Critical Parent gave her strong coping skills of independence, optimism, and an outward appearance of tenacity that she would fight this diagnosis. When her Adapted Child became discouraged or she showed visible signs of depression, her Critical Parent would kick in, and she would talk about "quit being a baby and just deal with whatever is to come." She refused to feel sorry for herself. As the treatments continued to exacerbate the side effects, her Adapted Child alternated between depression (Stage 4) and anger (Stage 2).

Finally, she was no longer coming to my office for our sessions, so I traveled to her home. Frequently, we sat out in her beautiful tranquil garden that she loved so much and talked about days gone when her Free Child planted so many of the bushes and flowers. Often these sessions were interrupted by bouts of nausea (5–10 minutes apart), and she would easily lose her train of thought. In response to my gentle inquiry, "Is this quality of living for you?" she cried and finally allowed her Adapted Child to admit what her Adult had already accepted. She was dying. She decided it was time to engage hospice services and asked me to meet with her family when she told them.

Both of her sons wanted to be supportive, but the youngest son's Adapted Child reacted and argued that she would be able to defeat the cancer. He became angry and insisted she was just "giving up," which was a clear response from his Critical Parent. His wife, Peggy, only cried softly, also a reaction of the Adapted Child. Roger and Nancy both asked thoughtful questions and listened carefully to Betty's responses. Initially, it appeared that their adult ego state was operational, but based on the stoic tenor in Roger's voice, I suspected this was how his Adapted Child was coping with the news. He and Nancy had been married for only 6 months, so her calm, questioning reaction could have been based on the brevity of the relationship rather than lack of emotional connection to Betty.

Betty patiently responded to their questions as best she could, but finally was exhausted from her weakened condition and asked me to talk to them while she went in to take a nap. These conversations are never easy, but it is best when I can fully engage my own Adult to answer questions truthfully and unemotionally and allow my Nurturing Parent to appropriately drive my empathic responses. Both sons asked for my opinion, which of course was not important and would have been inappropriate to share from an ethical perspective. I explained that Betty had been struggling with "being sick" for several months at that point, and the nausea associated with the treatments was getting worse. I always ask family members in this situation "Is this quality of living?" This usually helps me identify both emotions they are struggling with and also a hint of the ego state that is surfacing.

Bruce talked about how unfair life was for him and the fact that Betty would not be there to see his children born and grow up. Other examples he provided indicated to me that his Adapted Child was struggling with loss of his caregiver. Roger's stoic questions and reaction revealed that his role in the family was to be the "man of the house," but he did not know how to deal with a situation that he had no control over. Through this initial conversation, we were able to identify some ways to spend quality time with Betty while she received palliative care to deal with the advancing tumor. Certainly quality versus quantity is not an easy question, but finally they were able to admit that they were not ready for Betty to die, but they wanted to support her decision.

When Betty returned to the discussion, the family had accepted that it was time to make the call to hospice and asked that I be part of that discussion with the hospice team. While there was clear evidence of Adapted Child visible, most of the discussion came from the Adult ego state. Plans were made to discontinue the chemotherapy, which ended Betty's nausea and restored a fraction of quality to her days. The four family members divided caregiving responsibilities, and each took advantage of their personal time with Betty to create precious memories to sustain them in the future. They were able to have meaningful conversations about the past (AC), laugh about funny childhood times (FC, AC), and provide loving acts of kindness (NP) during her remaining weeks.

There were days and even moments when different family members were in different stages of their anticipatory grief. Roger and Nancy were expecting their first child and longed for Betty to live long enough to see the baby born (Stage 3), but they did not want Betty to suffer (NP). Betty desired that as well, however, she died 4 weeks before "Little Betty" was born.

Somewhere during the weeks that transpired between engaging hospice services and Betty's death, all five of them were able to reach a point of quiet resignation and acceptance. I was with the family as Betty, surrounded by their loving vigil, slipped quietly into a coma and died 72 hours later.

Certainly there were lots of tears at the funeral (AC), but there was also a quiet peace that the Adult had been able to process out of the journey (Worden's Task 1). Roger and Nancy named their daughter after his mother, but were able to find peaceful resolution because of the Adult processing of their emotions (Worden's Tasks 2, 3, 4). Bruce struggled with strong feelings of anger (AC) for about a year (Worden's Task 2). His anger came from his need to have his primary attachment figure since she was the only parent he remembered from his earliest childhood memories. In my professional opinion, he would have benefited from some counseling, but he was not open to that. Roger stepped in and was able to fill some of that void as a Nurturing Parent, and Bruce was able to accept that new role (AC) from Roger (Worden's Task 3, 4). Peggy's role throughout this whole journey was more of the Nurturing Parent for her husband and the Adult caregiver and dutiful daughter-in-law for Betty. Her own emotional needs were never very clear, but she was able to be the support her husband needed in order to deal with this difficult life transition.

My work with Betty lasted a little more than a year. Once it was clear the chemotherapy was not successfully treating the tumor, my role changed from "only" her counselor to working with her as part of the hospice team. It would be unrealistic to say that I did not get "emotionally hooked" by this family, because I was a significant part of their final journey together. They were open to my presence and support (NP), which allowed my Adapted Child to appropriately share personal emotions with the family.

I also sought my own consultation with this case and found appropriate outlets among my peer support group to prevent me from becoming tangled in my own emotional struggles. I was keenly aware of my Nurturing Parent tendencies, my own Adapted Child needs, and my Adult abilities to provide effective counseling. Although difficult for me to do at times, I made conscious decisions to limit my availability (A). I played with my grandchildren (FC) and focused on my hobbies (AC, FC). My spiritual beliefs are a constant source of encouragement and renewal to me, so my Adult chose to spend time in Bible study, prayer, and listening to Christian music. All these replenished my soul and renewed my spirit.

Case 2: Maggie and Tom

Maggie and Tom came to see me three months after their only son, age 32, died after a brief struggle with leukemia. Tom was silent through much of our initial sessions, but was very supportive of Maggie, as she struggled to come to a place of acceptance. Their son, Larry, had been a difficult teenager, and his rebellious personality led him into drugs and alcohol throughout high school. Eventually he was arrested for dealing drugs and spent 10 years in jail. During that time, he went through an intensive treatment program, plus he gained skills as a carpenter. In the 2 years since his prison release, he was gainfully employed and had a serious relationship with Jackie. This couple was referred to me by the local hospice, and we spent most of our time together in Worden's Task 2.

During the rebellious and prison years, Maggie and Tom reported they had been loving parents (NP) who were very confused about "what they did wrong" (CP), but convinced that their son would find his way (A). They described the past 2 years as the "best years of his life," full of fun adventures (NP, FC) and were grieving not only the death of their son, but so many other losses as well. They would never see him marry or be grandparents (NP, AC). They would never get to see Larry live up to his potential now that his life was clean and sober. Maggie also was angry that "we have been through so much, but now were the easy years" (CP, AC).

While both reported that they had a spiritual faith, they did not follow any organized religion. Their sense of existential meaning was challenged as they tried to make sense out of "why now" (AC). The emotional reactions they struggled with were similar, but different. Both Maggie and Tom struggled with bouts of depression (AC), which seriously impacted their ability to work or function in daily living. They reported that their friends had withdrawn, but reported that neither had "much energy or interest in social conversation anyway."

Our initial goal for the first 4 weeks was to get both of them out of bed every day (AC). While this may be a simplistic goal, it was a major accomplishment to move them toward experiencing the pain of their grief (Worden's Task 2). During most of the 10 months we worked together, we addressed and processed unfulfilled dreams (A, AC), resentments about past hurts from the troubled years of their relationship with their son (AC), and the anger toward others who voiced that the couple "should be over it by now" (CP, AC).

The strong emotions both were experiencing made it difficult for them to depend on each other for the support they needed (AC). Their respective

Adapted Child ego states were hurting and in such despair that it was a struggle to meet their own personal needs much less the needs of the other. Their marriage commitment to each other and love for the other were clearly evident in nonverbal expressions throughout our sessions. They sat close together on the couch, sometimes held hands, and sometimes just held each other as they cried together in anguish (NP).

In anticipation of difficult calendar dates, we made plans for what the day's activities would be, including meals to eat. (This was important because both of them reported they forgot to eat for lengthy periods of time.) As each date came and went, the grief dissipated, and they were able to focus on the present instead of being locked into past memories. We created rituals to mark different events, which proved helpful because it gave them a plan to follow. It was difficult for their Adult to function in this area of their lives because of the intense pain of the Adapted Child.

Tom adjusted to life more rapidly (A) than Maggie did, and they both attributed that to the fact that Maggie had been Larry's primary caregiver during his brief days in hospice. Both repetitively struggled with the fact that Larry had ignored the warning symptoms of his illness until it was too late to do more than provide palliative care (CP, NP). He had hidden the symptoms and the diagnosis from his parents until it could no longer be avoided. Therefore, it did not leave much time to prepare for his impending death.

As this couple moved forward into Worden's Task 3, more of their daily life routine began to return. Maggie still struggled some days at work and felt embarrassed by her tears, which she said, "were inappropriate, especially after 'this' long!" (CP). We established a "safe place" where she could find some quiet time to cry if needed, and she identified a co-worker whom she was comfortable enough to share her pain. Both seemed to help her ease back into work and begin to embrace a life that did not evolve around grief.

As more of their lives became focused on the present, they were able to have happy moments that did not center on their son's death (AC, FC; Worden's Task 4). They both begin to focus on making some changes in their lives that included early retirement (A). They were unclear what the future would bring as far as a second career, but they began to talk about the future (NP, A, AC). Larry was not erased, but they realized their relationship with him was more than just those last few weeks.

They accepted that their son would never return, and there was no need for his college fund. They decided to purchase a camper and begin to travel on the weekends (A, FC). They took quiet trips, which included spending time in nature. It was on one of these adventures that they found a mountain stream where they decided to spend the 1-year death anniversary weekend and spread Larry's ashes (NP, A, AC; Worden's Tasks 3, 4). This action seemed to bring a healing release for both of them, and when they returned to our next session, they were able to talk about Larry's life and death without the deep anguish or pain that had been so prevalent when they first came to counseling. Within 4 weeks, they terminated counseling and agreed to return if they needed additional help.

I did not make any part of the journey with this couple prior to Larry's death, so there was no clear evidence of Kübler-Ross' stages during our work together. Also, the work I did with them was a traditional counseling role within the confines of my office. My adult was the evaluation standard that determined my treatment planning and goals. However, I was aware of my Nurturing Parent being engaged, especially early on when this couple was in such deep pain. I was surprised to discover how often my thoughts would focus on this couple (NP). Therefore, I sought consultation with a peer, who does grief work, to explore any potential countertransference issues.

MENTAL HEALTH SERVICE PROVIDER, TRANSACTIONAL ANALYSIS (TA), AND SELF-CARE

A diagnosis of death is a crisis for both the patient and those who are significant family and friends. Caplan (1961), often referred to as the father of modern crisis intervention, identified a crisis as "an obstacle that is, for a time, insurmountable by the use of customary methods of problem solving" (p. 18). The crisis state usually only lasts about 4 to 6 weeks because people cannot tolerate psychological disequilibrium for more than a few weeks (Caplan, 1961; James, 2008; Kanel, 2012; Roberts, 1990). Kanel (2012) stated, "According to Caplan (1961, p. 19), growth is preceded by a state of imbalance or crisis that serves as the basis for future development. Without crisis, development is not possible" (p. 3.) Janosik (1984) suggested that it is this disequilibrium, and the anxiety it creates, that provide the opportunity for personal growth and change.

James (2008) reported that "people can react in any one of three ways to crisis" (p. 3). Some gain inner strength to cope effectively with the crisis situation and gain the strength to change and grow in a positive way. Others attempt to block the impact of the crisis, and the emotional reaction that accompanies it, only to have it surface in a variety of ways throughout the remainder of their life. The final group becomes impaired by this crisis and must have outside intervention to be able to move forward.

Using these cases as illustrations, we have identified a form of crisis, described reactions from one or more ego states, and offered a brief explanation of outcome in each case. The focus has been on the patients and their families. However, a brief explanation is necessary from the perspective of the hospice mental health service provider who works with this family through their journey. Depending on when the family enters hospice care, these providers may become emotionally as well as physically involved and may be overlooked in terms of their own mental health needs.

Transactional Analysis (TA)

Those who choose to become involved in a local hospice may be "more prone to burnout as a result of conflicts between an idealistic 'professional mystique' and the harsh realities of working in human services" (Leiter, 1991, as cited in Kanel, 2012, p. 38). This idealistic professional has a strong Nurturing Parent that seeks to help those in need. However, this need to help may also be driven by the Adapted Child in either a positive (own needs were met, so wants to help others) or negative way (no one was there to meet my needs, so I want to make a difference for others).

As long as personal balance between all ego states is maintained in life outside of the job, providers may be able to do their job effectively. However, Schneider (1984) challenged us that "it is not possible to be a facilitator of the growth aspects of bereavement if the helper is not also experiencing growth in relation to personal losses" (p. 270). Kanel (2012) suggested that many providers deal with their emotions by depersonalizing the intrapersonal connections; however, this can be incongruent with the caring nature that initially attracted the service provider into this profession. Therefore, the Adult ego state must process and reprocess our internal emotional struggles and find creative ways to meet our own physical, mental, emotional, and spiritual needs as we work in the field of dying and death.

COMPASSION FATIGUE

Burnout is not a catchall buzz word to describe job dissatisfaction and the emotions that accompany it. Billions of dollars are lost or expended to deal with this phenomenon in terms of lowered productivity, absenteeism, substance abuse, social withdrawal, and increased mental health issues (James, 2008; Kanel, 2012; Leiter & Maslach, 2005). "When many of the clients get worse instead of better despite all of the workers' skills and effort, burnout becomes a high probability" (James, 2008, p. 530). It takes a great deal of empathy to work in this heart-wrenching environment, and James stated "according to Figley (1995) between a very dedicatory ethic and at times an insatiable need to assist everyone with any of type of problem, the idealistic human services worker sees his or her job as a calling" (James, 2008, p. 539). Not only is the increasing emotional intensity between the mental health professional with the client and their family members a drain on the worker's resiliency and optimism, it also takes a toll physically.

The relationship that is created and solidified is a unique one that will always end in death for the client and sometimes continue with follow-up care for family members. Interactions are frequently linked to erratic hours, large case loads, lack of control of home or office counseling visits, and encounters with emotionally raw individuals. Clarke (2000) also suggested that lack of company support and poor staff cohesiveness were also contributors to burnout.

This repetitive exposure to the dying and death as a routine job description for extended periods of time can lead to *compassion fatigue*, a term coined by Figley (1995). He discussed this term in his work related to treating the stress response that can be clearly identified when working with a dying population (Figley, 1995, 2002). This is not a new concept. Figley (2002) suggested that the dedicated providers who genuinely care about their clients become fatigued physically, emotionally, interpersonally, behaviorally, and spiritually. Frequently, visible reactions of those experiencing compassion fatigue, or burnout, are personal emotional exhaustion, as well as depersonalization and deindividuation of clients (Vettor & Kosinski, 2000). Thus, mental health providers must find ways to alleviate their job stress and continually renew a sense of balance in their lives.

Self-Care

Farber (as cited in James (2008) purported that "Burnout occurs when the stress becomes unmediated and the person has no support systems or other buffers to ease the unrelenting pressure" (p. 532). James (2008) and Kanel (2012) provide a lengthy list of burnout-proofing. A partial list of suggested work-related coping management includes work viewed as a team approach and staffing as a routine part of the week; peer cohesion exists, and debriefing is scheduled to process emotions and monitor reactions, especially after someone has died; work time is limited to 40 hours a week or less; and the work environment is clean, brightly decorated, and conducive to mental wellness.

Personal coping strategies include emotional replenishment with routine significant physical and emotional activities that remove the worker completely from dying and death to create a balanced mindset. Another essentially critical coping skill is facing one's own mortality and the existential angst that can bring. Finally, seek mental health intervention in the form of personal counseling sooner rather than later. "Workers can deal with their own bereavement overload provided that they are aware of it while it is happening to them and that they act on their internal signals to get help" (James, 2008, p. 395).

CONCLUSION

Utilizing Transactional Analysis to understand the various ego states triggered by the dying process and the subsequent death can provide insights for understanding the family dynamics that often surface as a result of this disequilibrium crisis. Various ego states are triggered depending on how scripts are altered. As the individual's Adult processes these scripts triggered by the death of the significant person, new insights about life and living can be acquired, and individual ego states can be altered.

Each person touched by the death can find danger or opportunity. "Although the loss of a loved one may never be forgotten, the healthy progression through grief toward healing ends when, during what McKenna (as cited in James, 2008) identifies as the final (refocus) stage of grief, the survivor discovers that new dreams and opportunities may spring from the loss" (p. 363). When the sun refuses to shine, family members and mental health service providers can choose to ignore the warning signs and proceed toward danger, or they can embrace a new life of opportunity. The choice may require mental health counseling, but it certainly must include rediscovering balance in life that starts first with self-care.

REFERENCES

Adams, S. A. (2005). *Teaching the mourning song* (2nd ed.). Denton, TX: Author.

Becker, E. (1973). *The denial of death.* New York, NY: Free Press.

Berne, E. (1964). *Games people play: The basic handbook of Transactional Analysis.* New York, NY: Ballantine Books.

Caplan, G. (1961). *An approach to community mental health.* New York, NY: Grune & Stratton.

Clarke, R. D. (2000). Burned down to the wick? *Black Enterprise, 31*(5), 165.

Dennis, D. (2009). *Living, dying, grieving.* Sudbury, MA: Jones and Bartlett.

Doka, K. J., & Davidson, J. D. (Eds.). (1998). *Living with grief: Who we are, how we grieve.* Washington, DC: Hospice Foundation of America.

Dutro, K. R. (1994, April). *A dynamic, structural model of grief.* Paper presented at the Eighteenth Annual Convening of Crisis Intervention Personnel, Chicago.

Figley, C. R. (Ed.). (1995). *Compassion fatigue: Coping with secondary traumatic stress disorder in those who treat the traumatized.* New York, NY: Pergamon Press.

Figley, C. R. (Ed.). (2002). *Treating compassion fatigue.* New York, NY: Brunner-Routledge.

Gladding, S. T. (2000). Rational emotive behavior therapy and Transactional Analysis. In *Counseling: A comprehensive profession* (4th ed., pp. 233-257). Upper Saddle River, NJ: Pearson.

Harris, T. A. (1969). *I'm ok—You're ok.* New York, NY: Avon.

James, R. K. (2008). *Crisis intervention strategies* (6th ed.). Belmont, CA: Brooks/Cole.

Janosik, E. H. (1984). *Crisis counseling: A contemporary approach.* Monterey, CA: Wadsworth.

Kanel, K. (2012). *A guide to crisis intervention* (4th ed.). Belmont, CA: Brooks/Cole.

Kübler-Ross, E. (1969). *On death and dying: What the dying have to teach doctors, nurses, clergy and their own families.* New York, NY: Macmillan.

Kübler-Ross, E. (1975). *Death: The final stage of growth.* New York, NY: Touchstone.

Leiter, M. (1991). The dream denied: Professional burnout and the constraints of human service organizations. *Canadian Psychology, 32,* 547-558.

Leiter, M. P., & Maslach, C. (2005). *Banishing burnout: Six strategies for improving your relationship with work.* San Francisco, CA: Jossey-Bass.

Neimeyer, R. A. (2001). *Meaning reconstruction and the experience of loss.* Washington, DC: American Psychological Association.

Powell, J. (1998). *Why am I afraid to tell you who I am? Insights into personal growth.* Allen, TX: ThomasMore.

Rando, T. A. (1984). *Grief, dying, and death: Clinical interventions for caregivers.* Champaign, IL: Research Press.

Roberts, A. R. (1990). *Crisis intervention handbook: Assessment, treatment, and research.* Belmont, CA: Wadsworth.

Schneider, J. (1984). *Stress, loss, and grief: Understanding their origins and growth potential.* Baltimore, MD: University Park Press.

Vettor, S. M., & Kosinski, F. A., Jr. (2000). Work-stress burnout in emergency medical technicians and the use of early recollections. *Journal of Employment Counseling, 37,* 216.

Weiss, R. S. (1998). Issues in the study of loss and grief. In J. H. Harvey (Ed.), *Perspectives on loss: A sourcebook* (pp. 343-353). Philadelphia, PA: Brunner/Mazel.

Worden, W. (2009). *Grief counseling and grief therapy* (4th ed.). New York, NY: Springer.

http://dx.doi.org/10.2190/FATC11

CHAPTER 11

The Experience of Dying in Prison

Nicole Pizzini*

Victor Frankl wrote about the ghastliness of being imprisoned and discussed the concept of meaning in his book, *Man's Search for Meaning.*

> A man who let himself decline because he could not see any future goal found himself occupied with retrospective thoughts. In a different connection, we have already spoken of the tendency there was to look into the past, to help make the present, with all its horrors, less real. But in robbing the present of its reality there lay a certain danger. It became easy to overlook the opportunities to make something positive of camp life, opportunities which really did exist. Regarding our "provisional existence" as unreal was in itself an important factor in causing the prisoners to lose their hold on life; everything in a way became pointless. Such people forgot that often it is in just such as exceptionally difficult external situation which gives man the opportunity to grow spiritually beyond himself. Instead of taking the camp's difficulties as a test of their inner strength, they did not take their life seriously and despised it as something of no consequence. They preferred to close their eyes and to live in the past. Life for such people became meaningless. (2006, pp. 71–72)

The above passage describes concepts of hopelessness, having a meaningful life, and making the most of life circumstances, which may be helpful in understanding the experience of dying in prison. One does not usually stop to reflect on the meaning of one's life until that life is threatened. According to Corey (1996), meaning comes through interactions involving ongoing creation, building, work, and love. The ability to fully live out last days and months and to experience a "good death" is through meaning making (O'Connor, 2004).

The culturally based notion of a "good death" and "dying with dignity" are typically expressed by freely declining use of medical technologies that prolong death, pain management, and controlling the environment around you at the time of death (Kaufman, 2000). However, there are many reports of death that are

---

*This chapter is an abridgment of dissertation research conducted by Dr. Nicole Pizzini.

anything but "good and dignified." Due to the nature of the correctional environment, the cultural ideal of a "good death" and "dying with dignity" may be compromised for those who are incarcerated while dying. The correctional environment presents a distinctive situation for the dying experience.

BRIEF LITERATURE REVIEW

Inmates and Terminal Illness

According to the Bureau of Justice Statistics (BJS, 2012), state and federal correctional authorities had jurisdiction over 1,612,395 prisoners on December 31, 2010. This was a decrease of 5,575 prisoners from year end 2009. The federal prison population increased by 0.8% (1,653 prisoners), while the number of prisoners under state authority declined by 0.8% (10,881 prisoners). During 2010, prison releases (708,677) exceeded prison admissions (703,798) for the first time since the BJS began collecting jurisdictional data in 1977. According to the Bureau of Justice Statistics (BJS, n.d.), on December 31, 2004, there were 2,135,901 prisoners incarcerated in federal and state prisons and jails across the United States. The average growth rate from 1995 to 2003 was 3.4%. As of December 31, 2001, there were an estimated 5.6 million adults who had served time in a state or federal prisons.

As prisoners incarcerated in federal and state prisons serve long sentences and serve more time on their sentence, the average age of the prison population increases. The BJS (n.d.) estimated that 43% of inmates in state prisons were over the age of 35 in 2001. This aging prison population brings new challenges to prison administrators, staff, and incarcerated offenders. One challenge is managing the increasing number of prisoners who will die while incarcerated (Ratcliff, 2000).

Suicides, homicides, executions, deaths related to medical illnesses, and deaths related to natural causes are not unfamiliar to prisons (Ratcliff, 2000; Volunteers of America, 2003). The image of dying from medical illness or natural causes in prison might be depicted as lonely, with no family at your bedside, no last goodbyes, no reconciliations, and bleak, with walls all around you. Prisoners have a constitutionally protected right to medical care; however, dying in prison is different than dying in the free world (National Institute of Corrections, 2004).

O'Conner (2004) and Ratcliff (2000) identify several ways in which dying in prison is different from dying in the free world. In the prison environment, the ultimate control over a prisoner is by correctional staff, therefore, the level of control is different in prison. As one nears death, there may be loss of personal control, however, there is even fewer opportunities for control in prison. The second difference is the types of individuals who are available to provide care near the end of life. The prison environment has unique layers of involvement by prison administrators, prison staff, other inmates, and at times, the Board of Parole and the Governor. A third difference is the notion of trust. The correctional system is mistrusting of the inmates and the inmates are commonly mistrusting of the correctional system. Anger and burnout in correctional staff can be related to mistrust of inmates. Mistrust by inmates with terminal illness can lead to depression and helplessness. Pain and symptom management presents a fourth difference. Due to security concerns with medications related to use and abuse, theft and trafficking of drugs, and assurance of effective dosages, some medications are prohibited from being prescribed for inmate patients. Finally, corrections staff may have a difficult time seeing the prisoner as a patient, and as a human being. Attitudes of fear, anger, and prejudice can impact the ability to see beyond the label of criminal/offender/prisoner.

The rising awareness about the experience of dying in prison influenced prison programming aimed at assisting this life process. The debate about providing end-of-life programs was settled; the debate then became a matter of how programs should be offered. Palliative care, prison hospice programs, and other end-of-life care services were developed and implemented. The Federal Bureau of Prisons reported only 11 states that provided end-of-life programs to inmates in 1998 (Volunteers of America, 2003). By 2001, the number of states providing end-of-life programs and developing end-of-life care programs rose to 14 (Volunteers of America, 2003).

A Good Death

For the greater part of two decades, the United Sates has been discussing the notion of a "good death" in a variety of forums. These discussions have brought about the mobilization of hospice and other forms of compassionate care (Kaufman, 2000). In addition, research has focused on the description of a "good death." Themes related to pain and symptom management, clear decision making, preparation for death, completion, contributing to others, affirmation of the whole person, dignity, timing, place, personhood, spirituality, quality of life and meaning of life, as well as the meaning of "end of life" have been identified in relation to "a good death" (Chochinov, 2002; Long, 2003; Steinhauser, Christakis, Clipp, McNeilly, McIntyre, & Tulsky, 2000; Steinhauser, Clipp, McNeilly, Christakis, McIntyre, & Tulsky, 2000).

Dignity

The concept of dignity is central to the philosophy of palliative care and end-of-life issues (Brant, 1998; Madan, 1992). Dignity has been expressed through the perspectives of linguistics, philosophy, and attributes. The linguistics perspective identifies dignity as rooted in the Latin words *dignitus*, meaning merit; and *dignus*, meaning worth (Collins, 1991). Philosophers such as Kant (1948) describe dignity as worthiness that is intrinsic, unconditional, and incomparable.

The attribute perspective brings about a robust description of dignity. Some of the descriptions include privacy, communication, respect for patients, patient control, confidentiality, need for information, patient choice, patient decency, cognitive acuity, functional capacity, physical distress, psychological distress, role preservation, hopefulness, resilience, maintaining normalcy, spiritual comfort, living in the moment, burden to others, social support, giving and receiving love, having rights, and appearance and body image (Chochinov, 2004; Enes, 2003; Matiti & Trorey, 2004). The attributes describe by patient perspectives aided in the development of the Dignity Model (Chochinov, Hack, McClement, Kristjanson, & Harlos, 2002).

The Dignity Model incorporates a wide range of existential, social, physical, and psychological issues that may affect individual perceptions of dignity and is composed of three major categories that contain several themes and subthemes (Chochinov et al., 2002). Concerns that originate from or are linked to the illness itself and intrude on or threaten a patient's sense of dignity describes the first category, illness-related concerns. Two themes within this category are level of independence and symptom distress. Dignity-conserving practices and dignity-conserving perspectives comprised two of these in the second category, dignity-conserving repertoire. External sources or issues that enhance or detract from one's sense of dignity describe the final category, social-dignity inventory. This category is composed of five themes: privacy boundaries, care tenor, burden to others, social support, and aftermath concerns.

Dignity and Incarceration

The attributes identified above have unique connotations when the context of a correctional environment, in particular prison, is applied. At first glance, the notion of control appears to be directly contradictory to the prison environment. The basic premise of a correctional environment is loss of control. However, if options or choices are provided, a sense of control can be instilled (Taylor, 2002). When an individual is removed from society, relationships are directly impacted. People visiting inmates are limited to those who are approved by correctional administrators. They are also limited on how often they can visit. These limitations as well as financial impact of visits and location of prison can lead to isolation from family and friends and possibly termination of their family roles (National Institute of Corrections, 2004). Other prison inmates and even prison staff often describe "family." In addition, the use of psychopharmacology treatments is restricted, thereby impacting the use of social support and medication in the treatment of psychological and physical pain management (O'Conner, 2004). Finally, the lack of trust can impact communication between correctional staff and inmates (National Institute of Corrections, 2004). Due to a lack of understanding and mistrust of the prison system, an inmate may be reluctant to sign a "do not resuscitate" order (Dawes, 2002; National Institute of Corrections, 2004).

As the prison population ages, it is imperative for correctional settings to address the unique issues that arise. One issue that continues to grow is the issue of increasing number of prisoners who die while incarcerated. The notion of a good death and dignity are central to the experience of death. The Dignity Model describe above provides a framework within which to understand the notion of dignity. When considered in the context of a correctional environment, the attributes of dignity take on new meaning.

Need and Importance of Study

There were two main needs for this study. First, as the number of deaths in prison continues to increase, there is a need to have a better understanding of dying in prison. Even though there is the constitutional right to care, the availability of a "good death" in prison remains rare (National Institute of Corrections, 2004). The dilemma of providing a "good death" for inmates is facing correctional administrators. However, in times of tightening budgets, prison overcrowding, and a goal of retribution, focus on dying prisoners may be blurry (Dawes, 2002).

Second, there is an abundance of research on death and dying. However, the research on death and dying in correctional settings is sparse (Chochinov, 2002; Enes, 2003; Matiti & Trorey, 2004). In light of the fact that prison populations are growing at alarming rates, it is imperative for there to be a greater understanding of the experience of dying in correctional settings, particularly prison. As the prison population expands, new challenges to prisoner management are encountered. Some of these challenges include population management, security concerns, housing concerns, medical concerns, budgetary/fiscal concerns, and ethical and legal concerns. Exploration into the experience of dying in prison may impact inmate programming, the prison experience, and the management of inmates. Research on this topic is therefore necessary. This study is a stepping-stone in the literature dealing with end-of-life concerns, the concept of dignity, and prisoner studies.

"The purpose of this study was to explore the experience of dying in prison from the perspective of inmates who were terminally ill, medical prison staff, and security prison staff. In addition, their reflection on dignity and a 'good death' was explored" (Pizzini, 2008). The following research questions were explored (Pizzini, 2008):

1. What is the experience of prison inmates with a terminal illness who are dying in prison?
2. How do prison inmates with a terminal illness describe dignity?
   a. How do prison inmates with a terminal illness characterize dignity?
   b. What factors contribute to a sense of dignity for prison inmates with a terminal illness?
   c. What factors detract from a sense of dignity for prison inmates with a terminal illness?
3. How do prison inmates with a terminal illness describe a "good death"?

METHODOLOGY

This study utilized qualitative research methods to explore the research questions. A single-site, nested-case-study design, guided by phenomenology was employed. Data were collected through two semistructured interviews with inmates with a terminal illness. Medical prison staff and security prison staff completed one interview. The data were analyzed using the constant comparative method.

The setting of this research took place in a Midwest prison in the United States. The purpose of this housing unit is initial reception into the prison system and classification of offenders. This prison operates with an average daily population of 800 inmates. This prison has a hospice program in place and at the time of this research, there was construction of specialized medical units within the prison. Participants in this study were selected through purposeful sampling methods. The inmate participants were willing and able to participate, had a terminal illness, and had a Level of Service Inventory score less than 39. Three inmates agreed to participate and one inmate declined to participate in the research project. In addition, two medical corrections staff and two security corrections staff agreed to participate.

RESULTS

A brief description of the participants is necessary in order to provide a context for results. Fictitious names have been assigned and descriptions have been kept vague in an attempt to preserve confidentiality. Mike is an inmate, approximately 60 years old, diagnosed with cancer, and participating in the prison hospice program. During his interviews he was visibly suffering pain. Mike was unable to participate in his follow-up interview due to diminished mental capacity. Jim is an inmate, approximately 70 years old, diagnosed with diabetes and emphysema, a veteran of the Korean War, and not involved in the prison hospice program. He was not involved with the prison hospice program. Linda has been a correctional officer for approximately 30 years and has not been involved with the prison hospice program. Scott has worked in corrections for over 20 years and was intimately involved with the development of the prison hospice program. Ann is a correctional nurse providing care to inmates in the prison hospice program. Prior to working in corrections, Ann worked in a public hospice program. Sally is a correctional nurse providing care to inmates in a forensic mental health unit and has worked in corrections for over 25 years.

The themes that emerged in relation to research question 1, the experience of dying in prison, were impact of prison environment, programs, dying location, food, socialization, impact on staff, impact on patient inmates, impact on inmates, common experiences, planning, and continuation of self.

In relation to prison environment, one inmate said, "If I had been sent back here, I probably wouldn't have gotten that pneumonia like that . . . asbestos, cold and hot and not, heat, cold, no air conditioning, none . . . you get drafts coming in." With regard to programs, once security staff said, "Hospice care and what we do doesn't involve a person, place, or thing. It involves a way of thinking about end-of-life process and how best to adapt that individual for reaching his end of life." One inmate remarked, "If given the choice . . . I'd die outside of prison" as he was speaking about where he would like to die. As one inmate picked up a fresh slice of bread, he commented, "They get powdered slop." Another inmate stated, "I'd like to be around the people that give me the most joy and happiness." A medical staff member commented, "It has made me feel good." The impact on patient inmates was evidenced in the comment by an inmate: "My last dying days, all you can see is prison." A medical staff member in a discussion surrounding inmate hospice volunteers described the impact on inmates: "It's not that they've felt disconnected, but it's just something that they can't deal with themselves." A medical staff member also reflected on common experiences in this statement: "No one escapes death." One inmate showed concern around planning in his comment: "I'm waiting to sign the damn papers." One inmate commented on the continuation of self as evidenced in the statement, "I figure there got to be life after or something after."

In response to research question 2, description of dignity, dignity was characterized by autonomy, decision making, self-respect, modesty, and privacy. One inmate described how he would rather be sick and not go the hospital than to have shackles put on his ankles.

Themes that emerged that related to factors contributing to dignity were treatment of individuals, follow-through, making accommodations, empathy, having needs met, and self-identity. One medical staff member stated, "I see them as a human being, not as a convict, a con, a prisoner, an inmate, that type of thing. I see them as another person. I try to treat them as such." One security staff member commented, "Sometimes you forget what they are doing time for and you deal with the person."

Themes identified as factors detracting from dignity were inflexibility, rigidity to rules/procedures, and disrespect. One medical staff member commented, "They may pick them up more harshly or forcibly than someone would; they don't explain to the offender what they're going to do, they just do it."

In response to research question 3, a description of "good death," the emergent themes were pain managed, having people around, at peace and comfortable, die with respect and dignity, and hastening death. One inmate reflected, "A good death would be just laying down there and going to sleep, that's just dead and dying, that's it. Just dying, just going. A bad death is laying out on the bed in pain and suffering, and know you're dying and you can't get anybody to help you die." One inmate commented on wanting other inmates around, "and some of the inmates here, you know, not a bunch of them, but some of them."

DISCUSSION

This study had two central findings. First, the experience of dying in prison is shaped by environment and bio-psycho-social factors. These factors include cognitive and affective functioning, coping strategies, physical impact of disease, and interaction with others. The unique environment of a prison impacts the experience of dying. Participants discussed how prison is different than the free world, how relationships are impacted by the prison experience, and how prison programs and policies impact dying and death. Level of control and trust were the differences most noted by the participants.

Second, the results support the existing literature on dignity and a "good death." Prisoners describe dignity attributes as identified in the Dignity Model. Participants described the three categories in the model: illness-related concerns, dignity-conserving repertoire, and social dignity inventory. Participants described six components of a "good death" as identified by Steinhauser et al. (2000): clear decision making, pain and symptom management, preparation for death, completion, affirmation of the whole person, and contributing to others. In addition, they discussed how they are impacted in a holistic way, with mention of physical, emotional, mental, social, and spiritual domains. The main focus was on physical and social impacts, however all domains were discussed by the participants.

LIMITATIONS TO THE STUDY

Limitations to this study were fourfold:

1. Because this study had a low number of participants, the integrity and soundness of this study may be questioned. During the time of this research, only three inmates qualified to participate in this study. The rich descriptions provided by participants established this research as trustworthy.
2. Participant bias may be of concern. Participants may have altered their responses in order to have someone to speak with or in order to return to work duties. The similar descriptions provided by the participants support the credibility of this research.
3. Gender bias may also be of concern, as the voices of female offenders were silent, and the male voices were not diverse.
4. The researchers' intimate knowledge of the prison system, access to inmates, and attitudes toward inmates creates researcher bias. Researcher bias was limited through the use of triangulation, respondent debriefing, peer review, and use of an audit trail.

This research shed much light on the experience of dying in prison. The findings can serve to inform corrections professionals and others who provide services to inmates who are at the end of life about the experience of dying in prison. The benefits of the findings outweigh the limitations described above.

IMPLICATIONS

This study provides insight into the experience of dying in prison for prisoners with a terminal illness; more specifically, that the experience is impacted by environment and bio-psycho-social factors. There are three main implications as a result of this research. First, staff must be prepared to address the experience of dying in prison. Second, correctional administrators need to create and implement policies and procedures that provide for a "good death." Finally, correctional staff must have an understanding that dying in prison is different than dying in the free world. Understanding the experience of dying in prison will enhance the services provided to inmates who are dying.

CONCLUSIONS

The current study contributed to the literature on death and dying literature. This study provided an in-depth investigation into the experience of dying in prison from the perspective of inmates and correctional staff. Participants reported that the experience of dying in prison was influenced by the correctional environment and bio-psycho-social factors. In an effort to promote a sense of dignity for the inmate population, it is encouraged that service providers and correctional staff expand their understanding of dying in prison. This study provided a glimpse into the experience of dying in prison, and it must be remembered that this experience is individualized. More research needs to be completed so that the experience of dying in prison can be fully understood.

REFERENCES

Brant, J. M. (1998). The art of palliative care: Living with hope, dying with dignity. *Oncology Nursing Forum, 25*, 995-1004.

Bureau of Justice Statistics. (2012). *Data collection: National prisoner statistics*. Retrieved September 5, 2012 from http://bjs.ojp.usdoj.gov/index.cfm?ty=dcdetail&iid=269

Bureau of Justice Statistics. (n.d.). *Criminal offenders statistics*. Retrieved March 2, 2006 from http://www.ojp.usdoj.gov/bjs/crimoff.htm#inmates

Chochinov, H. M. (2002). Dignity-conserving care—A new model for palliative care: Helping the patient feel valued. *Journal of the American Medical Association, 287*(17), 2253-2260.

Chochinov, H. M. (2004). Dignity in the eye of the beholder. *Journal of Clinical Oncology, 22*(7), 1336-1340.

Chochinov, H. M., Hack, T., McClement, S., Kristjanson, L., & Harlos, M. (2002). Dignity in the terminally ill: A developing empirical model. *Social Science & Medicine, 54*, 433-443.

Collins. (1991). *Collins concise dictionary and thesaurus.* Glasgow: HarperCollins.

Corey, G. (1996). *Theory and practice of counseling and psychotherapy* (5th ed.). Pacific Grove, CA: Brooks/Cole Publishing.

Dawes, J. (2002). Dying with dignity: Prisoners and terminal illness. *Illness, Crisis & Loss, 10*(3), 188-203.

Enes, S. P. (2003). An exploration of dignity in palliative care. *Palliative Medicine, 17,* 263-269.

Frankl, V. (2006). *Man's search for meaning.* Boston, MA: Beacon Press. (A revised edition of *From death-camp to existentialism. A psychiatrist's path to a new therapy,* 1959, Boston, MA: Beacon Press.)

Kant, I. (1948). *Groundwork of the metaphysic of morals.* New York, NY: Harper and Row.

Kaufman, S. R. (2000). Senescence, decline and the quest for a good death: Contemporary dilemmas and historical antecedents. *Journal of Aging Studies, 14*(1), 1-23.

Long, S. O. (2003). Cultural scripts for a good death in Japan and the United States: Similarities and differences. *Social Science & Medicine, 58,* 913-928.

Madan, T. N. (1992). Dying with dignity. *Social Science & Medicine, 35,* 425-432.

Matiti, M. R., & Trorey, G. (2004). Perceptual adjustment levels: Patients' perception of their dignity in the hospital setting. *International Journal of Nursing Studies, 41,* 735-744.

National Institute of Corrections. (2004). *Correctional health care: Addressing the needs of elderly, chronically ill, and terminally ill inmates* (NIC accession No. 018735). Washington, DC: U.S. Department of Justice.

O'Conner, M. (2004). Finding boundaries inside prison walls: Case study of a terminally ill inmate. *Death Studies, 28,* 63-76.

Pizzini, N. J. (2008). *A qualitative analysis of the experience of dying for prisoners with a terminal illness.* Iowa City, IA: The University of Iowa.

Ratcliff, M. (2000). Dying inside the walls. *Innovations in End-of-life Care, 2*(3). Available at www.edc.org/lastacts

Steinhauser, K. E., Christakis, N. A., Clipp, E. C., McNeilly, M., McIntyre, L. M., & Tulsky, J. A. (2000). Factors considered important at the end of life by patients, family, physicians, and other care providers. *The Journal of the American Medical Association, 284*(19), 2476-2482.

Steinhauser, K. E., Clipp, E. C., McNeilly, M., Christakis, N. A., McIntyre, L. M., & Tulsky, J. A. (2000). In search of a good death: Observation of patients, families, and providers. *Annals of Internal Medicine, 132*(10), 825-832.

Taylor, P. B. (2002). End-of-life care behind bars. *Illness, Crisis & Loss, 10*(3), 233-241.

Volunteers of America. (2003). *Compassionate end of life care inside the walls: Transforming Death . . . and life, final report.* Alexandria, VA: Author.

http://dx.doi.org/10.2190/FATC12

CHAPTER 12

The "Other" Kind of Pain: Understanding Suicide in the Context of End-of-Life Care

Janet S. McCord

In his final book, Edwin S. Shneidman explored the criteria for what he called a "good-enough" death (Shneidman, 2008). Tired, ill, lonely for Jeanne, his life partner, the notion of imminent death had been on his mind for several years and, in fact, he died just two days after his 91st birthday, less than a year after the book was released. After celebrating his birthday with his four sons, he died quietly in his sleep in the home where he and Jeanne had raised their family. His caretaker told me that she had left his bedside for only 20 minutes to prepare herself a meal and, when she returned, he was gone. "Alone," I said. "It's the way he wanted it."

His death met, I think, all 10 of his own criteria (Shneidman, 2008, pp. 131–134)— it was a death by *natural causes*; at a *mature age*; *expected*; *honorable*; and *intestate* in the psychological sense, with one or more projects left unfinished. He had *accepted* his death and was at peace with it. He was *rueful* as well; I spoke to him earlier in the week for just a moment, promising to come to Los Angeles to see him. "Don't bother," he chuckled. "I'll be dead!" Never mind that he had said that for several years. This time it was true. I'm quite certain his death was *civilized*—in his home surrounded by the things he loved. In teaching and mentoring so many, he made quite sure his death was *generative*, and his post-self will live on in the program that bears his name and in the hearts of all of his students over the years, as well as in the memories of his sons, grandchildren, and great-grandchildren. Finally, it was *peaceable*—a time "marked by amicability and love, a coming together before falling apart and as much freedom from pain as contemporary pharmacology can provide" (Shneidman, 2008, p. 134). He was a hospice patient, and the days before his death were marked by coming together with his sons and with enough medication that he was not in pain. Although there were times when he was disappointed that he had survived an ambulance trip to hospital, I am certain that he neither killed himself nor planned to hasten his death.

The reality is, not all deaths are as peaceful and as "good enough" as his.

For those who work in hospice and end-of-life care, understanding suicide and bereavement after suicide will be of increasing importance. In a study conducted by Ferrell, Virani, Grant, Coyne, and Uman (2000), over 2,000 oncology nurses responded to a survey investigating, among other things, the experiences of nurses with terminally ill patients requesting medication with the intention to end their lives. The results indicate that 23% of nurses were asked to assist a patient to obtain medications for ending life, and 22% were requested by patients to administer a lethal injection. Lest we think this is a distinctly American issue, although assisted suicide is illegal in the United Kingdom, in an issue of *Nursing Older People*, Anguita (2011) reports on guidelines from the Royal College of Nursing on how to handle the increasing requests for assisted suicide. "Death with Dignity" laws have been passed in Oregon and Washington, and Montana's legislation protects physicians from prosecution after assisting the death of a terminally ill patient. There is no reason to think that this sort of legislation will not spread. In the meantime, the ethical questions on both sides continue to be debated, and some dying patients will continue to ask their caregivers to help them die. It is widely acknowledged that physicians and nurses have provided assistance secretly and below the legal radar (Quill, 2012). The question remains, how should professionals working in hospice and end-of-life care think about these matters, and how best to respond? Is it deliverance? Or is it suicide?

UNDERSTANDING SUICIDE

The facts about suicide are fairly well known: over 30,000 lives are lost every year in the United States to suicide, a number that has remained fairly constant for decades. What is not commonly known is that the demographic group at highest risk for suicide is the elderly. For Americans age 65 and older, both men and women, the suicide rate in 2009 was 14.8 per 100,000, a couple of points higher than the national average. This amounts to one elderly suicide every 90 minutes or so. Because more elderly men than elderly women kill themselves, the suicide rate among elderly men (over age 65) in 2009 was 31.2 per 100,000. But the highest risk of all was among non-Hispanic White men over age 85, for whom the suicide rate jumped to a whopping 45.6 suicide deaths per 100,000 (American Association of Suicidology, 2012).

For the most part, suicide has been considered in the dominant literature as a medical or psychiatric problem. Lists abound of demographic, clinical, and individual risk and protective factors. Care providers, teachers, counselors, and others are encouraged to pay attention to talk about suicide, a sense of purposelessness and anxiety, expressed hopelessness, withdrawal, anger, mood changes, substance abuse—clues to suicidal thinking—and the availability of means. The medical or epidemiological model for suicide and treatment-as-usual for an individual who attempts or discloses suicidal ideation includes psychiatric assessment, sometimes hospitalization, and frequently police involvement. In the assessment, imminent risk of suicide is determined, and an underlying psychiatric disorder is sought, since research has shown that 90% of suicidal attempts are associated with psychiatric disorders (Haw, Hawton, Houston, & Townsend, 2001; Isometsä et al., 1995; SAVE, 2012). The treatment protocol is normally linked to a diagnosed underlying psychiatric disorder with the assumption that, as a result of effective treatment, the suicidality will go away. This model inextricably links suicide with psychiatric disorders. Although sometimes effective, the link between suicidality and mental illness is not always relevant. As David Webb (2010) argues, sometimes it is not only irrelevant but dangerous. There may be a strong statistical correlation between psychiatric disorders and suicide, but correlation is not necessarily causal.

Edwin S. Shneidman was, perhaps, the first to recognize that the link between psychiatric illness and suicide is neither definitive nor inseparable. Not a fan of the Diagnostic and Statistical Manual, he would quip that millions of people live very long, unhappy lives with major depression but never consider killing themselves; therefore, suicidality was related to something else. From the beginning, Shneidman adopted a nontraditional approach. In his *Definition of Suicide* (1977), he set aside Freud and Durkheim, ignored demographics and psychiatric categories, assumed that all suicidal persons are perturbed or agitated, and approached the matter from a new direction. He was primarily interested in understanding suicide from the inside out. He wanted to know, what was suicide *like*? What made suicide a sensible choice to a suicidal person? What cut across all suicides? What was experienced by all suicidal individuals, not just those who suffered from depression or another mental illness? "I aim for a practical definition, guided by wisdom and common sense, that applies sensibly to almost every conceivable situation of self-destruction" (Shneidman, 1977, p. 122).

It was in this book that he examined in detail what he called the Ten Commonalities of Suicide—stimulus, stressor, purpose, goal, emotion, internal attitude, cognitive state, interpersonal act, action, and consistency (Shneidman, 1977). These 10 commonalities included personal elements related to decision making, internal state, relationships with others, and lifelong coping patterns. But already Shneidman had zeroed in on what he considered most important: the common stimulus in suicide is intolerable psychological pain; the common stressor is frustrated or thwarted psychological needs, perturbation or agitation; the state of "upsetness"—is the third essential element. "Suicides are born, negatively, out of needs. In this sense one may say aphoristically: There are many pointless deaths but never a needless suicide" (Shneidman, 1977, p.126). Then he went one step further: "The clinical rule is: Address the frustrated needs and the suicide will not occur. In general, the goal of psychotherapy is to decrease the patient's psychological discomfort. One way to operationalize this task is to focus on the thwarted needs" (Shneidman, 1977, p. 127).

A decade later, Shneidman offered the Cubic Model of Suicide (Shneidman, 1987) as another way to conceptualize suicide visually, illustrating that when stress/press, perturbation/agitation, and psychological pain converge at high levels, the result is a perfect storm of suicidality, but that if one or more of these three elements are relieved, usually the person will choose to live. Indeed, he suggested avenues for research, indicating that he himself would scour the literature of psychology and psychiatry for nonsuicide studies related to various elements of the cubic model, and ponder the interrelatedness of the variables. As for the clinical implications, he had this to say:

> The simply stated prescriptions are (a) reduce the hurt, (b) lift the blinders, (c) pull back from action, and (d) lighten the pressure, even just a little bit. (Get the person out of the 5-5-5 cubelet.) Any of these actions can save a life. In terms of this model, that is how suicide is prevented. The underlying rule is: Lower the pain, perturbation, and press, and the lethality will decrease with it. (Shneidman, 1987, 177)

Figure 1 illustrates Shneidman's 5-3-5 cubelet (1986, p. 175).

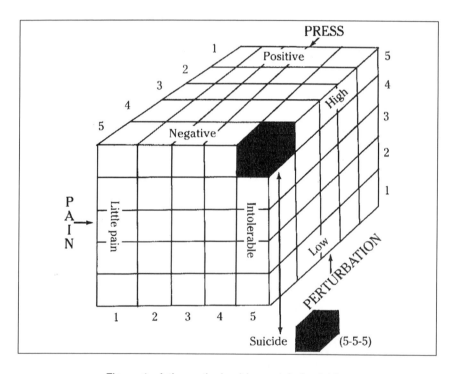

Figure 1. A theoretical cubic model of suicide.

Over the next decade, he refined these ideas, and in 1993, Shneidman published *Suicide as Psychache: A Clinical Approach to Self-Destructive Behavior*. The purpose was to summarize his thinking up to that point in a single volume and to assert the importance of *psychache* as a theoretical construct with great implications for suicide prevention and clinical intervention with suicidal individuals. He further explicated the notion of *psychache* and the Murray Need Form, a tool he created for assessment of psychological pain, in *The Suicidal Mind*, published in 1996.

The Murray Need Form is easy to use, though not, at first glance, so easy to understand. The 20 needs have rather archaic-sounding names like "Sentience" and "Succorance," and to think of human personalities in terms of needs is not an easy task. Yet the concept behind the task can help us to understand what makes an individual tick in a rather precise way. A full examination of the personality needs behind suicidality is beyond the scope of this chapter, but the notion Shneidman put forth is relevant.

The 20 needs Shneidman (1996) used in his Murray Need Form are:

- Abasement (to submit passively)
- Achievement (to accomplish something difficult)
- Affiliation (to adhere to a friend)
- Aggression (to overcome opposition)
- Autonomy (to be independent)
- Counteraction (to make up for loss)
- Defendance (to vindicate the self)
- Deference (to admire and support)
- Dominance (to control)
- Exhibition (to entertain others)
- Harmavoidance (to avoid pain)
- Inviolacy (to protect the self)
- Nurturance (to nurture another)
- Order (to achieve order)
- Play (to act for fun)
- Rejection (to exclude another)
- Sentience (to seek sensuous experiences)
- Shame avoidance (to avoid humiliation)
- Succorance (to be loved)
- Understanding (to know answers)

To profile a personality, rank the needs in terms of importance, focusing on the four to six needs that seem prominent, and assign numbers weighted with respect to a need's importance to that individual. The sum of all numbers assigned should total no more than 100. The array of needs, and the differences among them, offers a glimpse into the personality of the individual. Thinking about the constellation of needs can offer an opportunity to explore what is really important to an individual profiled in this way.

If we think about these 20 needs in terms of our own personality—what's important to us, how we operate in the world—four to six needs will arise as our operational needs, those we seek to fulfill on a daily basis by how we live our lives and how we move through the world. In crisis, a subset of those operational needs will bubble up as vital needs—those one or two needs that seem non-negotiable, the needs we would die for. To think of needs in another way, particularly the vital needs, identify an individual's reactions to all the losses, stresses, insults, humiliations, or embarrassments of life, and a constellation of vital needs will likely emerge.

Each case of suicide should be examined and understood on its own terms, but Shneidman identified the 12 needs that emerge most often in suicidal states. He grouped these needs into five clusters representing different types of psychological pain. These needs are most frequently associated with love (succorance, affiliation), control (achievement, autonomy, order, understanding), shame/humiliation (affiliation, defendance, shame avoidance), grief (affiliation, nurturance), and excessive anger (dominance, aggression, counteraction) (Shneidman, 1996, p. 25). To illustrate, he included examinations of three case studies, and followed this book with *Autopsy of a Suicidal Mind* (2004) in which he examined a single case study in depth.

Although psychiatric disorders are correlated with suicidality, the link is not causal, Shneidman argued. Instead, he theorized, mental illness was relevant only when the individual experienced mental illness as intolerably painful, when the psychiatric disorder upset the apple cart of personality needs, or made need-fulfillment impossible. Other life-altering experiences can also result in thwarted needs: job loss, grief, old age, terminal illness, traumatic experiences, and a host of others. Whatever thwarts a vital need can be experienced by an individual as psychologically painful. When the psychological pain escalates, the threshold for pain, unique to each individual, comes into play and the individual may conclude, "this far, no further."

Throughout his writings, Shneidman was clear:

> Suicide is not a psychiatric disorder. Suicide is a nervous dysfunction, not a mental disease. All persons who commit suicide—100 percent of them—are perturbed—but they are not necessarily clinically depressed (or schizophrenic, or alcoholic, or addicted, or psychiatrically ill). A suicidal crisis is best treated on its own terms. It is a deadly serious (temporary and treatable) psychache. (Shneidman, 1993, p. 55)

As for the clinical implications, he concluded that only two questions are needed: "Where do you hurt?" and "How can I help?" (Shneidman, 1996; personal conversations with Shneidman).

Potâto, Potãto: The Debate on Death with
Dignity and Physician-Assisted Suicide

The history of the debate on assisted suicide in the United States does not start with Jack Kevorkian but goes back at least to 1939, when the Euthanasia Society of America was founded. Of course, by that time a push for euthanasia of those whose lives were not considered worth living was well underway in Nazi Germany, and many were killed under *Aktion T4*, a program that claimed some 70,000 lives in two years before it went underground. The Euthanasia Society of America, a movement with roots in the eugenics movement of the 1920s, found its work trumped by news of the horrors of the Holocaust.

In the late 1960s, 1970s, and 1980s, a resurgence of interest in assisted suicide found its way to the forefront with the Society for the Right to Die and the Hemlock Society, both organizations that advocated for legalized mercy killing for the suffering. In the 1990s, Compassion in Dying was established, with a goal to challenge state laws banning physician-assisted death, beginning with Oregon and Washington. In 2003, the Hemlock Society changed its name to End of Life Choices, and a couple of years later, Compassion in Dying and End of Life Choices merged as Compassion & Choices. In 2009, a 4-2 Montana Supreme Court decision ruled that physicians need not fear prosecution for writing lethal prescriptions for mentally competent persons with terminal illnesses (O'Reilly, 2010).

Because the approach is interpretive and not a ruling on whether or not citizens in Montana have a constitutional right to physician-assisted death, some suggest that the Montana Supreme Court ruling will pave the way for similar rulings and laws in other states, leaving the window open wide for abuse. Susan Behuniak (2011) masterfully examines the use of the word "dignity" by those both for and against physician-assisted death, in particular Compassion & Choices on the one hand, and Not Dead Yet on the other. She rightly questions the notion of dignity, its definition, and its place in the debate, suggesting that the addition of the word "dignity" into the discourse about physician-assisted suicide muddies the waters and encourages a broad and naïve acceptance of the notion with little critical assessment. Criteria for impugned dignity, borne out by reasons given by individuals who have requested physician-assisted death in Oregon, include helplessness, incontinence, incoherence, dependence, drooling, and being a burden, while a peaceful death is strongly associated with one that is assisted or hastened (Behuniak, 2011, p. 22).

Not Dead Yet, a lobbying and advocacy group organized in 1996 following Kevorkian's acquittal in the assisted suicide of two women who had disabilities but were not terminally ill, also emphasizes the importance of dignity, but from a very different perspective. This organization has argued against physician-assisted suicide legislation on the grounds that it presents a risk of morphing into hastened death and euthanasia for those who live with disabilities. As easy as it may be to dismiss slippery-slope arguments, Behuniak (2011) argues that they may have a point. Depending on how the Fourteenth Amendment's Equal Protection Clause is interpreted, it is not beyond the realm of possibility that a right to physician-assisted death for a terminally ill individual could be extended by the courts to others perceived to be in an arguably similar situation (Behuniak, 2011, p. 26). Many disabled people live every day with helplessness, incontinence, incoherence, dependence, drooling, and being a burden.

On February 7, 2011, Diane Coleman, President and CEO of Not Dead Yet, presented testimony before the Hawaii Senate Health Committee opposing SB 803, legislation that would make physician-assisted death legal in the state of Hawaii. Coleman summarizes the concerns of the disability rights community and asserts that physician-assisted death legislation is not about rights for individuals but about legal protection for physicians, and results in physicians being set up as the gatekeepers for access to prescriptions to lethal doses of medication. She asserts,

> Some people get suicide prevention, while others get suicide assistance, and doctors decide who gets what. In effect, assisted suicide laws give physicians the power to judge whether a particular suicide is "rational" or not, whether judgment is impaired or not, essentially based on the doctor's prejudice or devaluation of the individual's quality of life. The proposed law allows doctors to actively assist certain suicides based on their subjective, quality of life judgment about whose suicides are rational, and whose aren't. This should be viewed as a clear cut and blatant violation of the Americans with Disabilities Act, which prohibits discrimination based on disability. (Coleman, 2011)

The Doctors for Compassionate Care Education Foundation was established in 1994 in direct response to the passing of the Death with Dignity legislation in Oregon, by physicians who viewed the legislation as in direct conflict with their oaths as physicians to do no harm. An article by Kenneth Stevens (2008) points out that Oregon now ranks sixth in the nation for suicides of individuals over age 65 and, as a result, the Oregon Department of Human Services has advised early screening of the elderly for depression. Yet, in at least one study, oncologists were found to be poorly equipped to assess their patients, accurately diagnosing depression only 13% of the time in patients whose cancer was advanced. In this study, patients whose depression was most often inaccurately classified were those experiencing very high levels of pain and disability (Passik et al., 1998).

> With that background, it is extremely troubling that *none* of the 49 patients, who were reported to have died of physician-assisted suicide in Oregon in 2007, were referred for psychiatric evaluation. Overall in the 10 years, 1998–2007 only 11% (36/341) of the reported physician-assisted suicide deaths in Oregon were referred for psychiatric evaluation. (Stevens, 2008; emphasis in original)

These facts indicate that patients in Oregon who request physician-assisted death are not receiving an acceptable standard of care and are actually being discriminated against because of their condition (Stevens, 2008).

Indeed, laws against physician-assisted death are being tested in many states across the United States with a push to shift the terminology of the discourse and encourage acceptance of the notion that a terminally ill person who chooses to die by their own hand is not "committing suicide" but rather rationally and reasonably choosing a "peaceful death" or "dying with dignity."

Dr. Timothy Quill (2012), a supporter of the legalization of physician-assisted death, has suggested that, for the most part, dying patients who request assistance in dying are not suicidal but are acting out of a genuine, well-thought-out and logical desire to be delivered from overwhelming suffering. There is another population of patients who have requested assistance who were, in Quill's estimation, "suicidal in the mental health sense of the word"; these individuals did not receive his help but would, if needed, be involuntarily hospitalized. Those individuals who warrant serious consideration for his assistance in dying would, he asserts, be insulted at any suggestion that they were suicidal and would have found such a label "preposterous and demeaning," since such a term denotes extreme "personal disintegration," a condition they are seeking to avoid (Quill, 2012). Dr. Quill offers a good example of the tone of argument that permeates the debate surrounding physician-assisted death in that he seeks to draw a clear line between elderly, sick, suffering individuals who have very little left of their lives and the garden variety, mentally ill suicidal person.

To be clear, Dr. Quill goes on to suggest that excellent palliative care and symptom control should always be the first line of treatment, and every option should be explored with primary care physicians, patients, and families to find ways to address pain and suffering other than hastened or facilitated death. He is sensitive to the fact that excellent palliative care is not available everywhere and that most dying individuals will not need any kind of physician-assisted death if they receive adequate palliative care. He does an excellent job of outlining the questions to explore and the options available, and in the end, he encourages legalization of physician-assisted death because without legislation, there are no safeguards to protect those for whom there might have been another way. And, when physicians and families carry out physician-assisted death in private, the postdeath burden of secrecy can have consequences during bereavement (Quill, 2012). Emily Jackson (Jackson & Keown, 2012) agrees, suggesting that the choice is not between legalizing physician-assisted suicide or not, but between legalizing it and having it continue being practiced secretly, with no safeguards, no second opinions, and no assessments.

The philosophical, psychological, ethical, and medical explorations of physician-assisted death have resulted in a varied literature that approaches the issue in a variety of ways. As the population ages, increasing numbers of requests for physician-assisted death are anticipated, and studies show that hospice nurses are regularly asked for assistance in dying (Ferrell et al., 2000; Schwarz, 2003, 2004). The dilemmas for those caring for the suffering and dying are immediate and difficult, and professional caregivers, not to mention family members, are not always sure how to respond.

Interestingly, over 93% of those who have used Oregon's Death with Dignity law between 2008 and 2010 were enrolled in hospice (Campbell & Cox, 2012), a situation that results in hospice employees and volunteers confronting further ethical dilemmas. This is primarily because hospice caregivers develop close relationships with their patients and families, and are frequently asked to be present for the ingestion and/or the death. There is nothing in the law that prohibits caregivers from being in attendance for ingestion or death, yet for 30% of hospices in Oregon, employees are prohibited from being present when a patient takes the prescribed lethal dose, and some even forbid them to be in attendance when death occurs. At the same time, hospices seek to provide the best end-of-life care possible, without regard to choices made by individual patients for physician-assisted suicide. This forces some professional caregivers to attend to patients on their own time or to do so in defiance of local hospice regulations (Campbell & Cox, 2012).

According to a study examining the effects of physician-assisted suicide on physicians who wrote the prescriptions, there is a measurable emotional impact on caregivers (Stevens, 2006). The study reveals that most physicians suffer a negative emotional toll, including pangs of conscience, mixed emotions, and a sense of giving in to significant pressure from patients and families. This negative emotional toll is, perhaps, reflected in the downward shift in the numbers of physicians who attend the ingestion and death of patients. In the first 4 years of the Death with Dignity law in Oregon, 52% of prescribing physicians were present at ingestion and death. By 2004, that number had declined to 16% (Stevens, 2006). And the negative emotional toll is not just reserved for the prescribing physician but extends to psychiatrists who are asked to evaluate patients who have requested physician-assisted death. Patients who have been disqualified frequently blame the psychiatrist, and the resulting anger directed toward the psychiatrist has its own impact.

Does physician-assisted suicide improve the death or dying experience? That was the question for at least one study, and the results suggest that the quality of death and dying for patients who made that request is not statistically significantly different from those who do not request it, but is marginally "better" (Smith, Goy, Harvath, & Ganzini, 2011). Using a Quality of Death and Dying Questionnaire, family members of deceased individuals were asked to rate the dying experience of their loved one, postdeath. Differences were reported in 9 of the 33 quality item indicators, indicating that those who requested physician-assisted suicide and carried it out experienced greater control over symptoms, bowel/bladder function, and surroundings, as well as higher ratings on preparedness for death. The researchers concluded that the dying experience for those who requested physician-assisted suicide was no worse, and in some cases better, than those who did not request it. The results are not surprising since death would most likely have occurred earlier in the disease trajectory, before the symptoms and discomfort of impending death progressed beyond the perceived tolerance of the deceased.

UNDERSTANDING SUICIDALITY IN THE CONTEXT OF END-OF-LIFE CARE

The high rate of suicide among the elderly in the United States, and the gradual increase in the number of states where terminally ill individuals can request and receive the means to kill themselves, suggests that it is important to understand suicide in the context of end-of-life care. Not all terminally ill patients will request assistance in dying or hastened death, but some will. Not all terminally ill patients will exhibit suicidality, but some will. The onus on caregivers is to determine how best to assess the suicidality of patients and how best to respond. If every suicide should be evaluated on its own terms, then each request for physician-assisted suicide or exhibited suicidal behavior should also be evaluated on its own terms, with an eye to understanding the underlying issues and setting aside vested interests and personal beliefs regarding the reasonableness and rationality of such a request.

A longitudinal qualitative study examining the motivations for requesting physician-assisted suicide suggests that there are three general sets of issues at play: the effects of the illness (physical deterioration, losses of functioning), the patient's sense of self (desire for control), and fears about the future (Pearlman et al., 2005). The researchers discovered that depression and hopelessness were not significant issues for their sample, but loss of the sense of self was prominent and described in terms of a loss of vitality, essence, and personal definition. This was interpreted by the researchers to highlight the threat of death to the social constructs of meaning (Pearlman et al., 2005 p. 238).

Similar results emerge from a meta-analysis of the literature on unbearable suffering (Dees, Vernooij-Dassen, Dekkers, & van Weel, 2010). The researchers found that the suffering of patients requesting physician-assisted suicide was described in terms of "pain, weakness, functional impairment, dependency, being a burden, hopelessness, indignity, intellectual deterioration, perception of loss of oneself, loss of autonomy, and being tired of life" (Dees et al., 2010, p. 342). In most respects, these are existential issues that are not optimally addressed by a medical or epidemiological approach. Further, the researchers found that the point at which suffering becomes unbearable is unique to each person and related to life history, social factors, culture, and personality. The researchers concluded that, in general, for those who chose physician-assisted suicide, the "circumstances of their illness brought all the patients to the point where they would rather die than continue to live under the conditions imposed by their illness" (Dees et al., 2010, p. 342).

Suicide occurs in the context of hospice even without physician assistance. Warren and Zinn (2010) wrote a letter to the editor of the *Journal of Palliative Medicine* in which they profiled five cases of suicide over 10 years of patients enrolled in a West Virginia hospice. All were retired White males and were between 64 and 78 years of age; four had advanced cancer and one had end-stage lung disease. Four had a history of military service. All five killed themselves with firearms and were alone at the time. Their concerns focused on high-lighting the need for everything from appropriate assessment tools to inquiry about firearm access to information on cleaning agencies that help families clean up after a firearm suicide.

Harwood, Hawton, Harriss, and Jacoby (2006) conducted a study in the UK in which semistructured psychological autopsies were conducted for 100 people age 60 and older who died by suicide. Similar psychological autopsies were conducted for 54 age- and gender-matched control subjects who died by natural causes. The study found that although physical illness, interpersonal problems, and bereavement are associated with suicide in the elderly, financial problems, living accommodations, and long-term bereavement were found to be more specific risk factors. Lisa B. Aiello-Laws (2010) suggests that cancer patients should be regularly assessed for suicidality, that health professionals must shift any personal perspective that cancer is an understandable reason for suicide and instead recognize that cancer has become a chronic illness. The crossover between elderly and the terminally ill is an important one that needs attention both in research and in assessment protocols.

The various motivations cited in the literature for requesting physician-assisted suicide or suicide can be listed as follows: loss of control, hopelessness, indignity, loss of sense of self, loss of autonomy, dependency, incontinence, incoherence, drooling, helplessness, being a burden, fear of suffering, fear of pain, discomfort of symptoms, shame, desire to control circumstances of dying, fear of the future, inability to enjoy pleasurable activities of life, (Behuniak, 2011; Pearlman et al., 2005; Schwarz, 2004). The list is not exhaustive, but certainly broadly represen-tative. Interestingly, extreme physical pain is not in the list.

The mitigating factor is the notion that these motivations are couched in the context of terminal illness and the end of life. All of the motivations relate to specific conditions brought about by a terminal illness and the level of suffering experienced by an individual and connected to life history, social factors, culture, and personality (Dees et al., 2010) and, of course, to the individual's threshold for that suffering. The debate around hastened death or physician-assisted suicide or even active euthanasia turns on this one element, in a culture that has not been particularly open to discussing death and has tended toward a preference for able-bodied youth, vitality, autonomy, and control. There is no doubt that death is, at best, inconvenient and, at worst, messy and painful and packed full of suffering for all concerned. But the notion of hastened death as somehow more dignified than, shall we say, a more "natural" approach, is one that needs to be questioned. It is important to think critically about the notion that, since death is coming soon anyway, it is becoming more socially acceptable to choose the date, time, and method.

I admit that my years of study with the man who created the field of modern suicide studies have influenced my thinking that a self-inflicted death is, regardless of the circumstances, suicide. My years of study with another mentor, Elie Wiesel, have similarly instilled in me with the importance of life as sacred and holy and the notion that there are only three circumstances in Jewish Law that make suicide acceptable or even necessary: as a response to rape, involuntary conversion, or being forced to kill another. So, while hastened death or physician-assisted suicide is, for some, tolerable, understandable, acceptable, or even welcome, another perspective may add to the conversation.

Perhaps the issue is not one of rational versus irrational suicide; suicide-because-of-intractable-mental-illness versus a choice for death with dignity. If Shneidman is correct, that suicide is the result of intolerable (for that person) psychological pain, then it may be fruitful to apply this theory to desires and requests for physician-assisted death. Let's explore how the Murray Need Form may be used as a simple tool to understand the underlying motivations to such a request.

To review, there are 20 personality needs listed on the Murray Need Form, but Shneidman's work suggests that the needs operative in most suicides can be organized into five primary clusters of needs: those needs most often affiliated with love (succorance, affiliation); control (achievement, autonomy, order, understanding); shame/humiliation (affiliation, defendance, shame-avoidance); grief (affiliation, nurturance); and excessive anger (dominance, aggression, counteraction) (Shneidman, 1996, p. 25). Two clusters stand out as most relevant for physician-assisted suicide decision making: fractured control and avoidance of shame/humiliation.

The kind of psychological pain that Shneidman identified as "fractured control" (1996, p. 25) includes frustrated needs for achievement (to accomplish something difficult), autonomy (to be independent), order (to achieve order), and understanding (to know answers). Of the motivations listed above, loss of control, loss of autonomy, being a burden, incoherence, inability to enjoy pleasures of life, incontinence, dependency, fear of pain, and fear of the future stand out as indications that one or more of these needs have been thwarted. The need to "die on one's own terms" speaks to a need for control and for achievement—to accomplish the kind of death that does not involve the loss of the ability to care for oneself. To choose death before becoming totally helpless and dependent on others indicates a strong need for autonomy and independence. The need for order, closely related to the need for control, can be a motivating factor as well—the progression of symptoms at the end of life can throw families into a sense of chaos that a dying person may find intolerable to confront and wish desperately to avoid. In such a situation, the suffering experienced can be perceived as insurmountable, frightening, and best averted by planning death in a controlled environment.

The type of psychological pain that Shneidman (1996) called "assaulted self-image and the avoidance of shame, defeat, humiliation and disgrace" includes frustrated needs for affiliation (to adhere to a friend), defendance (to vindicate the self), and shame-avoidance (to avoid humiliation). Within the list of motivations for physician-assisted suicide, the needs for affiliation and defendance do not emerge significantly, but the need for shame-avoidance figures strongly. Loss of control, indignity, loss of a sense of self, incontinence, incoherence, drooling, helplessness, shame, hopelessness, and being a burden can generate in many a strong sense of shame, humiliation, and disgrace. This sense of shame can extend to caretakers. When my grandfather was ill and hospitalized, my father communicated through his body language and facial expression a decided sense of disgust at having to spoonfeed his helpless father a cup of tapioca. His own sense of shame in the face of leaving the hospital years later with an oxygen tank for emphysema (something he had once declared he would never, ever do) may have led to his premature death (not by his own hand—he just died) the night before discharge.

The motivations offered by someone requesting assistance in dying or a hastened death can be explored through examining the "need profile" of the individual. Identifying operative needs as well as the vital needs—the needs an individual would die for—can provide inroads for a discussion of the meaning of suffering, death, suicide, and fears of living through to the end. A conversation around what makes life and death "dignified" (or its converse) can lead to helpful insights. Shneidman has rightly stated that there is "no handy morphine drip for psychological pain that, to be effective, does not, at the same time, alter who we are" (Shneidman, 1996, pp. 161–162). Nevertheless, there are interventions that could prove helpful for individuals confronting the end of life, whether or not they are suicidal or requesting physician-assisted suicide.

Shneidman's two questions, "Where do you hurt?" and "How can I help you?" can be important first questions when a terminally ill individual requests assistance in dying. Shifting the focus from the desire for death or suicide to an exploration of what hurts (and why) can lead to a fruitful conversation in which the dying individual can contribute meaningfully to the treatment plan. Follow-up questions can elicit more information that can then be acted upon by a savvy hospice or palliative care team, but the spirit of inquiry should always be collaborative, in the spirit of working together to find an alternative to suicide as an answer to pain and suffering. At least four interventions can be helpful: developing a "hope kit," a crisis card, expanding social relationships, and exploring the past.

One intervention that can be used is the generation of a "hope kit" (a box filled with trinkets, mementoes, photos, which when examined, can elicit hope). An intervention developed originally by Beck and his colleagues (as cited in

Jobes, 2006, p. 83), a hope kit can be used to help a dying person and family members remember what's important and what's worth living for as they make their way through the disabling elements experienced by most individuals at the end of life. An intervention such as this can assist families to soothe themselves in moments of crisis.

Jobes (2006) also suggests that a "crisis card" can be helpful when an individual is in treatment for suicidality. The idea here is to have five protherapeutic ideas or activities that an individual can use when in a suicidal crisis—taking a walk, doing some artwork, meditating, writing a letter to an old friend—activities that can redirect an individual away from the crisis and toward life-enhancing alternative coping skills. A similar crisis card can be developed for a terminally ill individual, listing coping activities in place of suicidal thinking, which can help the individual and family move through a crisis state.

Increasing social supports can be an invaluable intervention. Many elderly and dying individuals are alone, and many more feel alone even if they are surrounded by loving family. Joiner (2005) has argued that social influences are central to the suicidal state. According to Joiner, a suicidal individual is simultaneously overwhelmed by the notion that they are a burden on others on the one hand, and unloved on the other hand. The burdensomeness, dependence, helplessness, and hopelessness that figure so strongly in the list of motivating factors of those requesting physician-assisted suicide are both sides of this coin. Jobes agrees: "The absence—or presence—of certain key relationships can be suicidogenic" (2006, p. 84). Quill (2001) has argued convincingly for the importance of humanistic end-of-life care that involves caring relationships among care providers, patients, and family members (p. 17). Helping the elderly and the terminally ill to expand the social support system, even if this means developing new relationships, can be essential to reducing isolation and thus the existential suffering that can feed the fire of suicidality at the end of life.

Finally, psychotherapy can be helpful. Considering what it is that leads to some individuals experiencing more psychological pain than others, Shneidman suggested that childhood is the culprit. Although he acknowledged that suicide does occur in adults confronting intolerable pain in a decisive and impulsive moment and not connected in any way to a tragic past, he leaned toward a conclusion that suicide was more common among individuals who had measurably unhappy childhoods. "Suicide never stems from happiness—it happens because of the stark absence of it" (Shneidman, 1996, p. 163). Thus, in addition to examining the motivations for a suicidal state, an examination of the life histories and the lifelong coping strategies of those who request physician-assisted suicide or euthanasia can illuminate the issues.

Indeed, systematic life review can be helpful for anyone at the end of life, suicidal or not. For the last few years of his life, Shneidman went back into therapy with a hospice social worker—something he referred to as "thanato-therapy" or "death therapy" (Shneidman, 2008, p. 159). Citing George Valliant's book *Aging Well*, Shneidman's therapist, Ethel Oderberg, reminds us that the "task of Integrity forces us to reflect upon human dignity in the face of disability" (Shneidman, 2008, p. 162). For Shneidman, this was the purpose and scope of his therapeutic relationship with Ethel. He was not terminally ill, just old and cognizant of the fact that he may die on any day, at any moment. In her chapter, included in what became his final book, she shares in print what Shneidman shared with me in countless telephone conversations: that he enjoyed, all things considered, a fairly contented existence in which he was both ready to die and still planning for the future. She reflects on this relationship and suggests that writing that book, not knowing if he would live to see it published, testified to the "idea that being creative and productive at the end of one's life, whatever form that might take, is the antidote to the depression that can surface when one feels that his or her life lacks purpose" (Shneidman, 2008, p. 170).

Thinking about how Shneidman's approach to suicide can illuminate suicidality at the end of life brings us full circle. In his book *Caring for Patients at the End of Life*, Quill (2001) presents a case study of "Diane," a woman diagnosed with leukemia. This woman, Quill tells his readers, was raised in an alcoholic family, survived vaginal cancer, struggled with depression and alcoholism, and worked hard to overcome all of these obstacles to life, only to be diagnosed with yet another life-limiting disease and one that would require aggressive chemotherapy to overcome, with no assurance of success. Quill presents her story as an example of someone who decided not to pursue treatment and who, when the "time" came, wished to control her own death. Quill reflects that although pharmacology provides many ways to control pain, "to think that people do not suffer in the process of dying is an illusion" (Quill, 2001, p. 39). He shares with his readers that he provided the means for Diane to die at a time and place of her choice. Although married and close to her husband and son, she ultimately chose to die alone while they waited in another room. The case study lends itself to an alternative understanding. Her needs for control, independence, and fear of suffering are prominent motivating factors. Her sense of fractured control and assaulted self-image in the face of leukemia led to a level of psychological pain for which she determined that death on her terms was the only answer. Her suffering ended. Whether or not she was "suicidal" is a matter of interpretation. In the "normal mental health sense of the word" she was not (Quill, 2012). In the Shneidman sense, perhaps she was.

Anyone who has attended the death of a loved one knows that, indeed, death sometimes involves suffering—extreme suffering—and helplessness, incontinence, incoherence, dependence, drooling, and being a burden. Suffering in this context is not limited to the dying person but often extends to caretakers and family. There are no easy answers. For every "Diane," there are countless others who suffer as much or more but who do not take their own lives. Instead of holding up the deaths of the Dianes of the world as admirable and "dignified," the question needs to be asked, Why? What is underneath the expressed motivating factors? Steps can be taken to address the factors, relieve the suffering, and offer supportive comfort and care for the dying. Then, dying with dignity can mean something closer to Shneidman's concept of a "good enough death"—natural, mature, expected, honorable, intestate, accepted, civilized, generative, rueful, and peaceable. Shneidman's thoughts?

> Sometimes the most difficult thing in the world is to choose to endure life. But even when there is no choice, as in a natural death in old age, dying *well* is among the most challenging feats of life: To die with some sense of grace, panache, good manners, or thanatological breeding—especially when frightened and in pain—can be the crown of one's life. . . . To die naturally will, in the course of time, occur to most of us, but to die "well," to accept one's mortality and not hasten one's death may be the most difficult act in life. (Shneidman, 1996, pp. 161–162)

REFERENCES

Aiello-Laws, L. B. (2010). Assessing the risk for suicide in patients with cancer. *Clinical Journal of Oncology Nursing, 14*(6), 687-691.

American Association of Suicidology. (2012). *Elderly suicide fact sheet.* Retrieved October, 2012 from http://www.suicidology.org/c/document_library/get_file?folder Id=262&name=DLFE-264.pdf.

Anguita, M. (2011). Nurses given unequivocal advice on assisted suicide. *Nursing Older People, 23*(10), 6-7.

Associated Press. (2012). U.S. military suicide rate doubles for July. Retrieved October 2, 2012 from http://www.cbsnews.com/8301-201_162-57494963/u.s-military-suicide-rate-doubles-for-July/

Behuniak, S. M. (2011). Death with "dignity": The wedge that divides the disability rights movement from the right to die movement. *Politics & The Life Sciences, 30*(1), 17-32.

Campbell, C. S., & Cox, J. C. (2012). Hospice-assisted death? A study of Oregon hospices on death with dignity. *American Journal of Hospice & Palliative Medicine, 29*(3), 227-235. doi: 10.1177/1049909111418637

Coleman, D. (2011). *Testimony Before the Hawaii Senate Health Committee Opposing SB 803,* presented by NDY President Diane Coleman February 7, 2011. Retrieved September 17, 2012 from http://www.notdeadyet.org/testimony-opposing-hawaii-sb-803

Dees, M., Vernooij-Dassen, M., Dekkers, W., & van Weel, C. (2010). Unbearable suffering of patients with a request for euthanasia or physician-assisted suicide: an integrative review. *Psycho-Oncology, 19*(4), 339-352.

Ferrell, B., Virani, R., Grant, M., Coyne, P., & Uman, G. (2000). Beyond the Supreme Court decision: Nursing perspectives on end-of-life care. *Oncology Nursing Forum, 27*(3), 445.

Harwood, D., Hawton, T., Harriss, L., & Jacoby, R. (2006). Life problems and physical illness as risk factors for suicide in older people: A descriptive and case-control study. *Psychological Medicine, 36*(9), 1265-1274.

Haw, C., Hawton, K., Houston, K., & Townsend, E. (2001). Psychiatric and personality disorders in deliberate self-harm patients. *British Journal of Psychiatry, 178,* 48-54.

Isometsä, E., Henriksson, M., Marttunen, M., Heikkinen, M., Aro, H., Kuoppasalmi, K., et al. (1995). Mental disorders in young and middle aged men who commit suicide. *British Medical Journal, 310,* 1366-1367.

Jackson, E., & Keown, J. (2012). *Debating euthanasia.* Oxford, UK: Hart Publishing.

Jobes, D. A. (2006). *Managing suicidal risk: A collaborative approach.* New York, NY: The Guilford Press.

Joiner, T. E. (2005). *Why people die by suicide.* Boston, MA: Harvard University Press.

O'Reilly, K. B. (2010). Physician-assisted suicide legal in Montana, court rules. Retrieved from http://www.ama-assn.org/amednews/2010/01/18/prsb0118.htm

Passik, S., Dugan, W., McDonald, M., Rosenfeld, B., Theobald, D., & Edgerton, S. (1998). Oncologists' recognition of depression in their patients with cancer. *Journal of Clinical Oncology: Official Journal of the American Society of Clinical Oncology, 16*(4), 1594-1600.

Pearlman, R. A., Hsu, C., Starks, H., Back, A. L., Gordon, J. R., Bharucha, A. J., et al. (2005). Motivations for physician-assisted suicide. *JGIM: Journal of General Internal Medicine, 20*(3), 234-239. doi: 10.1111/j.1525-1497.2005.40225

Schwarz, J. (2003). Understanding and responding to patients' requests for assistance in dying. *Journal of Nursing Scholarship, 35*(4), 377-384.

Suicide Awareness Voices of Education (SAVE). (2012). *The link between depression and suicide.* Available at https://www.save.org/index.cfm?fuseaction=home.view Page&page_ID=70489B01-CDA6-EC10-E40B95178144A08F&r=1

Schwarz, J. (2004). Responding to persistent requests for assistance in dying: A phenomenological inquiry. *International Journal of Palliative Nursing, 10*(5), 225-235.

Shneidman, E. S. (1977). *Definition of suicide.* Northvale, NJ: Jason Aronson.

Shneidman, E. S. (1987). A psychological approach to suicide. In G. R. VandenBos & B. K. Bryant (Eds.), *Cataclysms, crises, and catastrophes: Psychology in action* (pp. 147-183). Washington, DC: American Psychological Association.

Shneidman, E. S. (1993). *Suicide as psychache: A clinical approach to self-destructive behavior.* Northvale, NJ: Jason Aronson, Inc.

Shneidman, E. S. (1996). *The suicidal mind.* New York, NY: Oxford University Press.

Shneidman, E. S. (2004). *Autopsy of a suicidal mind.* New York, NY: Oxford University Press.

Shneidman, E. S. (2005). *A commonsense book of death: Reflections at ninety of a lifelong thanatologist.* Lanham, MD: Rowan & Little Field Publishers, Inc.

Smith, K. A., Goy, E. R., Harvath, T. A., & Ganzini, L. (2011). Quality of death and dying in patients who request physician-assisted death. *Journal of Palliative Medicine, 14*(4), 445-450. doi :10.1089/jpm.2010.0425

Stevens, K. R. (2008). Depression and physician-assisted suicide in Oregon. Retrieved September 17, 2012 from http://www.pccef.org/articles/art66.htm

Stevens, K. R., Jr. (2006). Emotional and psychological effects of physician-assisted suicide and euthanasia on participating physicians. *Issues in Law & Medicine, 21*(3), 187-200.

Quill, T. E. (2001). *Caring for patients at the end of life: Facing an uncertain future together.* New York, NY: Oxford University Press.

Quill, T. E. (2012). Physicians should 'assist in suicide' when it is appropriate. *Journal of Law, Medicine & Ethics, 40*(1), 57-65. doi: 10.1111/j.1748-720X.2012.00646.x

Warren, S. C., & Zinn, G. L. (2010). Review of completed suicides in a community hospice. *Journal of Palliative Medicine, 13*(8), 937-938. doi: 10.1089/jpm.2010.0107

Webb, D. (2010). *Thinking about suicide: Contemplating and comprehending the urge to die.* Herefordshire, UK: PCCS Books, Ltd.

http://dx.doi.org/10.2190/FATC13

CHAPTER 13

The End of Life: Two Perspectives

Robert G. Stevenson

In this chapter, I thought to draw on personal experience in looking at two perspectives on the end of life that are not often examined in terms of their impact on the individuals and their attitudes toward this time. The two perspectives regarding the end of life are that of adolescents and those shown in a military ceremony used in the 18th and 19th centuries, *Feu de Joie* or Fire of Joy.

ADOLESCENTS AND THE END OF LIFE

Going back half a century, I was a student in Catholic school. At that time, the afterlife was often discussed (usually in terms of Heaven, Hell, etc.). We were told how to live a Christian life, but little was mentioned about the end of life, the final hours of life. It was not that the topic was taboo, it simply was not mentioned, other than to describe the sacrament known as Extreme Unction (the Last Anointing). This was Confession (now referred to as the Sacrament of Penance) and a special blessing to prepare the soul for death and the transition to the afterlife. I saw the final hours as a time of change, certainly change for the dying person but also change for those who care about them. Knowledge about what those changes might be, or how people act/react at such times, might have been useful, but such topics were not discussed. Instead, adolescents were often left to their own devices to work out why this time seemed so chaotic. End of life did not come up in schools, even in religious education.

There was no place for adolescents to speak about fear of death or fear of the end of life. This was part of my motivation in starting a death education course. The course was not in a religious school, but a public school. For 25 years, it was the most popular elective at my high school. Students even petitioned to have the course expanded from 9 weeks (an academic quarter) to 18 weeks, a full semester. Part of the course was an initial assessment of death-related attitudes. There was a simple instrument used as part of that assessment. Students were asked to answer this question: If you had to choose one (and only one) of the following, which would you pick?

1. A short, exciting life
2. A long, dull life with a peaceful death
3. A long, exciting life with a painful death

Adults most often pick choice 3. This was true as recently as the fall of 2012 in the answers of students at Mercy College (average age = 32). Adolescents, on the other hand, choose "1" as the most common answer, followed by "2." That was true when I started the death education course in the early 1970s, and it is still the case today.

Choice 3 generally reflects a fear of death, that is, the state of being dead. Those who make this choice often want to live as long as they can, packing as much living and excitement as possible into that time even if it means a painful death (Stevenson, 1991). Choice 1 offers only one guarantee: life will be short and the subject will never grow old. Here, the fear of old age is greater than either the fear of death or of dying.

With the reduction of the extended family, many young people do not have prolonged contact with older family members. Grandparents, especially those in good health, often engage in sports and outdoor activities, and they are not seen as "old." Those who do become ill are often cared for outside the home. Where do adolescents learn about old age?

Well, the image of *The Golden Girls* has been replaced by shows like *Hot in Cleveland*, offering a very different view of "old age." Betty White seems to have become a national "grandparent" figure. However, such shows still do not often look at the final hours of life.

As a nation, the people of the United States are still not comfortable with the process of aging. As Baby Boomers continue to grey, age becomes more visible (despite the many ads for hair color and plastic surgery). Age is becoming a topic that must be addressed. And when aging is examined, what will young people want and need to know about its conclusion?

What About Adolescents and the End of Life?

We have not yet looked at Choice 2 of our exercise. Choice 2 reflects a fear of dying (the "act" of dying more than the state of being dead). Those who choose this answer are concerned with the transition from life to death—with the final hours and the end of life. It is often based on events connected to a particular death that the person remembers. This is especially true if that death is one of the few times the person looked and/or thought about the end of life. Adolescents traditionally ask questions about what happens when someone is dead or, in fewer cases, about aging, but there are not many questions about dying itself or about the final hours of life. Do they not ask because the topic is too frightening or because there is no place in which it is acceptable to ask the questions? That is a question worth examining.

Adolescents often cope with their concerns in one of two ways: through avoidance and/or with humor. Avoidance tries to stay away from the topic entirely. This takes a good deal of energy, and the person must be constantly on guard against allowing the topic to intrude. Humor allows the topic to be dealt with indirectly (Stevenson, 1991). In effect, we joke about what we fear. If we become aware of the true motives behind this dark humor, we can perhaps find greater sympathy for those who use this coping strategy.

Children often tell jokes about tragedies that they experience. It was well documented back at the time of the Challenger disaster. When the space shuttle exploded, killing all of the crew, children told "jokes" for weeks afterward that were related to the event. The jokes reflected concern about bodily integrity, disintegration, and dying, which the children did not know how to process in any other way. The pattern reoccurs with each new tragedy.

Adults exhibit similar coping with humor. One need only listen to the "jokes" that follow major events and tragedies on late night and weekend comedy shows. It is almost automatic. The jokes and stories are then retold over and over. Some of the classic stand-up comics of the late 20th century (Bob Newhart, Shelley Berman, Robert Klein, and George Carlin) created extended routines about death, suicide, and funerals. The recipe of "tragedy plus time equals comedy" is an old one. The one change that has taken place is that the time between the event and the humor has grown much shorter. It has become an almost immediate reaction. Adults regress to coping patterns of their childhood and try to use humor as a way to externalize what they otherwise might hold inside. This is especially true when a death is sudden and unexpected. The assassinations of Lincoln and the Kennedy brothers; the deaths of the crew of the space shuttle Challenger; and entertainers like Elvis Presley, Michael Jackson, Amy Winehouse, Selena, Brittany Murphy, and Whitney Houston brought on jokes related to the death. If these events scared or upset adults, imagine how traumatic they were to children and adolescents. Sudden death allows no time for people to adjust, as might be the case with a period of time after illness or an accident.

Much of the humor of young people speaks of the death of a loved one, dying, or telling a person about the death of a loved one. These are issues that adolescents may believe cannot be discussed in any other way. Humor can tell us what it is that concerns young people, what they are thinking about. And, if they are thinking about it, perhaps that topic deserves attention. How will adolescents learn about the end of life, about the final hours, or about the hour of death? Do we, for example, allow young people to be present when someone is dying?

Today, children and adolescents are often allowed to attend wakes and funerals if they wish to do so. However, are they allowed to be with loved ones as they approach the end of life? Hospitals still restrict access of children and younger adolescents to loved ones in some of their wards. This was not always the case.

From the earliest years in the United States, people approaching the end of life were typically cared for at home. When the person died, the wake was held in the parlor of the home, and it was from there that the body of the deceased was taken to be interred. In the 20th century, the funeral industry created homes apart from the family residence to relocate the body for funerals. The modern funeral industry started in the late 18th century when Dr. Thomas Holmes developed the process of preserving the body through arterial embalming. Soon the parlor in the home was no longer being used for visitation to see the body after death. A separate building—a funeral parlor—was created. One magazine editor, Edward Bok of the *Ladies Home Journal*, decreed in his publication in 1910 that the main room in the home would no longer be referred to as a "parlor." It would henceforth be called a "living" room to separate the living in the home from the dead (Farrell, 1980). The body of the deceased would be placed in the funeral parlor—a separate building—away from home and family. Traditions that had seen young people witness the end of life and even had them help in the home to prepare a person for death and then for burial were abandoned. The jobs were now taken over by professionals—doctors, nurses, morticians, and others—always outside the home.

If we look back just a few years, it was not unusual for adolescents to have seen one or more dead bodies before they entered their teens. These dead may have been younger siblings (since more people in a given age group die in the first year of life than in the next 40 years). Young people helped to prepare the body for the wake or other memorial ritual, which often took place in the home. At that time, death was not seen as unnatural, and the end of life was not seen as something strange or remote. These young people knew about death and dying. Death was the natural end of the life process, and the end of life was not as fearful or strange as it came to be seen in the latter 20th century. Illness was sanitized and taken from the home to hospitals. The elderly were taken from the home to nursing homes and "senior residences." Death became strange and remote. Young people seldom see real death, only its images or its reflections on television or in the movies. For many years, death was taken from the "normal" experience of the young. Most young people didn't see it, didn't experience its effects, and had little on which to build their own attitudes and feelings when death finally entered their lives. It should not be surprising that, as adults, these same people sought to maintain their denial and avoidance when these two methods of coping were only a logical reflection of the role that had been adopted by society as a whole. Adolescents coped in one of the few ways they felt society allowed them to.

What was needed was to find a way to help people lower the defenses that were used from their early years to shield themselves from the awareness of death. The hospice movement, which seeks to bring better quality to the end of life, helps the dying to leave the sterile atmosphere of hospitals and to return home. The hospice movement, which owes so much to Dame Cicely Saunders, is described in detail throughout this book, *Final Acts*. One of its biggest lessons for family and other loved ones was that even if all they felt they could do at the end of a person's life was to be there, that was still important. They learned to *be there*, and by their presence, added to the quality of those final weeks, days, and hours. The mere presence of another person represents *connection* at a time of transition and letting go. It is a living reminder of something my maternal Irish grandmother often said: *Happiness shared is happiness multiplied, and sorrow shared is sorrow divided.* Two things we can give to those at the end of life are our time and our presence. This is an example worth following and may be one of the most important gifts we can give to the young.

ONE MILITARY VIEW OF LIFE AND DEATH

One place in which death is no stranger is in the military. All soldiers know that by going in harm's way for their country, they may at any time lose their lives, or see the lives of comrades ended in sudden and violent ways. Modern soldiers, like the adolescents described earlier, often attempt to cope with the presence of death through denial and through dark humor. The American military in the 18th and 19th centuries was not a group of "professionals" sent far away for training and then service. The military was composed of large numbers of local or state militia. They trained locally and often were seen by local people in their military capacity. When a soldier died, his death was a major event for the entire community. The funeral procession was long, and entire towns turned out to take part in the memorial. Local papers carried detailed accounts of the military units that were there, often with long descriptions of the uniforms and the procession route from a church to the cemetery. General Enoch Poor, one of General George Washington's top officers, died in New Jersey. There were accounts of the crowds that attended his funeral procession from the Old Stone Church in Paramus to the burial site at the county seat in Hackensack, several miles away. Military music with muffled drums beat a slow, sad cadence for the marchers. At graveside, there was a ceremony that was used by the military throughout the late 18th and 19th centuries. It was known as the "Fire of Joy" or, in the original French, the *Feu de Joie*. This took place at the end of the burial. It linked the sadness over the death with the celebration of continued life. It was carried out by a select group of soldiers, but it involved the entire community.

FEU DE JOIE—THE "FIRE OF JOY"

The soldiers were lined up in one or two ranks. Muskets were brought to present arms, and at the command to "Mourn Arms," each would slowly lower the musket until the muzzle touched down on the shoe of the soldier. Each soldier then placed his left hand on the butt of the musket and covered it with his right hand. The head was then bowed (forehead touching the hands). The regimental flag was waved back and forth as it too was lowered until it touched the ground. The officer in command then removed his hat, bowed his head, and saluted with his sword. After a moment of silence, the muskets and the colors were raised and brought to the shoulder. On command of the officer, each man loaded his weapon (with a blank charge of black powder). The regiment came to the position of "ready," and the command was given to execute "running fire" from the right to the left. At the command "Fire!" each man, one at a time, would fire his musket going along the line. The muskets were reloaded, and the running fire was then done from left to right in the same manner. Finally, every man loaded his musket, and there was a mass "volley fire" of all weapons. It is most impressive to behold, and it would have been observed by the entire community.

The symbolism of that ceremony was first, a time to honor the deceased and his life (Present Arms) and to mourn his loss (Mourn Arms). The Fire of Joy, with each man firing three times, was a salute to the fallen given individually and then as a group to mark that point in time. The men would then march off to a faster march, with loud drums and joyful fifes as a celebration of continued life.

That ceremony mirrors the attitude that was present throughout society—remember and honor the life of the deceased, mourn the death, and move on with life. The State of Israel went one step further and established within its armed forces a Ministry of Bereavement. That office helped families of the fallen and the entire nation to acknowledge the sacrifice of each soldier who died and to help with the grief that followed. However, in the United States, the military tried to move away from the open acknowledgement of death. Reporters were kept away from seeing returning caskets bringing fallen warriors back home. No photographs were allowed. The military stopped automatically sending an honor guard to the burial of veterans, detailing one man to accompany the fallen on his or her final trip home. Buglers were no longer made available. The Mourn Arms was abandoned—partly for the practical reasons that weapons were now too short. The Fire of Joy was changed to three volleys instead of the earlier ceremonial firing. The rifle salute was also discontinued for most military burials, as was music at the burial, except on rare occasions. Mainly, the event became one only for family and friends and was no longer, in many cases, something that brought a community together. In a sense, the change in the military was a reflection of the change in attitudes toward death in society as a whole.

A TIME OF CHANGE

Change is taking place for adolescents. From a few isolated cases starting as early as 1972, adolescents can now learn about death in schools. Death education moved into what had become a missing component in adolescent development. After being unanswered for many years, adolescents now had a place to ask their questions and to get informed answers. Even if there was sometimes no single "correct" answer that all could embrace, the discussion helped them to examine the topic and to better understand their own thoughts and feelings related to death. Since it was no longer a taboo subject, the balance of life and death could now be spoken about openly in their lives. It has come to be seen as a positive change.

Change is taking place for the military as well. Moving away from its reluctance to mark each death as important, the Army now acknowledges it has a duty that goes beyond the burial of those who have given their lives. It has created the Tragedy Assistance Program for Survivors (TAPS), which draws upon the Israeli experience and is again connecting with families of the fallen to perform the tasks of remembrance, honor, and moving forward with life. The people who work in TAPS are there for the survivors to help with the emotional and psychological issues that follow a military death. They also assist with some of the practical issues that survivors must address as they attempt to move on with life. One might say that, in some ways, they have become a living embodiment of the principles represented in the *Feu de Joie*.

It appears that for both groups touched on here—adolescents and the military—change is taking place. No longer are "denial and dark humor" the only ways to address issues related to dying and to death. No longer is one expected to address this alone. As hospice has tried to bring comfort to travelers on their final journey, and to their families, there can be seen a national movement to try to bring the same sense of connection to American society as a whole.

REFERENCES

Farrell, J. J. (1980). *Inventing the American way of death, 1830-1920*. Philadelphia, PA: Temple University Press.

Stevenson, R. G. (1991). Adolescents and the final hours. In *The final 48 hours*. Philadelphia, PA: Charles Press.

The Tragedy Assistance Program for Survivors, Inc. (TAPS). e-mail: info@taps.org; website: www.taps.org/

SECTION 3

Cultural Considerations

CHAPTER 14

Palliative Care is a Human Right

Stephen R. Connor

Over one million people die each week worldwide. In North America, Western Europe, Australia, and a few other exceptional countries, palliative care has now become integrated to varying degrees into mainstream healthcare systems. However, almost everywhere else, palliative care and relief from pain is still an unrealized dream. About 80% of the world's population lacks adequate access to opioid medications for pain control. Australia, Canada, New Zealand, the United States, and several European countries accounted for more than 90% of the global consumption of opioid analgesics (INCB, 2010). In the developing world, getting any health care, let alone palliative care, is difficult and depends mainly on whether you have financial resources; if you do, you can get treatment; if you don't, you likely won't.

In most of the world, the right to health care is not well established. In spite of the fact that most countries are signatories to the International Human Right to Health from the International Covenant on Economic, Social, and Cultural Rights (ICESCR) Article 12.1 (United Nations, 2000) calling for the "right of everyone to the enjoyment of the highest attainable standard of physical and mental health." This right is aspirational and not enforceable, except that signatory countries are expected to work toward its fulfillment.

While palliative care is not specifically mentioned in the statement, the committee overseeing the ICESCR issued a general comment on the right to health that includes a number of core obligations of all signatory nations, irrespective of resources (United Nations, 2000). These obligations include access to health facilities, goods and services on a nondiscriminatory basis; the provision of essential drugs as defined by the World Health Organization (WHO); and the adoption and implementation of a public health strategy. When it comes to palliative care, it is clear that patients with life-limiting illness should have access to appropriate health care, basic medications for symptom control and terminal care, as well as inclusion of palliative care in national healthcare policies.

STATUS OF PALLIATIVE CARE AVAILABILITY INTERNATIONALLY

In 2006, the Worldwide Palliative Care Alliance (WPCA) commissioned the International Observatory on End-of-Life Care at Lancaster University in the United Kingdom to conduct an analysis of Palliative Care Development using a 4-level description of palliative care progress. The report and subsequent publication (Wright, Clarke, Woods, & Lynch, 2006) revealed that palliative care was not being provided at all in half of the countries of the world. Palliative care had reached some level of integration in only 35 countries (15%). Moreover, in 80 countries (35%), there was at least one palliative care service, though this ranged from one service in Pakistan with 160 million people to one service for every 63,000 inhabitants in Australia.

At the time of this report, there were 41 countries with interest in providing palliative care but no service delivery and 79 countries, mainly in Africa and the Middle East, where no one could be found expressing an interest in palliative care.

Subsequently, the WPCA commissioned a repeat of this report, and there has been some improvement in that the percentage of countries providing some palliative care has increased from 50% to 58% (Lynch, Connor, & Clarke, 2012). A new, more detailed measurement scale was used so that the original 4-level measure has now become a 6-level system with levels 3 and 4 broken into two parts. Level 3 includes countries that are just beginning service provision versus those that have more extensive service delivery, and Level 4 comprises those countries beginning to integrate into national healthcare systems versus those few where palliative care is reasonably well integrated (see Figure 1).

The WHO (2011) estimates that there were about 57 million deaths from all causes worldwide in 2008. This number is projected to double in the next 50 years. Of these, it is believed that between 45% and 60% would benefit from palliative care (Stjernsward, Foley, & Ferris, 2007). Diagnoses appropriate for palliative care include, but are not limited to, cancer, heart failure, chronic obstructive pulmonary disease, kidney failure, liver failure, dementia, motor neuron diseases, stroke, HIV/AIDS, tuberculosis, debility or frailty of old age, and various childhood conditions. Those not likely to need or to be able to access palliative care are generally those who die suddenly from injury or an acute

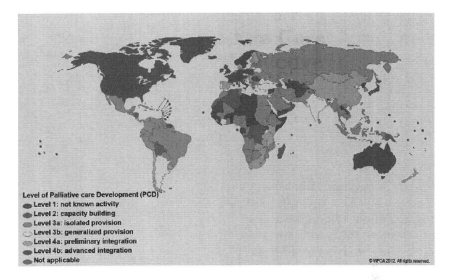

Figure 1. Levels of palliative care development worldwide.

condition not preceded by a period of disability, including sudden heart attack or stroke, and those with infectious diseases other than HIV or TB.

The WPCA estimates that there are approximately 16,000 specialized palliative care teams worldwide. About 6,000 of these teams are in North America. A rough estimate of those receiving specialist or intermediate palliative care is 3 million patients or less than 12% of the need worldwide. Palliative and hospice care also always treat "family," conservatively, at least 2 to 3 per patient. This puts the need for palliative care worldwide at around 100 million people annually, and this need will grow considerably in the next 30 years, especially in the developed world.

Prior to 2012, we were in a period of calm before the storm in that the first "Baby Boomers" of the post-World War II generation has now begun to die in significant numbers, starting in that year. The demand for hospice and palliative care will continue to grow in the decades ahead. However we are having a difficult time expanding palliative care in countries where it is lacking.

MAJOR GAPS AND OBSTACLES

As noted in the previously discussed reports, there are major gaps in the ability to access palliative care services worldwide. These gaps exist because of some persistent obstacles that continue to interfere with the growth of palliative care. These obstacles include many policy-related barriers as well as psychological barriers. The policy-related barriers are summarized in the public health model for palliative care that was developed at WHO. Figure 2 illustrates this model:

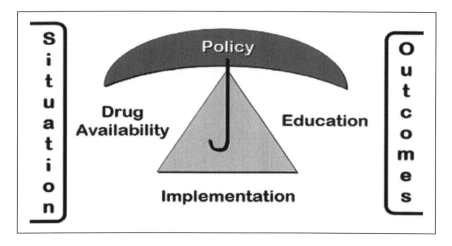

Figure 2. The public health model for palliative care development.

Policy

Without policy support for palliative care, nothing else can make much progress. Policies include a legal basis for the existence of palliative care, standards of palliative care, recognition of palliative care as a health service and an area of specialization, the development of a needs assessment and national strategy for palliative care implementation, and methods for budgeting or funding for palliative care.

Drug Availability

Essential palliative care medications need to be available to all providers. Globally, lack of access to opioids, especially oral morphine, is an endemic problem. Overly strict policies have emphasized control of illicit use of opioids at the expense of medical and scientific use. When the UN Single Convention on Narcotic Drugs (1961) was signed, countries agreed that equal emphasis would be placed on prevention of illicit use with access to opioids for medical and scientific use. This principle of "balance" has not been achieved, as almost all emphasis has been on control rather than access.

Recent efforts to bring balance to the control of opioids have begun to yield results. The UN Commission on Narcotic Drugs passed a resolution in 2011 titled, "Promoting adequate availability of internationally controlled licit drugs for medical and scientific purposes while preventing their diversion and abuse." This came about after a concerted effort by international NGO's, including the WPCA and Human Rights Watch, became concerned with the appalling lack of pain relief worldwide.

The International Association for Hospice and Palliative Care (IAHPC), in cooperation with WHO, also published a list of Essential Palliative Care Medications that list those specific drugs, including opioids, which at minimum, need to be available to provide even basic palliative care.

Education

Education is at the heart of palliative care development. We think of professional education as including basic, intermediate, and advanced or specialized levels. All healthcare professionals need a basic understanding of palliative care. Those who work regularly with patients who have advanced chronic or life-limiting illnesses need further training, usually at least several months. Those needing the skill to attend to the most complex patients need specialized training of at least 1 year.

Most developing countries lack specialized training centers for palliative care, and language barriers make education in palliative care very challenging. Most curricula are in English, which is not commonly understood in Asia, Latin America, most of Africa, and the former Soviet republics. Translation into local languages is expensive and time-consuming.

Implementation

As noted in the report on "mapping levels of palliative care development," implementation of palliative care services is uneven and skewed toward developed countries and those with a higher Human Development Index. In the public health model, implementation is only possible when the proceeding elements are in place, including drug availability, education, and policy support. Hospice and palliative care have been transplanted in some places prior to broad development of these systems, but only with significant philanthropic support. It is often critical for there to be at least one model program or a series of pilot projects in a country in order to demonstrate that palliative care can be provided in the cultural milieu. Palliative care cannot be successfully developed from the top down. It is necessary that there be strong community involvement and support so that it can be both bottom up and top down at the same time.

Psychological Obstacles

In addition to the problems of implementing palliative care from a public health perspective, there are many psychological barriers that persist. While we acknowledge that other people die, we continue to face difficulty in believing that this applies to ourselves and those closest to us. While the public is fascinated with unnatural death, there is a strong avoidance of natural death. Death anxiety is pervasive, and efforts to educate the public on the need for palliative care are very challenging.

There is a misguided belief that to openly acknowledge the possibility of impending death will itself hasten death. Up until 1991, it was against the law in Albania for a physician to tell a cancer patient their diagnosis and prognosis, based on the belief that such information would lead a patient to become depressed and to die sooner with poorer quality of life, even though there was no evidence to support this belief. We now know that, while patients may respond to such news with initial distress, this is more than offset by enhanced opportunities to come to terms with the illness and to have more opportunities to resolve unfinished business with oneself and with loved ones.

There are also a number of myths about palliative care that persist. Not only the fear that it means "giving up" and dying sooner but the idea that somehow using morphine hastens death. There is growing evidence that for many patients, palliative care may even improve survival (Connor, Pyenson, Fitch, & Spence, 2007; Temil et al., 2010).

QUALITY OF HOSPICE AND PALLIATIVE CARE

Recently, the Economist Intelligence Unit published a report titled "The Quality of Death: Ranking End-of-Life Care Across the World" (2010). The United States tied Canada for ninth place out of the 40 developed countries measured. The reason the United States ranked lower than the UK, Australia, New Zealand, Ireland, Belgium, Austria, The Netherlands, and Germany was that the overall cost of dying in the United States was unusually high, and there were too many people dying without health insurance.

A quality-of-death index was developed for this report, which was made up of four main categories, including basic end-of-life healthcare environment, availability of end-of-life care, cost of end-of-life care, and quality end-of-life care environment. The main findings of the report included

- While all countries had weaknesses and need to improve, the UK led the world in quality of death, and many developed nations must work to catch up.
- Combating perceptions of death and cultural taboos is crucial to improving palliative care.
- Public debates about euthanasia and physician-assisted suicide may raise awareness but relate to only a small minority of deaths.
- Drug availability is the most important practical issue, and improved access to opioids is urgently needed.
- Government funding of end-of-life care is limited and often gives priority to conventional treatment over palliative care.
- More palliative care may mean less health spending, yet better, more appropriate care.

- High-level policy recognition and support is crucial. Without palliative care policy at a national level, palliative care cannot grow.
- Palliative care is mainly home-based care. More training is key to increasing the capacity of caregivers.

An article in *JAMA* looked to summarize what we know about measuring quality in palliative care (Teno & Connor, 2009). Five C's were used to understand what is most important in palliative care: care that is Competent, Coordinated, patient and family Centered, Compassionate, and Committed to quality. There is a growing consensus that the domains of quality palliative care include symptom palliation, emotional support, promoting shared decision making and advance care planning, meeting the needs of patients and those who care for them, addressing grief and spirituality, and coordination of care.

CONCLUSION

The availability of palliative care is improving in the developed world while the challenges of expanding to developing worlds are being recognized. Pain relief and palliative care are practically unavailable to 80% of the world's population. Access to palliative care is increasingly seen as a fundamental human right and an important measure of the moral development of individual countries.

For palliative care to develop, a public health approach is needed that addresses the need for policy development, access to essential palliative care medications, as well as professional and public education that leads to the implementation of services. Beyond public health barriers, there remain many psychological and cultural barriers that limit acceptance of the principles of palliative care. Many myths persist that reinforce these barriers that need to be dispelled, including the belief that palliative care means giving up hope, which may hasten death. The determinants of quality of palliative care are just beginning to be understood and vary greatly throughout the world.

REFERENCES

Connor, S., Pyenson, B., Fitch, K., & Spence, C. (2007). Comparing hospice and non-hospice patient survival among patients who die within a 3-year window. *Journal of Pain and Symptom Management, 33*(3), 238-246.

Economist Intelligence Unit. (2010). The quality of death: Ranking end-of-life care across the world. Retrieved March 22, 2011 from: http://www.eiu.com/site_info. asp?info_name=qualityofdeath_lienfoundation&page=noads&rf=0

International Narcotics Control Board (INCB). (2010). Report on the availability of internationally controlled drugs. Retrieved March 22, 2011 from www.incb.org/pdf/annual-report/2010/en/supp/AR10_Supp_E.pdf

Lynch, T., Connor, S., & Clarke, D. (2012). Mapping levels of palliative care development: A global update. *Journal of Pain & Symptom Management.*

Stjernsward, J., Foley, K., & Ferris, F. (2007). The public health strategy for palliative care. *Journal of Pain Symptom Management, 33*(5), 486-493.

Temil, J., Greer, J., Muzikanski, A., Gallager, E., Admone, S., Jackson, V., et al. (2010). Early palliative care for patients with metastatic non–small-cell lung cancer. *New England Journal of Medicine, 363*(8), 733-742.

Teno, J., & Connor, S. (2009). Referring a patient and family to high quality palliative care at the close of life: "We met a new personality, with this level of compassion and empathy." *Journal of the American Medical Association, 301*(6), 651-659.

United Nations. (2000). Substantive issues arising in the implementation of the international covenant on economic, social and cultural rights: The right to the highest attainable standard of health. Retrieved March 22, 2011 from http://www.unhchr.ch/tbs/doc.nsf/%28symbol%29/E.C.12.2000.4.En

World Health Organization. (2011). The top 10 causes of death. Retrieved March 22, 2011 from http://www.who.int/mediacentre/factsheets/fs310/en/index2.html

Wright, M., Clarke, D., Woods, J., & Lynch, T. (2006). Mapping levels of palliative care development. *Journal of Pain Symptom Management, 35,* 469-485.

http://dx.doi.org/10.2190/FATC15

CHAPTER 15

Spirituality in End-of-Life Care: A Roman Catholic Perspective

Gerry R. Cox and Rev. Christopher W. Cox

A visit to any congregation reveals something about that congregation, whether a mosque or a synagogue, whether a storefront church or a Gothic cathedral. Perusing a Christian hymnal, seeing some common songs and some peculiar to a tradition, reveals something of the faith and spirituality of the congregation. Such diversity reflects the old Latin maxim: *lex orandi, lex credendi*. The law of prayer is the law of belief. Put more simply, our prayer reveals and forms what we believe. Understanding distinctive features of Roman Catholic prayer and practice reveals the beliefs of Catholics and assists the caregiver in accompanying Catholics in the end-of-life encounter.

A visit to a Catholic church makes evident that the structure, with its prominent placement of the altar and dedicated space for the tabernacle, was built for the celebration of the Eucharist. While a certain breed of more modern architecture has fewer images, most Catholic churches have a remarkable number of statues and stained glass and murals depicting the life of Christ (especially the crucifixion), Mary and the saints, and angels. Peruse a Catholic hymnal and one will find, ordinarily, songs predominantly invoking the first-person plural—we, us, our—instead of the first-person singular—I, me, mine—more common in a Protestant hymnal. These undergird a Catholic worldview that is particularly grounded in a communal experience of God, centered around the Eucharist and other sacraments. The community is not just the flesh and blood of members of a congregation, but also includes those who have gone before us, sinner and saint alike, as well as the angels. While the Catholic Church, a historic and ancient faith, has certain well-defined practices and beliefs, modern trends of diminished catechesis and adherence complicate the matter. Nonetheless, the Catholic, whether practicing or lapsed or ex-Catholic, engages in some dialectic with the faith in facing the end of life. Not just a medical issue, the end of life is social, communal, psychological, and economic as well, but, even more, it is a spiritual issue. Understanding the spiritual and religious approach of Roman Catholics and

191

the strengths that come from this approach should become a resource used in giving end-of-life care.

For Catholics, spiritual development begins with a genuine and personal encounter with God. Each person is a child of God, with the ability to be transformed and respond to God's call (Miscamble, 2000, p. 18). The presence of God—grace—is in and around everyone. God's grace informs daily life and transforms it. Work, play, objects, art, sense of place, beauty of encounters can all be the time and place for an encounter with God. Spirituality reflects one's relationship with God while facing challenges of everyday life in a given historical and cultural environment (Svoboda, 1996, p. 5).

The Sacraments are also fundamental places to encounter God. In the words of the Catechism of the Catholic Church (1994), sacraments are "efficacious signs of grace" (#1131), privileged moments of encounter with God. Catholic belief in the Communion of Saints joins "those who are pilgrims on earth, the dead who are being purified, and the blessed in heaven, all together forming one Church," and, hence, believe "that in this communion, the merciful love of God and his saints is always [attentive] to our prayers" (#962). Catholics acknowledge the presence and seek the aid of the Communion of Saints and angels in daily living. Some examples of prayers of petition or intercession asking for the aid of saints would include the Hail Mary, *Memorare*, Prayer to St. Michael, Hail Holy Queen, Prayer to Our Lady of Perpetual Help, Prayer of St. Anthony, the Litany of the Saints, the Litany for the Dying, A Prayer to Our Lady of Guadalupe, Prayers to the Angels, Prayer of St. Jude, and Prayer of St. Joseph. A common prayer, taught to children and repeated by adults is *"Angel of God, my guardian dear, To whom God's love commits me here, Ever this day be at my side, To light and to guard, to rule, and to guide, Amen."* Catholics pray to find lost objects, for health, for their children, for the dead, to ask saints to intercede for them, to be able to go to Heaven, to have their loved ones become saints, and for all sorts of other hopes and dreams. The belief in sacraments and in the Communion of Saints is built on the experience of prayer, the *lex orandi*, of regular practice.

The idea that spirits inhabit the world is not unique to Catholics. Native Americans believe that spirits are a part of the world as well. Phyllis Swifthawk suggests that her grandfather appeared to her telling her that she needed to walk again because she had much to do in her life. Her spiritual nature and prayers led him to come to her when she was paralyzed and unable to walk and allowed her to walk again without treatment (Cox, 2010, p. 95). The Hopi ask the dead to bring them rain and help them in other ways in life.

DYING PREPARATIONS

In the face of death, the Catholic Church teaches that God has created each person for eternal life, and that Jesus, the Son of God, by his death and resurrection, has broken the chains of sin and death that bind humanity, giving perfect glory to God, principally by the paschal mystery of his blessed passion, resurrection from the dead, and glorious ascension (Krisman, 1990, p. 2). The funeral rites commend the dead to God's merciful love and pleads for the forgiveness of their sins, reaffirms the unity of the Church on earth with the Church in Heaven, the great communion of saints, the spiritual bond that still exists between the living and the dead, and the belief that all the faithful will be raised up and reunited in the new heavens and a new earth where death will be no more (Krisman, 1990, p. 3). The Catholic Church teaches that death does not end nor does it break the bonds formed in life (Krisman, 1990, p. 2).

The role of the ministry of consolation rests with the community of believers who are expected to offer faith and support, acts of kindness, assist in routine tasks of daily living, help plan funeral liturgy, attend vigil, be part of the funeral liturgy, reconcile differences with the living, help the bereaved adjust to loss, celebrate the sacrament of penance, and to encourage the family to take an active role in the ministry; but be sure to not make it burdensome for them (Krisman, 1990, pp. 4–5). As a community of believers, Catholics are expected to be present for the entire process. The pastoral care of the sick and dying means having a relationship with them that they may know sings of God's presence.

Catholics have a threefold series of sacraments for initiation: Baptism, Confirmation, and Eucharist. Likewise, Catholics have three sacraments in preparation for death: Reconciliation, Anointing of the Sick, and Eucharist. The three sacraments together form the viaticum, which together constitutes the end of Christian life. The sacrament of Reconciliation has traditionally been viewed as allowing the remission of eternal punishment, if necessary, due to our sins. The effects of the sacrament are to reconcile us with the Church, and by doing so, the person is able through penance and faith to pass from death to life and not come into judgment (Catechism of the Catholic Church, 1994, p. 369). Illness and suffering are part of life. Not only the dying, but those who are sick may receive this sacrament. The elderly or the sick who have received this sacrament may receive it again. Like all sacraments, the Anointing of the Sick is a liturgical and communal celebration. It is typically celebrated with the sacrament of the Anointing of the Sick, and with the Eucharist. Together, they form the last sacrament of the earthly journey, the "viaticum" for "passing over" to eternal life (Catechism of the Catholic Church, 1994, p. 379).

Before one dies, the family will typically notify the priest of the seriousness of the illness or malady. If the seriously ill person is conscious, the priest will ask if he or she would like to receive the Sacrament of Reconciliation. If the person says yes, then all but the priest are expected to leave the room. Confession is between the person and God, the priest being the instrument for hearing the confession. The confession may occur before or after the anointing, although it is preferred that the confession be heard prior to the other sacraments. The priest will administer the Sacrament of the Sick to the dying person. Before the Second

Vatican Council (1962–1965), the sacrament was administered at a critical time as death was imminent. Now, the sacrament is administered at relatively early stages of any serious illness, including those from which one can be reasonably expected to recover. The priest administers the sacrament by the laying on of hands, the prayerful recitation of a ritual formula. The seriously ill and the homebound are given the sacrament of Communion even though they are unable to attend the Mass at the church. As time and people permit, communion is brought to the seriously ill on Sundays, Holy Days, and as often as is feasible on other days. In the last hours of life, the dying person will be given his or her last communion with a special ritual called "Viaticum." The Viaticum essentially is Eucharistic Food for the final journey. The purpose is to fortify the individual with the sacramental sign of Him who the dying is looking forward to meeting. It is also viewed as a way to help the community of believers to more fully understand and identify with the Paschal Mystery in a more personal way. Roman Catholics are ritualistic and sacramental. It is common for those receiving end-of-life care to have missals, books of prayer, holy cards, crucifixes rather than crosses, holy water, medals around their necks, rosaries, pictures of saints, and other religious artifacts as part of their religious experience in facing dying and death. Inviting the priest to be a part of the process is typically quite important to them.

Apart from the Sacrament of Reconciliation, the other sacraments are explicitly communal. All present are invited to take part in the prayers. Those who choose to not take part in the prayers are encouraged to remain silent and observe or pray or otherwise to show respect for the rituals. Only Catholics in good standing may receive communion. It is certainly encouraged to approach the priest with those receiving communion, but Catholics who are not allowed to receive communion and those who are not Catholic are expected cross their arms, placing their hands on the opposite shoulder as they approach the priest so that he will know to give them his blessing rather than communion. It is the only part of the ritual other than confession that is restricted to non-Catholics. Before the priest leaves, he will bless the person, those present, and the home. All may take part in the blessing including sprinkling holy water over the seriously ill person. This includes those who are not Catholic as well. Because Catholicism is based upon a theology of hope, there is little focus upon repenting or changing one's ways before death. Rather, the focus is upon behaving as a person with purpose and meaning in life. One is called to live a life of Christ. Catholics do not despair for anyone. The concept of even those who have done great evil possibly being in Heaven is accepted. God's mercy is infinite. Gospel stories of the wedding feast in which many were invited, good and bad, from the highways and byways illustrate the belief in God's divine mercy. Only one guest did not have on the proper wedding garment, which could be interpreted as having a soul that was not filled with sanctifying grace (Crock, 1948, p. 39). Catholics generally believe that anyone can go to Heaven. When a person dies, the general statement is that "a new saint is in Heaven."

Upon death, the priest is called as soon as possible. The funeral director will also be called. In the United States, the funeral director is often called first. If the person has been in hospice, the hospice staff will often manage the phone calls and notices for the family. The family will make arrangements with the funeral director to plan the funeral process. In some areas, little real planning is required because the Roman Catholic rituals follow rubrics from the Order of Christian Funerals. The liturgy, the pall bearers, which priest the family wants to officiate, which newspapers need to be notified, who will notify family/friends, and so forth need to be decided.

As a traditional and ancient religion, the Roman Catholic dying and death management practices have not changed much over the centuries. The Roman Catholic practices do no vary much from place to place or over time. The basic structure follows the same pattern regardless of time or place. The structure includes a wake or vigil, the funeral mass, and a closing ritual at the place of interrment or at the cemetery.

The theology of the Roman Catholic is one of hope upon death and a belief in an afterlife. Like the even more ancient Jewish religion, Roman Catholics belief that human life is a gift from God that is to be cherished and protected. Roman Catholics protect all life, including that of the unborn, the elderly, and even those awaiting execution on death row. When one's life has achieved its purpose, it is one's time to die. The death of a loved one is to be a joyous occasion because a saint has been born. The loved one is united with God.

Each person was created by God for eternal life. The death and resurrection of Jesus ended the chain of sin and death for humankind. Baptism is our journey into the tomb with Jesus and as we join him in death, we join him as He was raised to life; we too, will imitate him in His resurrection. This union with Jesus is strengthened through the Eucharist. The Eucharist is part of the Roman Catholic funeral ritual as well.

The funeral ritual becomes a thanksgiving to God for the gift of life, which has been returned to God, the author of life and hope. The Mass, the memorial of Jesus' death and resurrection, is the principle celebration of the Roman Catholic funeral. The rituals of the funeral are designed to commend the dead to the love and mercy of God and to plead for forgiveness of the sins of the deceased. The celebration of the Mass is the community reaffirming and expressing the union of the Church on earth with the Church in Heaven and the communion of saints. It is also an honoring and farewell that allows the living to recognize the loss of the deceased and to commend him or her to God. It also recognizes the spiritual bond between the living and the dead that continues after death. The Roman Catholic theology does not view death as the end of the relationship between the living and the dead. There is also a belief in resurrection for all, including the living. The funeral rituals remind the living that they too will face final judgment and to expect God's mercy and judgment. Humans need to turn to God in times of crisis.

As the Roman Catholic rituals involve the community of believers, the funeral rituals include the entire community. This suggests that in the Roman Catholic tradition, the question of whether or not to include children is a moot point. Rather than ask should children attend, the Roman Catholic tradition expects children to be a part of the ritual. If children are noisy or cry, it is not considered to be a problem. The energy and enthusiasm that they bring to the ritual adds to the ministry of the community. Being full of life, children add to the ability of those grieving to better manage their grief.

MEANING AND RESEARCH

Roman Catholics, like other religious groups, expect to have answers to their questions that remain unanswered in life. In her research, Janice Winchester Nadeau suggests that "revelation, reunion, and reward include meanings of what will happen in the after-life" (Nadeau, 1998, p. 184). Revelation is the concept that answers will be given in Heaven. Reunion is that the loved one will be reunited in Heaven. Reward is the concept that by going to Heaven, one is rewarded with eternal life. Nadeau also found that respondents saw death as both the deceased and the bereaved testing their faith, their strength and courage, and their sense of purpose (Nadeau, 1998, pp. 186–187). Rabbi Earl Grollman suggests that spirituality, combined with faith, prayer, and ritual, enhances mental and physical health, reduces hostility and stress, aids grief and loss, and helps in seeking meaning and purpose in life (Grollman, 2000, p. 101). Elisabeth Kübler-Ross (1991) argues that it can be a blessing to have cancer or a heart attack because it will allow you to grow in understanding, love, learning, and the opportunity to use the end of your life to love and finish unfinished business (pp. 18–19). Kübler-Ross also suggests that as a scientist, she has verified that in the time of transition, one will have guides, guardian angels, and those who passed on before you to guide you and to help you (1991, p. 31), which is in keeping with Roman Catholic tradition.

SUMMARY

While end-of-life care today is usually provided by teams with clergy of different faiths, Roman Catholics cling to the sacraments and rituals that involve having a priest present. While deacons and lay people can be a major part of the care, some rituals can be provided only by priests. The spirituality of Roman Catholics is a critical part of end-of-life care. As members of an ancient and traditional religion, Roman Catholics are steeped in rituals and tradition that must be included in end-of-life care. Accepting the beliefs in life after death, spirits, guardian angels, and communion of the saints aids in the process. Catholics generally believe that life has purpose and that all can be transformed to live the life to which one was called.

REFERENCES

Catechism of the Catholic Church. (1994). Ligouri, MO: Ligouri Publications.

Cox, G. R. (2010). *Death and the American Indian.* Omaha, NE: Grief Illustrated Press.

Crock, C. H. (1948). *Paths to eternal glory: Consolation for the bereaved.* New York, NY: Joseph F. Wagner.

Grollman, E. A. (2000). *Living with loss, healing with hope: A Jewish perspective.* Boston, MA: Beacon Press.

Krisman, R. F. (1990). *Order of Christian funerals.* Chicago, IL: Liturgy Training Publications.

Kübler-Ross, E. (1991). *On life after death.* Berkeley, CA: Celestial Arts.

Miscamble, W. D. (2000). *Keeping the faith: Making a difference.* Notre Dame, IN: Ave Maria Press.

Nadeau, J. W. (1998). *Families making sense of death.* Thousand Oaks, CA: Sage.

Svoboda, M. (1996). *Traits of a healthy spirituality.* Mystic, CT: Twenty-Third Publications.

http://dx.doi.org/10.2190/FATC16

CHAPTER 16

Grief and the American Indian

Gerry R. Cox and Andrea R. Sullivan

The experience of grief is different for each individual. However, each person's grief experience is culturally influenced and can be somewhat predictable because of their culture. By gaining knowledge of various cultural practices relating to grief and bereavement, one can learn successful grief management practices and apply them to other groups. One can also better understand how people of other cultures respond differently to grief and thereby learn to provide better services and care. American Indian burial and bereavement practices are similar to those of other cultures, but they are also different enough to puzzle and stifle caregivers who work with them. This chapter attempts to outline cultural differences among American Indians to assist the caregiver in helping indigenous peoples deal with their grief.

The cultures of the Americas before the arrival of the Europeans included the islands in the Caribbean, South and Central America, and North America. In just the area north of what is now Mexico, over 700 distinct languages were spoken (Schaefer, 2008, p. 167). While it is not possible to discuss over 700 cultures, the death management practices of the larger surviving cultures will be presented here.

For those who work with American Indians who are grieving, an understanding of the culture and attitudes of the particular clan with whom one is working is required. Non–American Indians often have inaccurate or potentially offensive preconceptions of indigenous cultures that can get in the way of successful grief management practices. For instance, instead of defining success by the dominant cultures' terms, the caregiver must understand what successful grieving means for the American Indian. The emphasis must be upon the positive, the good things that can be done to help the grieving person. Many speak of American Indians as being disadvantaged, lacking skills that prepare them to survive in modern culture. Looked at differently, one could say American Indians have a double advantage of living and knowing in two cultures. They may be more aware of the caregiver's attitudes and values than the caregiver is of theirs. Most non–American Indians also define their cultures as dying. Instead, one can see the cultures as greatly modified; but often these modified cultures are thriving and developing. Caregivers often are not aware of the difficulties of being American Indian in a non–American Indian world. When asked about their grieving practices, the typical response is to answer what the American Indian thinks the caregiver wants to hear rather than explaining the rituals and traditions they follow after a death or a loss.

To get to know American Indian cultures, one must understand that culture is not just buildings, places, objects, or environment, but it is the way of life of a group of people. Attitudes, values, customs, beliefs, assumptions, expectations, behaviors, artifacts, and the buildings compose culture. For American Indians, spirituality is integral to their culture. It is not a separate part of their lives, but rather it is present in everything. While the names vary—for the Dakota, *Wakan Tanka*; for the Algonquin, *Manito*; for the Iroquois, *orenda*; for the Ojibwa, *Kitche Manitou*—a supernatural force exists in everything in the world. Spirits are in everything—the mountains, the trees, animals, streams, rocks, plants, Father Sun, Mother Earth, the moon, the stars, and all other things found in the world. Rituals often are designed to invite the spirits to look favorably upon the living, to aid them in battles, growing crops, healing the sick, to have love, and most other human desires and wants. The spirits have to be thanked and honored through prayers, offerings of food and tobacco, and often through a shaman (Bial, 2000, p. 72).

Dreams and visions are also important to most clans. Many American Indians believe that if they can understand their dreams, they can understand themselves. Those who work with grieving American Indians need to be aware of the power of dreams and their importance in the grieving process.

Many groups commune with the spirits of the dead through rituals that involve masks, false faces, and kachinas. The False Face Society of the Iroquois carved faces into trees and made a mask that held the power of the disease spirit as well as the life power of the tree, which could be used for good, but the danger of harm was always there if the spirit was offended (Hanson, 1992, p. 138). It was generally believed that the more grotesque and ugly the mask was, the more power it held! It was thought that when a person wore the mask, the spirit of the ugly flying head entered his body and his own personality was gone. The False Face Societies of the Iroquois were known for their ability to cure people in crowds by driving out evil spirits. Their approach is more acceptable today because modern medicine recognizes the relationship between illness and the mind. For the Hopi, kachinas are supernatural beings and spirits of the dead. Children are given carved wooden dolls as images of them to help them learn about the Hopi religion. Like the False Face Society, the Hopi believe that when they dress as a kachina, their spirit leaves and is replaced temporarily by that particular kachina. Clearly, the Hopi believe that the dead are still with us. Caregivers need to understand this. The Zuni also wear masks. At the winter solstice, the masks worn by the Zuni make them appear 10 feet tall or more.

While the caregiver may not see the value of the ritual, such as wearing the mask, it may be a powerful tool in the grief process. American Indians who grieve have many rituals available to them: to cleanse, to release the deceased, to purify, to aid in the journey, or to appease the spirit world. Even long after a person has died, the griever may feel the need to do a particular ceremony because of a dream or vision. Caregivers need to understand the importance of encouraging whatever rituals or ceremonies are sought by the grieving American Indian.

Another cultural experience common among many American Indians of the plains is medicine lodges and sweat lodges. Most lodges would have the door facing the east into the rising sun. They would contain a sacred fire, an altar, and often four pillars. Four is an important number for most groups; there are four winds, four seasons, and so forth. For the Arikara, the four pillars represented the sunrise, thunder, wind, and night. While sweat lodges have become popular among non–American Indians, their purpose is primarily religious. For most groups, the purpose is to purify spiritually and physically. While most benefits are mental, it also is beneficial for health and hygiene. Lodges may have medicine bundles around the walls along with special symbols and other artifacts. Medicine bundles are collections of objects that vary greatly from one group or individual to another but are generally made from animal skins and contain stones, grasses, tobacco, the sacred pipe, skulls or bones, and other sacred objects. Many groups have tribal medicine bundles as well as individual bundles. It can be expected that most groups will have some sacred objects and places that may or may not be open to the caregiver.

Another cultural aspect to be noted is that, for the most part, American Indians are concerned with the joys and problems of life and do not focus upon what happens to them when they are dead. This is not to say that they do not believe in an afterlife. Instead, they follow burial practices and grieve so they can move on with life after a loss. The practices followed after a death vary from group to group. The Ojibwa bury their dead in the ground with food and tobacco for the 4-day journey to the land of the souls. The Iroquois fast for 10 days after a death, and the family grieves for an entire year, wearing mourning clothes and carrying the spirit bundle. The widow sleeps next to the spirit bundle and places food before it (Bial, 2000, p. 43). The widow does not remarry for a year. At the end of the year, a special ceremony is held in which mourners are given gifts and comforted, which signals the end of their time of grief and allows them to rejoin the daily activities of the village (Bial, 2000, p. 43). For the Dine (Navajo), after the burial, there are 4 days of restricted behavior (Leighton & Kluckhohn, 1969, p. 92). The Navajo are noted for their repulsion of contact with dead bodies. They have ceremonies for people who have touched dead bodies to remove the evil effects of such contact, but interestingly, they also will use the same Blessingway ceremony to neutralize the evil effects of contact with white people (Allen, 1963, p. 59). For the Navajo, grief is part of life. Each Navajo is reminded that the symbols and expression of the unknown power of the Supreme Being are everywhere in all of creation; it surrounds one's life and gives meaning and purpose to life (Greenberg & Greenberg, 1996, p. 128). To survive grief, one must remember where one came from and who one is. Grief keeps a person from performing his or her purpose in life. For the Navajo, one must return to what being a Navajo means to be able to manage grief. At the Sun Dance, the Lakota feed a ritual meal to mourners who have lost someone in the last year; this is to reincorporate them back into the ordinary activities of the Lakota society (Medicine, 1987, p. 168). The Lakota are expected to restrict behavior for 4 days and at the end of the year, to feed the ghost for one last time, distribute the belongings at a feast or Giveaway, which releases them from their period of mourning and allows them to begin life anew (Grobsmith, 1981, p. 66).

Clearly, the caregiver who is instructed in only the stages of grief or even the process theory of grief will find that the usual methods of guiding people through grief do not work so well for American Indians unless they have been fully acculturated in the dominant society. While there may very well be anger, depression, lack of wanting to go on with life, denial, and other common reactions, the means to helping the person through their grief is not group therapy, counseling, or medicine. Rather than therapy, the focus should be upon ritual, tradition, and return to what is important. The Lakota may want to "keep the ghost" of a dead relative, but they would still be expected to end their mourning, conduct a Giveaway, and so forth. They are also expected by their culture to end their mourning after a year and begin life anew (Grobsmith, 1981, p. 66). For American Indians, cultural expectations are more powerful and important than feelings.

How does one learn cultural expectations? Caregivers should study information about the cultural group of the individual with whom they are working. If there is a community available, the caregiver can become involved in that community and learn valuable ideas about the culture: things that work with grieving people, the role of elders, the role of spirituality, and the importance of ritual and ceremonies. Visiting with the people in the community at every opportunity is very valuable, as well as listening to them rather than talking to them; particularly, visiting with the elders and with parents; visiting with the attitude of learning, respect, and value of the cultural group and the community.

While visiting, a caregiver will find there are some cultural components that hold true across clans. For instance, in most American Indian communities, life and thought are centered around people and not things. People are more likely to be respected for their contributions to the group than for their status, possessions, or other individual accomplishments. Standing in the community is generally based upon helping others and contributing to the group rather than getting a job or achieving fame. The successful person is the wise elder, a good model for others, or one who has benefited his or her people. Deep trust and reliance upon others is important. Sharing and cooperation are important. Defeating others or getting better grades or a bigger house is not considered a positive goal. Sharing includes sharing grief. The caregiver is expected to grieve with the griever and not just offer advice or comfort. When another is unhappy, so are you! If one is hungry and another has food, all will eat! For caregivers, this is often a problem. Some groups have the Giveaway in 6 months rather than waiting a year. They may have given away all of their food. The caregiver has food but does not share! How can a selfish person aid those who share everything?

Most clans are relatively quiet. While being quite hospitable, friendly, and fun-loving, a traditional Navajo will typically enter a room where there are many friends but will show them no sign of recognition for several minutes. After a socially acceptable length of time, he will touch hands with all of them. Navajos are seldom loud or demonstrative in public. They may cry on each other's shoulder if there are no strangers present, but public displays of affection are rare. Navajos rarely speak louder than is necessary to make themselves heard by the person to whom they are speaking. Caregivers who are loud or speak when they walk into the room or hug when they meet the Navajo are generally looked upon as not showing respect, and their ability to work with Navajos is compromised greatly.

Caregivers must exercise tremendous patience when working with American Indians. For a culture that focuses upon billable hours, having too large of a caseload, and little time for anything, it is extremely difficult to meet the needs and values of American Indians. A caregiver might want to have several visits with the family when he or she is simply there before offering any kind of professional support. Certainly the caregiver would want to visit neighbors, elders, and others in the community before offering professional advice. If the caregiver is well established in the community, it may not be necessary to spend so much time with others in the community. Nevertheless, elders need to be respected and should be consulted even if their advice or counsel is ignored.

To be able to work with American Indian communities, caregivers must show respect for people, especially the elderly. Respect for people and their feelings are very important in American Indian societies. Relationships between family members are based upon mutual respect and care. People get great satisfaction in helping others. For the caregiver, these are the positive relationships that care can be based upon. The American Indian will go to great lengths to avoid doing anything that will disrespect others. Children are taught restraint and self-control. They are taught particularly to respect the elderly. Caregivers must learn to show respect as well. As children are not to interrupt or speak before spoken to, so should caregivers.

Caregivers typically are from a society that honors children. In American Indian societies, people anticipate and celebrate reaching the age of 50, when they can become an elder. Having "snow on the mountain" (white or gray hair) is a good thing. It is also important to know that respect is earned and not just the result of age. Being a respected elder is based upon gaining wisdom, humility, calm judgment, and becoming a model for others, particularly those who are younger. Non–American Indians can be respected if they show the same traits.

American Indians are generally taught to respect the privacy of others. They should not interfere in other people's affairs. Personal dignity is highly valued. One does not give advice unless the other person asks for it. Most American Indians resent freely given advice that most caregivers offer. One should not make decisions for others. One is to fulfill one's duties to the family, clan, and community. One should be generous, control oneself, and mind his or her own business! The nature of caregiving is often counter to this approach. The extended family is also very important. Children spend far more time with extended family, including grandparents, than in the larger society.

Caregivers are typically under a time constraint. The hospice program will allow them to work with a family for only a limited period of time. The government will pay for only so many visits. The management will not allow for non-billable hours. Time is viewed differently in American Indian cultures, in which one should not rush through life. If there is work to do, then do it. If not, spend time with your clan and friends. There is no rush to manage grief or anything else! Patience is normal, not expected in only certain situations.

Caregivers who work with American Indians need to better understand the cultures of the people they are serving. It is important to show respect for the values and way of life of the people they serve. Gaining cultural knowledge is an important step in gaining respect for those cultures and receiving respect from those you are serving. Indeed, without mutual respect, assisting an American Indian in successful grief management will prove elusive.

REFERENCES

Allen, T. D. (1963). *Navahos have five fingers*. Norman, OK: University of Oklahoma Press.

Bial, R. (2000). *The Ojibwe*. New York, NY: Benchmark Books.

Greenberg, H., & Greenberg, G. (1996). *Power of a Navajo: Carl Gorman: The man and his life*. Santa Fe, NM: Clear Light Publishers.

Grobsmith, E. S. (1981). *Lakota of the Rosebud: A contemporary ethnography (Case studies in cultural anthropology)*. Austin, TX: Holt, Rinehart & Winston.

Hanson, A. S. (1992). *Indians of Wisconsin and the surrounding area*. St. Croix, Wisconsin: Ashanson.

Leighton, D., & Kluckhohn, C. (1969). *Children of the people*. New York, NY: Octagon Books.

Medicine, B. (1987). Indian women and the Renaissance of traditional religion. In R. J. DeMallie & D. R. Parks (1987). *Sioux Indian religion*. Norman, OK: University of Oklahoma Press.

Schaeffer, R. T. (2008). *Racial and ethnic groups*. Upper Saddle River, NJ: Prentice Hall.

http://dx.doi.org/10.2190/FATC17

CHAPTER 17

"It Will Do When I Am Dying": Navigating the Nuances of Fundamentalist Christianity's Understandings of Death and Dying

Harold Ivan Smith

> Precious in the sight of the Lord is the death of his saints.
>
> Psalms 116:15, KJV

THEOLOGY PACKAGED IN SONG

Christianity, given the illiteracy of adherents in earlier centuries, communicated theology through music (Fischer, 2005) and art. In 20th-century America, spirited congregational singing was a vital element in Protestant worship. The gospel song, *Old Time Religion*, gained popularity because of a snappy tune and lyrics promising that "the old-time religion" would moderate the dying process:

> It will do when I am dying,
> It will do when I am dying,
> It will do when I am dying,
> And it's good enough for me! (Tillman, 2012)

A RESPONSE TO THE UNIVERSAL FEAR OF DEATH

Frye (2011) insists that "humans everywhere are interested in religion . . . because they all die, and are afraid of oblivion" (p. 39). As he was dying, Lipsenthal (2011), a physician, observed that the fear of dying is "the most basic fear all humans share" (p. 1). Spong (2009) identifies religion as a means to diminish the fear of death "which accompanies our knowledge of mortality" (p. 98). Thus, many Christians believe in an afterlife "not because we are convinced that [the promises] are true, but because we have a deep need for them to be true" (p. 120).

Aries (1981) describes a "tamed death" facilitated by clergy through the rituals of the church to influence the dying process and prepare for death.

Death shapes Protestant religion because of a residual fear, Klass (2002) argues, "that the individual might not survive death" (p. 136). This life *might be* "all there is." For fundamentalists, confidence in salvation diffuses that fear. Nevertheless, Klass laments, "In counseling we see people for whom the fear of death is linked to the fear of punishment for real or imagined shortcomings" (p. 138).

Theological constructs of personal salvation elevate and diffuse death anxieties. Theological beliefs, particularly about the meaning of suffering or limitation of medications that inhibit conversation, may influence medical decisions. Belief-based behaviors may intrude on the dying, family members, friends, hospice personnel, and volunteers. Conflict stirs, or erupts, when a family member (particularly a fundamentalist Christian) does not want the individual to die without having the/another opportunity to "invite Jesus into her heart." The fundamentalist may even insist, "[Name] is *not* dying!" The hospice environment may be challenged when the dying individual and family members do not share theological beliefs. A patient, family members, or hospice staff and volunteers who may *once* have embraced particular theological interpretations experience discomfort when involved in or overhearing such conversations.

THE EMERGENCE OF FUNDAMENTALISM

"Fundamentalism" identifies a group within Protestant Christianity in 21st-century America who shares "an intense affirmation of biblical authority" and allegiance to Christian doctrines they deem "essential" (Melton, 1996, p. 105). In the face of threatening societal changes, fundamentalist Protestants "earnestly contend for the faith that was once delivered unto the saints" (Jude 1:3, KJV) against the challenge of modernity, science, and higher criticism of the Bible and, more recently, outspoken atheists in the public square. Admittedly, while some prefer a broader excusive agenda (6 to 14 nonnegotiable doctrines), 5 "we-can-agree-on" doctrines draw the widest support: the inerrancy of the Bible, the virgin birth of Jesus, substitutionary atonement, bodily resurrection, and the return of Jesus to earth (Zehner, 2009).

In the latter quarter of the 20th century, fundamentalists abandoned a long tradition of separateness and emerged in the public arena to battle for cherished religious beliefs. They embraced political agendas and mastered modern media, technology, Republican Party politics, and fundraising (Marty & Appleby, 1992). The explosion of American fundamentalism, Marsden (2006) contends, was a response to the perceived decline—and the predicted demise— of a "Christian culture" in America. In *Bad Religion*, Douthat (2012) argues, "America has indeed become less traditionally Christian across the last half century" (p. 3). For fundamentalists, "the old-time religion" is *the* defining conviction in their lives.

Who Are the Fundamentalists?

Some identify "fundamentalist" with public figures like Jerry Falwell, Pat Robertson, or James Dobson; indeed, Falwell zealously cultivated the media seeking to diffuse stereotypes of fundamentalists and to communicate *his* interpretation of Scripture and its political implications. Falwell distinguished between "small f and capital F fundamentalists" (Harding, 2000, p. xv); the small "f's," often younger, softened their public presence to attract converts and defuse intolerance. Many Christians do not identify themselves as fundamentalists, preferring "evangelicals, Bible-believing Christians or simply Christians" (Harding, 2000, p. xv) or conservative evangelicals.

Hardcore fundamentalists (the capital F's) reject all "fellowship" (cooperation) with individuals who do not share their rigid theological interpretations. Billy Graham, after migrating from fundamentalism to evangelicalism (which some consider fundamentalism "lite"), drew the antagonism of hardcore fundamentalists for partnering in his urban crusades with "nonevangelical" mainline denominations (Sweeney, 2005).

How Many Fundamentalists Are There?

Determining an accurate count of fundamentalists is a challenge since some who are fundamentalists do not self-identify as such; others who define themselves as evangelicals are, in fact, fundamentalists. Based on the Fourth National Survey of Religion and Politics, conducted at the University of Akron and financed by the Pew Forum on Religion and Public Life, John C. Green (2007, offers what he calls "a good estimate" of 10.8% of the adult population (p. 30) or 24,547,878 (DemographicsNow, 2011). However, not all of these subscribe to *all* five factors of fundamentalism. So, he suggests that "true" fundamentalists number 4.5% of adult Americans (p. 30) or 10,118,282. He concludes, "This group is hardly trivial" (p. 30). Unger (2005) estimates that there are some 70 million "evangelicals" (p. 206)

A Companion Development

Paradoxically, at the same time the fundamentalists were transitioning, the American religious landscape was diversifying rapidly. Melton (1996) insists that America is "a microcosm of world religion. Every major religious community is now present in strength" (p. 17), with well-known adherents. Although a significant majority of Americans still self-identify as "Christians" of some type, "the climate of mutual respect and honor demanded by pluralism" (p. 17) threatens fundamentalists.

There is a third factor as well. As transition and diversification were taking place, a third element was gaining acceptance: hospice. The Hospice Movement, birthed at St. Christopher's in South London, migrated to the United States to challenge the traditional medical model of dying. Over time, hospice has emerged as the dominant agency providing care for the dying.

A Word About Language

Borg (2012) identified *Christianspeak* as a functioning secondary language or shorthand. *Fundamentalistspeak* is a subspecies. Any words, terms, and phrases in the fundamentalist Christian lexicon, admittedly *dear* or *precious* to adherents, are neither easily understood nor valued by other Christians nor easily "packaged" to potential converts or to those who interact with fundamentalists in hospice settings. Nevertheless, Volf (2011) notes that "speaking in a Christian voice" (p. 132) is linked to identity and to an affirmation of particular doctrines, traditions, or rituals.

The word *conversion,* from the Latin *conversio* (meaning "turning toward") is the "bedrock" of fundamentalist faith. Conversion is a definite and decisive transformation from sinfulness to salvation. Balmer (2004) notes that conversion "is instantaneous" and "a databale experience of grace that signals the movement from death to life" (p. 187). By "accepting Jesus as personal Lord and Savior" the individual gains the right to eternal joy in heaven (and a "get out of hell free" card).

The term *Christian* is an "umbrella," covering a wide palette of beliefs, rituals, and practices for the 80% of Americans who identify themselves as such (Wuthrow, 2008, p. 287), and in particular, for the 33% who believe that Christianity "is the only true religion" (p. 293). Given the fluidity of *Christian,* fundamentalists drafted definitive qualifiers such as *"born again* Christian" or *"born from above"* to distinguish the "true" believer "from a 'liberal' or 'nominal' Christian who claims the designation falsely" (Balmer, 2004, p. 93). Zehner (2009) notes that many believe that "only fundamentalists are true Christians" (p. 292).

How Does Fundamentalism Impact Hospice?

Boston and Mount (2006) report, "The existential or spiritual domain is an important determinant of quality of life in the palliative care setting" (p. 13). Spirituality was an intentional element in conceptualizing hospice. Given the holistic focus of hospice, all dimensions of the individual's life are interpreted, appraised, and valued. Unfortunately, the assumptions, words, ideas, or methods fundamentalists use in religious-focused conversation may confuse or trouble hospice staffers and volunteers, a reality compounded by the diversity within "Christian" culture. Boston and Mount report, "Not having a shared language with which to discuss spiritual concepts" (p. 16) complicates assessment and care in hospice. So, how do hospice employees and volunteers "receive" religious ideas, particularly if these constructs are thought to intensify the angst of the dying, challenge the patient's autonomy, and complicate dying? How can staff respect "the *this*ness" of this patient or *this* fundamentalist Protestant (Rohr, 2011)?

Given that "the goal of Protestant religion is salvation" (Klass, 2002, p. 136), fundamentalists insist that the need for salvation is universal. "For *all* have sinned, and come short of the glory of God" (Romans 3:23, KJV; emphasis mine). Thus, *all* humans are appropriate objects for evangelization. Indeed, hospice patients are prime. Grudem (1994) observes,

> The knowledge of one's impending death often will bring about genuine heart searching on the part of the dying persons, and sometimes words of Scripture or words of Christian testimony that have been heard long ago, will be recalled and the person may come to genuine repentance and faith. (p. 815)

Individuals who practice other religions—the Jews, the Sikhs, the Buddhists, the Hindus, New Agers—may be "good people" but nevertheless need Jesus as personal savior! Billy Graham (2005) appeals to Jesus' assertion:

> "No one comes to the Father except through me." The way to God is through Jesus, for only He died and rose again to take away our sins. The Bible says, "Neither is there salvation in any other: for there is none other under heaven given among men whereby we must be saved." (Acts 4:12, KJV)

Jerry Falwell adds, Jesus "did not say that he was a way among ways" but rather "I am the way, the truth and the life" (1986, p. 46). Insert *only* after each *the* and you have fundamentalist Christianity in a nutshell.

OBJECTIVE ONE: DESCRIBE COMMON ELEMENTS IN A FUNDAMENTALIST UNDERSTANDING OF A "GOOD" DEATH AND THE AFTERLIFE

Identifying what is a "good death" and facilitating that is the *modus operandi* of hospice. Hospice's goal is providing a "good death from the perspective of both the dying person *and their family,* with the period before death being characterized by the best possible quality of life" (Randall & Downie, 2006, as cited in Watts, 2012, pp. 105–106; emphasis mine).

Fundamentalist Protestants, however, assert the *only* "good death" is being "ready" to meet God by having accepted Jesus. This world is, they conclude, the anteroom for the afterlife. Indeed, a common strategy in "witnessing" or "sharing one's faith" is asking, "*If* you were to die tonight, do you know for sure that you would go to Heaven?" or "*Where* would you spend eternity, Heaven or Hell?" *Christianity Today* (The question that died, 2012) identifies these questions as the most widely used technique in Christian evangelism. Some shrink the question to, "Are you saved?" (Grossman, 2007) Meacham (2012) reports that 85% of all Americans (and apparently 100% of fundamentalist Christians) believe in Heaven. Moreover, "Most of us are apparently confident—or at least say we are—that life does not end at the grave" (Meacham, 2012, p. 32). A dean at the hyper-fundamentalist Southern Baptist Theological Seminary astounded readers by an article published in that institution's alumni magazine entitled, "Christopher Hitchens Might be in Heaven" (Moore, 2012, p. 24). How, some sputtered, could Hitchens, "the world's most famously caustic atheist," (p. 24) *be* in Heaven?

A key element in fundamentalist theology is that an individual must, at all times, given the precariousness of life, be "ready to meet his/her Maker." One song frequently used during an "invitation" (a time in fundamentalist worship when the unsaved are given an opportunity to "accept" Jesus) repeatedly asks, "Are you ready?" for the "great day coming . . . when the saints and the sinners shall be parted right and left?" (Thompson, 1972, p. 186). Death comes to some like "a thief in the night" (1 Thessalonians 5:2); to others, as a slow process offering more opportunities to become "ready."

One can be "ready," according to the fundamentalist construct, *only* through believing in the *substitutionary* atonement of Jesus dying on a cross in 33 CE. Fundamentalists confidently quote, "For God so loved the world, that he gave his only begotten Son, that whosoever believeth in him should not perish, but have everlasting life" (John 3:16, KJV). Fundamentalists primarily accept *only* the King James Version, (1611 CE) as *the* most accurate version of the Bible, because it is believed to be without *any* error (Schimmel, 2008). Wellum (2012) contends,

> From Genesis to revelation , Scripture is clear that conversion is absolutely necessary for individuals to experience salvation and know God. . . . Unless we turn from our sin and turn to God . . . we will not know God savingly and will stand under his judgment and wrath. (p. 25)

Fundamentalists' belief that "all have sinned and come short of the glory of God" (Romans 3:23, KJV); that *all* motivates the doctrine of "original sin." Every human inherits the consequences of Adam and Eve's rebellion against God. Grudem (1994) cites the Apostle Paul's assertion that "sin came into the world through one man," that is, Adam (Romans 5:12, KJV).

> When Adam sinned, God thought of all who would descend from Adam as sinners. Though we did not yet exist, God, looking into the future and knowing we would exist, began thinking of us as those who were guilty like Adam. (pp. 494–495)

Although the Apostle Paul distilled conversion to one sentence: "If thou shalt confess with thy mouth the Lord Jesus, and shalt believe in thine heart that

God hath raised him from the dead, thou shalt be saved," (Romans 10:9, KJV), some fundamentalists demand a "turning *from* sin and turning *to* Christ" as "proof" of salvation. Colson and Fickett (2008) postured that believing *correct* doctrines is essential for true salvation. Wellum (2012) clarifies the point:

> In many of our churches, we find people who profess to have been converted, but they exhibit merely an intellectual assent to the gospel apart from any evidence of real change in their lives. Scripture clearly regards this kind of mere mental assent as false conversion. (p. 25)

Indeed, Barna (as cited in Grossman, 2007) suggests that 25% of "self-identified evangelicals" have "not even accepted Christ as their savior" (p. 6D). Thus, fundamentalists insist that individuals who have been "self-professing" Christians all their lives and been active in a "soul-saving, Bible believing" church, will, nevertheless, be damned to an eternity in hell. Graham (2005) explains, "We are Christians outwardly; we go to church; we've been baptized or confirmed—but deep inside we need something else. We need to be born again, spiritually reborn, which only Jesus can do for us" (p. 47).

Charles Stanley, a leading fundamentalist pastor and media personality, explains, "Our entrance into heaven has nothing to do with how good we are; what matters is how good Jesus is, and what He did for us" (as cited in Meacham, 2012, p. 34) So, by accepting Jesus' atoning sacrifice, one gets "a ticket to heaven which can never be revoked" (as cited in Meacham, 2012, p. 34). Billy Graham (2005) urged listeners to "make a decision for Christ" and accept God's generous gift of salvation; grace is *not* blanketedly dispensed. To expedite conversion, fundamentalists formulated "a sinner's prayer." After preaching to 50,000 people in New York City on June 25, 2005, and extending an invitation to those who "had come forward," Graham instructed, "By a simple prayer of faith, you can make a commitment to him [Jesus] today" (2005, p. 125) and gain eternal life. Graham asked individuals to repeat after him:

> O God, I am a sinner. I am sorry for my sin. I am willing to turn from my sin and I want to receive Jesus as my Savior. I want to confess Him as Lord. From tonight on, I want to follow Him and serve Him in the fellowship of His Church. In Jesus' name, Amen. (p. 93)

Graham declared that everyone who had sincerely prayed "*those words*" instantly became "a child of God."

How Does Fundamentalism Impact Hospice?

Many mainline Christians expected that, over time, as educational and economic standards in America were elevated, fundamentalism would fade away. Historian and theologian Martin Marty insists that fundamentalism "is back with a vengeance" (as cited in Armstrong, 2010, p. 886), especially propagated through sophisticated technology and a spirit of unapologetic, at times arrogant, certainty.

Spong (2009) notes that Americans historically have looked to three professions to explain death: clergy, physicians, and undertakers. Since no one escapes death, there must be someone to answer questions and address anxieties. Spong concedes, "The ordained ones in our society" have long been "cast in the role as death's interpreter in leading, in pastoral care, in dealing with the diagnosis that announces someone's impending doom" (p. 4). Clergy have been authorized to preside over funerals and memorial services and, in some cases, to refuse to conduct services. In fact, some pastors see the funeral sermon as an opportunity to "present" the gospel to the mourners.

Christians have long been involved in financing, building, and administering hospitals in response to the narratives of Jesus healing the sick (Anderson, 2001; Koenig, 2005). In the Middle Ages, some priests were excused from parish responsibilities "to deal exclusively with the spiritual and pastoral needs of patients" (Klessman, 2005, p. 260) and particularly the dying. Legions of orders of nuns have been (and many still are) devoted to nursing and running hospitals. In urban centers, a denominational affiliation was once part of many hospitals' identities or was a recognizable feature in a particular hospital's culture. Large cities had a Presbyterian *and* a Methodist *and* a Baptist *and* a Lutheran *and* a Jewish *and* one or more Catholic hospitals.

Hospitality, hospital, and hospice all developed from the Latin *hospitum*, which traces to *hospes*, a Latin word meaning "guest" and "host." Koenig (2005) notes that the word means "the stranger who receives a welcome, or less frequently, acts as a welcomer of others" (Koenig, 2005, p. 4138).

Hospice, according to Watts (2012), has relied "heavily" on "a significant volunteer workforce" to provide care for patients (p. 105), an essential element in making hospice financially viable. Moreover, "Some of those efforts were inspired through religious belief, and the development of the modern hospice movement has primarily been born out of a Christian tradition imbued with the principle of duty to others" (p. 105).

Hospice is emerging in 21st-century American society as the dominant interpreter of death. Certain questions once addressed to (and answered by) ministers, rabbis, imams, and priests/nuns are increasingly directed to hospice staff. Student (2009) observes, "As a rule, workers in a hospice are influenced in their work by religion and are predominately guided by a Christian view of humanity" (p. 260). Some staff who are ordained have trained in particular fundamentalist traditions; some chaplains and lay volunteers' first loyalty is to their religious tradition and secondly to hospice. Watts (2012) points to Connor's (2009) caution that some individuals become involved in hospice "with the goal of converting others to a faith before they die" (p. 109); this author would add, to a *particular* faith perspective. Fundamentalists in hospice, in some cases grudgingly, acknowledge that "the turf" is shared with individuals who prefer "spirituality" over religion. Thus, Student (2009) insists that preparation of and supervision of "these helpers" is critical.

Many Americans believe that, as death approaches, hospice will "know *what to do*" or "be there for us." Consequently, some religious dilemmas will be navigated (or negotiated) in hospice settings. At times, hospice staff must navigate theological land mines, balancing religious thoughts, interpretations, inklings, and longings with the patient's needs. Indeed, heightened by the immediacy of death, fundamentalists may see hospice patients as an enhanced venue for "witnessing" or "presenting Jesus"; hospice staff may be a secondary target. Evangelization, even if disguised as pastoral care, distracts from primary tasks or alters the environment in which the individual is dying and in which staff perform their responsibilities.

A Fluid Definition

Within hospice, the meaning of *Christian* presents barriers for clear communication. Patients, and staff, might label themselves Christian because they are *not* Buddhist, Jewish, or Hindu. Individuals might define themselves as Christian because they were baptized as babies or were confirmed as children or adolescents in Christian churches. Fundamentalists discount those rites as a true conversion.

While some in hospice might contend, "We all worship the same "God" or "We're all trying to get to the same place," fundamentalists dismiss that conclusion. A conversation between Humpty Dumpty and Alice illustrates the confusion factor in the word *Christian*. When Alice protests, "I don't know what you mean," Humpty Dumpty snaps, "Of course you don't—till I tell you. . . . When *I* use a word . . . it means just what I chose it to mean—neither more nor less." Alice retorts, "The question is . . . whether you *can* make words mean so many different things" (Carroll, 1993, p. 125; emphasis in original),

Although hospice has developed precise terminology for charting and documentation, the patient's spiritual preference may be framed in less precise lexicon. Thus, we might wonder, "Do *you* mean what *I* mean?"

OBJECTIVE TWO: EXPLORE WAYS TO NEGOTIATE FAITH UNDERSTANDINGS THAT COMPLICATE END-OF-LIFE CARE AND COMFORT

Protestant fundamentalists have two agendas: to witness to their own experience of salvation and to make certain that others, particularly the dying, and individuals with whom they come in contact, have an opportunity to pray "the sinner's prayer."

A friend of this author, who weighed almost 300 pounds, although dying, summoned enough energy to grab a male nurse at bedside and demand, "Are you *saved*?" The nurse sputtered, "From . . . *from what*?" When my friend expounded particulars, the nurse fled the room and asked to be reassigned. At my friend's funeral, the eulogist pointed out that the deceased had been "a soul winner to his dying breath." The eulogist suggested that his friends should exhibit that same zeal in sharing the Gospel "with the lost" and "making the most of *every* opportunity to present the claims of the Gospel." For fundamentalists, the sense of immediacy is driven by the Bible: "Behold, now *is* the accepted time; behold, now *is* the day of salvation" (2 Corinthians 6:2, KJV; emphasis in original).

Given the awareness of approaching death, fundamentalists may be blunt: "Do you know Jesus as personal Lord and Savior?" If yes, fundamentalists will follow up with narrowing questions: "When?" Fundamentalists a "punticular experience" or moment when the individual chose to accept Jesus (G. T. Smith, 2011, p. 374). Fundamentalists push for a specific date and place, as expressed in the lyrics of *Amazing Grace*, "the hour I first believed."

The Deathbed as Spiritual Battlefield

Historically, the deathbed was a "spiritual battleground" or theater. Some find a Biblical precedent for *ars moriendi* (the art of dying) in "When Jacob had finished giving instructions to his sons, he drew his feet up into the bed, breathed his last, and was gathered to his people" (Genesis 49:33, KJV). Family, neighbors, friends, strangers, even enemies, gathered at the bedside to witness the dying and, as James W. Green (2008) reports, "To receive the dying commending them all to God's care" (p. 5). This sometimes led to a "deathbed conversion" for the dying individual or for someone observing the death. According to Nuland (1994), the "art of dying" was "to let it happen . . . but to die the best way possible, at peace with God" (p. 265). Kehl (2006) insists "There is no clear, shared understanding of what the characteristics of good death are" (p. 277) and that any definition "may change after that family member has witnessed a death" (p. 278). Kehl adds, "The concept of a good death is highly individual and dynamic" (p. 280). Fundamentalists cannot imagine a "good death" without being "at peace with God"; but that phrase needs clarification. Given the circumstances of dying these days—hooked to machines, medicated, and alone—some raise concerns about the competence of an individual at "death's door" to repent sufficiently to be "at peace with God." Green (2005) describes the death environment:

> When the bedside ceremonies were completed, everyone waited patiently for the death to occur, now tamed because it came under ritual (and God's) control. At the end the priest performed absolutions, evoking the authority of the church on behalf of the departed and the bereaved . . . [which] took the nasty sting out of death. (p. 6)

Indeed, the worst death was to die instantly, without any opportunity to make amends, receive the sacraments of the church, and to be supported by family and friend. As early as the 15th century, a genre of books on good dying provided guidance to the clergy. The illiterate relied on religious art, particularly woodcuts, for instruction. It must be considered that at that time, Christians believed "that a soul's fate was often decided during the last hour on earth" when "the devil's forces" would intensify efforts to "to get hold of the soul that was about to depart." Final temptations included despair, impatience, pride, and arrogance, which could cause the dying "to forfeit the heavenly splendors and suffer in eternal hell" (Imhoff, 1996, p. 116).

Admittedly, in those days, dying primarily took place in homes. Given the shift of venue to hospitals, nursing homes, and hospice, many individuals die alone; some *prefer* to die alone. For many fundamentalists, a deathbed conversion is "the last hope" for unsaved relatives and friends, although Moore (2012) cautions, "We shouldn't count on last-second repentance" (p. 24).

Not surprisingly, some family members deny the prognosis or delay hospice care, perhaps subconsciously, hoping for some medical reprieve to give the individual more time to repent. Moore (2012) addresses "death bed conversion": "rarely, it does happen, and who knows? Perhaps you have relatives who in the last seconds of breath, breathed out a silent prayer of repentance and faith" (p. 24). But will your family know of your repentance and be assured of your salvation?

OBJECTIVE THREE: IDENTIFY WAYS TO COMFORT INDIVIDUALS MARGINALIZED IN THE DYING BECAUSE THEY DO NOT SHARE THE THEOLOGICAL UNDERSTANDING OF THE DYING

Individuals may be "burdened," in fundamentalist parlance, about the eternal "fate" of the dying individual—a discomfort that intensifies as the patient's ability to make rational decisions accelerates.

Student (2009) reminds practitioners that "the dying person *and* his or her relatives are the focus of treatment" in hospice (p. 259). Thus, "the needs of those affected, with attention to their physical, psychological, social, and spiritual dimensions, constitute the starting point of services" (p. 259) and acts of spiritual care. The issues of the dying or concerned family become the issues hospice care providers have to navigate in providing care.

In reality, given the expanding religious diversity in American culture as well as the migration of individuals from a faith of origin to a faith of choice, an individual may resist, even reject, what Douthat (2012) calls "radical literalism" of fundamentalism. Green (2005) notes,

> America contains many visions of what happens to us after we die and where we go, if anywhere, after that. The historical imagery of Christian eschatology [the doctrine of the future] now competes with revived Native American traditions; vigorous imports from Hinduism, Buddhism, and Islam;

and the late twentieth-century shift from formal, denominational "religiosity" to all-purpose "spirituality." (p. 84)

While the dying may be "at peace" with her beliefs, some may be dismayed by those beliefs. Many leaders in contemporary liberal Christianity, such as Elaine Pagels (2003), John Spong (2009), Clark Pinnock (1990), Peter Gomes (2003), Howard Thurman (1979), and Martin Luther King Jr. (as cited in Hodgson, 2009), rejected the fundamentalism of their childhood and adolescence and migrated to a faith of investment. While Pagels (2003) initially found joy in "the assurance of belonging to the right group, the true 'flock' of God" (p. 30), she overlooked "disturbing undercurrents." However,

> after a close friend was killed in an automobile accident at the age of sixteen, my fellow evangelicals commiserated but declared that, since he was Jewish and not "born again," he was eternally damned. Distressed and disagreeing with their interpretation—and finding no room for discussion—I realized that I was no longer at home in their world and left the church. (p. 31)

The behavior, or intensity, of fundamentalists may challenge the objectivity and hospitality that create what Brener (1993) terms *mekom hanekhama* or safe place of comfort. Hospice should be a "safe" environment for patient, family, and staff. One hospice bereavement worker, a gay man, after several close encounters with fundamentalists and many inquiries about his own "salvation," snapped, *"Those* people make me nervous," especially given their insistence that "accepting Jesus" would require that he abandon homosexuality "as if I had chosen to be gay."

Bass (2012) notes that some 44% of Americans do not practice the faith of their parents or of their baptism (p. 59). Some pointedly identify themselves as *"ex*-fundamentalists" or *"recovering"* fundamentalists. Yao (as cited in Evans & Berent, 1988) contends that "at least six million out of an estimated 60 million fundamentalists in the United States want to break away from their fundamentalist beliefs and environment" (p. 7).

Sullivan (2012) reports of the "nones": "The fastest-growing religious group in the United States is the category of people who say they have no religious affiliation" (p. 68). These individuals, some of whom grew up fundamentalist, compose 16% of the American population (p. 68). Some nones have "given up on organized religion . . . but not on faith" (p. 68). As Jonathan Callard, a none, confesses, "I may be done with the church, but I'm not done with Jesus" (2011–2012, p. 102).

Conversation with some fundamentalists is challenging, especially with those who are aggressively evangelistic or who want to argue religion or, more pointedly, question the patient, staffer, or volunteer's faith. On the other hand, having worshipped in fundamentalist Protestant culture for many years, this author has some sensitivity to their mindset and fears. Certainly, in some settings, this author can "speak" fundamentalspeak and catch subtle "nuances" that other individuals miss. Working as a thanatologist, this author bypasses opportunities to argue or debate religious dogma or doctrine, at times terminating conversations with, "We will just have to agree to disagree" or "I *choose* not to interpret the Bible *that way*." One friend working in hospice replies, "*My* God is *not* like yours!"

For some, despite hospice's bereavement care for a year , spiritual angst may impede integration of the death. One griever confessed, "How can I anticipate the joys of heaven, if *they're* right that my husband is burning in hell? *Forever!*" Given the intense desire of many to be "reunited with their loved ones," Burke (2012) includes this distress in the construct, "*complicated* spiritual mourning."

Responding with Narrative

Appreciating narrative in thanatology, this author sometimes attempts to diffuse spiritual angst or distress by telling a story. When someone says, "I don't believe in God!" this author responds, "Tell me what kind of God you do not 'believe in.' I *might* not believe in that God either."

A narrative attributed to John Newton, the famed British former slave trader who wrote the beloved *Amazing Grace,* has proven effective. Newton suggested that Heaven has three surprises. First, that one is in Heaven (especially if death was sudden or unanticipated). Second, who is in Heaven that one *cannot* believe is there! ("Who let *him* in?") Third, who is absent that one thought would be present (Pentecost 24C, 2010).

OBJECTIVE FOUR: STARTING POINTS FOR SHARING HOSPICE TURF WITH FUNDAMENTALISTS

Starting Point One: Recognize That Protestant Christianity is an Elastic Term

Klass (2002) notes that "Protestantism is a diverse and fragmented religious tradition" (p. 129). The doctrine of "the priesthood of the believer" declares "each Protestant has a direct and personal relationship with God unmediated by priest or sacrament" (p. 133). The Reformers insisted that believers need no intermediary and can approach God confidently and can know God through reading the Bible. Admittedly, this freedom has resulted in an entrenched individualism, notably in interpreting the Bible—"*My* Bible says. . ."—and constructing dogma that results in schism: "I am starting *my* own church to reflect *my* interpretation of the Bible!"

Even if one has some awareness of what Christians believe (or, in fundamentalist perspective, *should* believe), what does *this* patient or family member believe? Hospice staff must be slow to assume *this* particular Christian's beliefs are true for all Christians. Paradoxically, encounters sometimes offer a "reverse" witness: the individual with a loving, tolerant God may offer a clear witness and "something to consider" to individuals suffering the restrictive heart-numbing of theological certainty and arrogance.

Starting Point Two: Be Tolerant of Inconsistencies

Klass (2002) reminds, "No matter how hypocritical" or philosophically incoherent "to the outsider," religious interpretations and beliefs "always seem genuine to those who order their lives by its map" (p. 128). A belief is a cherished, perhaps entrenched, reality that offers some degree of certainty to the fundamentalist. Indeed, the loss of that certainty causes grief. The certainty of fundamentalism—what Daniel Taylor (1999) terms "the myth of certainty"—offers existential security to individuals to mitigate the discomforting realities of contemporary life, especially the death of a child or young adult.

Starting Point Three: Use Questions in Conversations with the Patient or Family Members

The author has developed a series of question to enhance conversation on spiritual issues:

- Did you love [Name of dying/deceased]?
- Is love one of the chief attributes of *your* God?
- Is it possible that God loves [Name] more than you?
- Is mystery a characteristic of God? Is it possible to know everything about God?
- If God loves [Name], why would He be reluctant to show mercy to her/him?

Based on the responses to the questions, the author could move to this question: Is it possible that an all-knowing, all-loving God could see into the depths of [Name's] heart and accept her/him? Douthat (2012) offers a comforting caveat, "There are no doubt many holy men and women whose sanctity is known to God alone" (p. 292). In dialogue with some fundamentalists, this author appeals to the lyrics of Frederick William Faber's (1972) hymn, *There's a Wideness in God's Mercy*.

> For the love of God is broader
> Than the measure of our mind;
> And the heart of the Eternal
> Is most wonderfully kind. (p. 15)

Faber based the hymn text on this Scripture: "See what great love the Father has lavished on us, that or the likes of us should be called 'children of God!'" (1 John 3: 1, author's adaptation). This author also points out that "*whosoever* believeth in him has eternal life" (John 3:16, KJV; emphasis mine) has no asterisk limiting God's generosity. On occasion, the author has appealed to an Old Testament Scripture narrating King David's estrangement from his son, Absalom:

"For we must needs die, and *are* as water spilt on the ground, which cannot be gathered up again; neither doth God respect *any* person; yet doth he devise means, that his banished be not expelled from him" (2 Samuel 14:14, KJV; emphasis in original).

Perhaps, hospice may be one of God's "devised ways" to facilitate reconciliation with an estranged human or between family members. Some attributes of God are beyond human imagination or comprehension.

Lindvall (2012) insists, "What we know of God is proportional to the incomprehensible mystery of the divine being, the transcendent reality that moral minds can never fully plumb" or comprehend. orthodoxy " (p. 13).

Starting Point Five: Dialogue About Committal

For centuries, the key funeral ritual has been "the committal" or burial. As the body is committed to the soul, fire, or water, the soul is committed to its Creator! The funeral did not develop within Christian communities until the 7th century (Long, 2009). The historical Anglican and Episcopal ritual (other denominations use some variation of this phrasing) reminds grievers,

> In sure and certain hope of the resurrection to eternal life through our Lord Jesus Christ, we commend to Almighty God our *brother N., and* we commit *his* body to the ground, earth to earth, ashes to ashes, dust to dust. (The Book of Common Prayer, 1979, p. 501)

For some fundamentalists, this author suggests reflecting on lyrics Don Moen composed for his nephew's funeral:

> God will make a way,
> Where there seems to be no way.
> He works in ways we cannot see,
> He will make a way for me. (2003)

At other times, the author appeals to the words of the lay theologian Dolly Parton, "I am not God. I do not judge" (as cited in Buck, 2012, p. 16).

Starting Point Six: Appeal to Just as I Am

The hymn, *Just as I Am*, written in 1835 by Charlotte Elliott, was popularized as an invitation in the Billy Graham Crusades. Fundamentalists sing their belief that when one comes to Jesus "just as I am," God accepts the individual "just as she is." With some fundamentalists, this author points to particular lyrics, "fightings and fears, within, without, O Lamb of God, I come, I come" (Elliott, 1972, p. 232). Thus, some may accept Jesus and reject some, perhaps much, of what she assumes Christianity or the Christian church stands for, particularly given the polarization of theological constructs.

Starting Point Seven: Navigate the "Hot Button": Spirituality vs. Religion!

In recent decades, there has been a significant migration from religion to spirituality, another "umbrella" term (Bass, 2012; Eck, 2011). Many adults declare, "I am *not* religious, but I *am* spiritual." Specifically, some want to experience the transcendent but reject constricting filters such as doctrines, dogmas, and creeds. Douthat (2012) protests, "A choose-your-own-Jesus encourages spiritual seekers to screen out discomforting parts of the New Testament and focus on whichever Christ they find most congenial" (as cited in Balmer, 2012, p. 13). Fundamentalists are particularly skeptical of "spirituality" because it incorporates practices that they do not consider Christian, particularly meditation.

Starting Point Eight: Examine Personal Religious and Spiritual Beliefs

Taylor (2011) poses this question: "How do you see God differently now than you once did? What caused the change?" (p. 204). The assumptions of "the hour I first believed" may have significantly evolved and merit exploration now. One might ask, "What do you *now* believe?" Schafer (2011) reminds, "Each person has unique spiritual values and a personal language to describe them as each teaches me about his or her interior universe" (p. 13).

Starting Point Nine: Recognize That Evangelism is a Means for Some Fundamentalists to Demonstrate Caring

"Believe this" in order to "get to Heaven" may lead some individuals to conclude that Christian faith is "fire insurance." Indeed, one common cliché in fundamentalism is "Turn or burn!" As one hospice chaplain poignantly told this author, "The patient got 'the main thing' taken care of . . . and got some of that hell insurance." Many fundamentalists genuinely care about the eternal destiny of individuals. Many believe that "the old-time religion" *will do* when crossing "Jordan's chilly waters" in death.

Starting Point Ten: Acknowledge That Many Individuals Have Spiritual Wounds From Previous Encounters With Fundamentalists

Certain conversational streams—even words—may trigger anxiety or irritate those wounds. One dying patient informed a chaplain, "I am ready to meet my Maker. I am at peace. But thank God, I am not going to meet *their* maker!" Thus, the hospice staffer may want to reflect: Can hospice staff isolate particular elements in this spiritual desire to convert, or resist, that are particularly distressing?

Starting Point Eleven: Audit the Suitability of Volunteers

Hospice has a responsibility to ensure that personal religious dogmas "do not negatively impact" hospice care (Watts, 2012, p. 109). Thus, in hiring staff and recruiting volunteers, "an ounce of prevention" may prove beneficial to all.

CONCLUSION

Marsden (2006) contends that the rise in fundamentalism at the end of the 20th century is one significant religious movement that cannot be ignored, especially by those who work in hospice and thanatology. The movement's ability—through skilled spokesmen, polished media, and a wide social network—to advocate "a biblically based worldview" (or, some would counter, a biblically *biased* worldview) gives individuals a confident sense of belonging. That community is a shelter, or fortress, in the darkness of a culture they find increasingly hostile to Christianity and dismissive of Christian beliefs on death and dying.

Hospice and fundamentalism both reject modernity; some within each movement suspect the other's motives. Perhaps, with exploration, there may be ways to work together to ensure "a good death."

REFERENCES

Anderson, M. (2001). *Sacred dying: Creating rituals for embracing the end of life.* Roseville, CA: Prima Publishing.

Aries, P. (1981). *Western attitudes toward death from the Middle Ages to the present.* Baltimore, MD: Johns Hopkins University Press.

Armstrong, C. R. (2010). Fundamentalism. In C. H. Lippy & P. W. Williams (Eds.), *Encyclopedia of religion in America* (pp. 886-694). Washington, DC: CQ Press.

Balmer, R. (2004). *Encyclopedia of evangelicalism.* Waco, TX: Baylor University Press.

Balmer, R. (2012, April 29). Breaking faith: Ross Douthat laments America's departure from its 'Christian center.' *The New York Times Book Review, 59*(10), 13.

Bass, D. B. (2012). *Christianity after religion: The end of church and the birth of a new spiritual awakening.* San Francisco, CA: HarperOne.

Borg, M. J. (2011). *Speaking Christian: Why Christian words have lost their meaning and power—and how they can be restored.* New York, NY: HarperOne.

Boston, P. H., & Mount, B. M. (2006). The caregiver's perspective one existential and spiritual distress in palliative care. *The Journal of Pain and Symptom Management, 32*(1), 13-26.

Brener, A. (1993). *Mourning & Mitzvah: A guided journal for walking the mourner's path through grief to healing.* Woodstock, VT: Jewish Lights.

Buck, L. (2012, April). Two brothers' quest to land Dolly Parton. *Camp,* p. 16.

Burke, L. A., Neimeyer, R. A., McDevitt-Murphy, M. E., Ippolito, M. R., & Roberts, J. M. (2011). Faith in the wake of homicide: Religious coping and bereavement distress in an African American sample. *The International Journal for the Psychology of Religion, 21*(4), 289-307.

Callard, J. (2011-2012, Winter). Ritual. *Image, 72,* 95-108.

Carroll, L. (1993). *Through the looking-glass and what Alice found there.* New York, NY: Morrow.

Colson, C., & Fickett, H. (2008). *The faith given once, for all.* Grand Rapids, MI: Zondervan.

Connor, S. R. (2009). *Hospice and palliative care.* New York, NY: Routledge.

DemagrapicsNow. (2011). Data retrieved March 31, 2011, from http://library.demograpics now.com

Douthat, R. (2012). *Bad religion: How we became a nation of heretics.* New York, NY: Free Press.

Eck, D. L. (2001). *A new religious America: How a 'Christian country' has now become the World's most religiously diverse nation.* San Francisco, CA: Harper San Francisco.

Elliott, C. (1972). Just as I am. In Lillenas Hymnal Committee (Eds.), *Worship in song hymnal* (p. 232). Kansas City, MO: Lillenas Publishing.

Evans, R. L., & Berent, I. M. (1988). *Fundamentalism: Hazards and heartbreaks.* LaSalle, IL: Open Court.

Faber, F. W. (1972). There's a wideness. In Lillenas Hymnal Committee (Eds.), *Worship in song* (p. 15). Kansas City, MO: Lillenas Publishing.

Falwell , J. (1984). Introduction. In M. K. Selvidge (Ed.), *Fundamentalism today: What makes it so attractive?* (pp. 7-8). Elgin, IL: Brethren Press.

Falwell, J. (1986). *If I should die before I wake.* Nashville, TN: Thomas Nelson.

Falwell, J. (1982). *Finding inner peace and strength.* New York, NY: Doubleday.

Fischer, M. (2005). Hospitality. In L. Jones (Ed.), *Encyclopedia of religion* (Vol. 46, Rev. ed., p. 229). Detroit, MI: Thompson-Gale.

Frye, R. N. (2011, Spring/Autumn). Answering death. *Harvard Divinity Bulletin, 39*(3&4), 7.

Gomes, P. (1996). *The good book: Reading the Bible with mind and heart.* New York, NY: William Morrow.

Graham, B. (2005). *Living in God's love: The New York crusade.* New York, NY: G. P. Putnams.

Graham , B. (2011). *Nearing home: Life, faith, and finishing well.* Nashville, TN: Thomas Nelson.

Green, J. C. (2007). *The faith factor: How religion influences American elections.* Westport, CT: Praeger.

Green, J. W. (2008). *Beyond the good death: The anthropology of modern dying.* Philadelphia, PA: The University of Pennsylvania Press.

Grossman, C. L. (2007, January 23). Can the 'E-word' be saved? *USA Today,* p. 6D.

Grudem, W. (1994). *Systematic theology: An introduction to biblical doctrine.* Grand Rapids, MI: Zondervan Publishing House.

Harding, S. F. (2000). *The book of Jerry Falwell: Fundamentalist language and politics.* Princeton, NJ: Princeton University Press.

Hodgson, G. (2009). *Martin Luther King.* Ann Arbor, MI: The University of Michigan Press.

Imhoff, A. E. (1996). *Ars Moriendi for our time: To live a fulfilled life; to die a peaceful death.* In H. M. Spiro, M. G. McCrea-Curnen, & L. P. Waldel (Eds.), *Facing death: Where culture, religion, and medicine meet* (pp. 114-128). New Haven, CT: Yale University Press.

Kehl, K. A. (2006). Moving toward peace: An analysis of the concept of a good death. *The American Journal of Hospice and Palliative Medicine, 23*(4), 277-286.

Kirkpatrick , W. J. (1972). Lord, I'm coming home. In Lillenas Hymnal Committee (Eds.), *Worship in song hymnal* (p. 249). Kansas City, MO: Lillenas Publishing.

Klass, D. (2002). Spirituality, Protestantism, and death. In J. D. Morgan & P. Laungani (Eds.), *Death and bereavement around the world. Volume one: Major religious traditions* (pp. 127-146). Amityville, NY: Baywood.

Klessmann, M. (2005). Hospitality. In L. Jones (Ed.), *Encyclopedia of religion* (Vol. 6, Rev. ed., p. 260). Detroit, MI: Thompson-Gale.

Koenig, J. (2005). Hospitality. In L. Jones (Ed.), *Encyclopedia of religion* (Vol. 6, Rev. ed., pp. 4158-4142). Detroit, MI: Thompson-Gale.

Lindbergh, A. M. (2012). *Against wind and the tide: Letters and journals, 1947-1986.* New York, NY: Pantheon.

Lindvall, M. L. (2012, April 18). Truth is proportional: The limits of what we can know. *Christian Century, 129*(8), pp. 12-13.

Lipsenthal, L. (2011). *Enjoying every sandwich: Living each day as if it were your last.* New York, NY: Crown Archtype.

Long, T. G. (2009). *Accompanying them with singing: The Christian funeral.* Louisville, KY: Westminster John Knox Press.

Marsden, G. M. (1990). Defining American fundamentalism. In N. J. Cohen (Ed.), *The fundamentalist phenomenon: A view from within; A response from without* (pp. 22-37). Grand Rapids, MI: Eeerdmans.

Marsden, G. M. (2006, March/April). The sword of the Lord: How 'otherworldly' fundamentalism became a political power. *Books & Culture, 12*(2), 44-46.

Marty, M. E., & Appleby, R. S. (1992). *The glory and the power: The fundamentalist challenge for the modern world.* Boston, MA: Beacon Press.

Meachem, J. (2012, April 16). Heaven can't wait. Why rethinking the hereafter could make the world a better place. *Time*, 31-36.

Melton, J. G. (1996). *Encyclopedia of American religions* (5th ed.). Detroit, MI: Gale.

Moen, D. (2003). *God will make a way.* Retrieved from http.//.www.allthelyrics.com/es/lyrics/don_moen/god_will_make_a_way

Moore, R. D. (2012, April). Do you know when you were saved? *The Pathway, 10*(7), 7.

Neimeyer, R. A., & Burke, L. A. (2011). Complicated grief in the aftermath of homicide: Spiritual crisis and distress in an African American sample. *Religions, 2*(2), 145-164.

Nuland, S. B. (1994). *How we die: Reflections on life's final chapter.* New York, NY: Alfred A. Knopf.

Pagels, E. (2003). *Beyond belief: The secret gospel of Thomas.* New York, NY: Random House.

Pentecost 24C. (2012). Pentecost 24C Scriptures for Sunday November 7, 2010. Retrieved from http://home.roadrunner.com/-lyndale/ Pentecost 24C./hmt

Pinnock, C. H. (1990). Defining American fundamentalism: A response. In N. J. Cohen (Ed.), *The fundamentalist phenomenon: A view from within; A response from without* (pp. 38-55). Grand Rapids, MI: Eeerdmans.

The Holy Bible: Authorized King James version. (1611). Cleveland, OH: The World Publishing Company.

The question that died. (2012, May). *Christianity Today, 56*(5), p. 9.

Randall, F., & Downie, R. S. (2006). *The philosophy of palliative care: Critique and reconstruction.* Oxford: Oxford University Press.

Roberts, L. C. (1981). *Memorial acclamation.* Chicago, IL: GIA Music.

Robertson, P. (1992). *Answers to 200 of life's most probing questions.* Nashville, TN: Thomas Nelson.

Rohr, R. (2011). *Falling upward: A spirituality for the two haves of life.* San Francisco, CA: Jossey-Bass.

Schafer. K. (2011 June). Death as spiritual teacher: End-of-life lessons for the living. *Presence: An international journal of spiritual direction, 17*(2), pp. 11-18.

Schimmel, S. (2008). *The tenacity of unreasonable beliefs: Fundamentalism and the fear of truth.* New York, NY: Oxford University Press.

Selvidge, M. K. (Ed.). (1984). *Fundamentalism today: What makes it so attractive?* Elgin, IL: Brethern Press.

Spong, J. S. (2005). *The sins of scripture: Exposing the Bible's texts of hate to reveal the God of love.* San Francisco, CA: Harper San Francisco.

Smith, G. T. (2011). Conversion. In G. G. Scorgie (Ed.), *Dictionary of Christian spirituality* (pp. 374-375). Grand Rapids, MI: Zondervan.

Smith, H. I. (1990). History of the AIDS epidemic. In M. Malloy (Ed.), *Am I my brother's keeper?* (pp. 11-26). Kansas City, MO: Beacon Hill Press.

Student, J. C. (2009). Hospice movement. In C. H. Lippy & P. W. Williams (Eds.), *Encyclopedia of religion in America* (Vol. 6, pp. 259-260). Washington, DC: CQ Press.

Student, J. C. (2010). Care of the dying. In C. H. Lippy & P. W. Williams (Eds.), *Encyclopedia of religion in America* (Vol. 4, pp. 228-229). Washington, DC: CQ Press.

Sullivan, A. (2012, March 12). The rise of the nones. *Time*, p. 68.

Sweeney, D. A. (2005). *The American evangelical story: A history of the movement.* Grand Rapids, MI: Baker Academic.

Taylor, D. (1999). *The myth of certainty: The reflective Christian and the risk of commitment.* Colorado Springs, CO: IVP Press.

Taylor, D. (2011). *Creating a spiritual legacy: How to share your stories, values, and wisdom.* Grand Rapids, MI: Brazos.

The book of common prayer and administration of the sacraments and other rites and ceremonies of the church. New York: Church Hymnal Corporation.

The question that died. (2012 March). *Christianity Today*, p. 9.

Thompson, W. L. (1972). There's a great day coming. In Lillenas Hymnal Committee (Eds.), *Worship in song hymnal* (p. 186). Kansas City, MO: Lillenas Publishing.

Thurman, H. (1979). *With head and heart: The autobiography of Howard Thurman.* San Diego, CA: Harvest/Harcourt Brace & Company.

Tillman, C. D. (2012). Old-time religion. Retrieved from http:www. Cyberhymnal.org/htm/o/l/oldtimer.htm

Unger, C. (2005 December). American rapture. *Vanity Fair*, 204-222.

Volf, M. (2011). *A public faith: How followers of Christ should serve the common good.* Grand Rapids, MI: Brazos Press.

Watts, J. H. (2012). Working as a hospice volunteer. *Illness, Crisis & Loss, 20*(2), 101-117.

Wellum. S. J. (2012 Spring). Conversion, God, and the whole self. *Southern Seminarian, 80*(2), p. 25.

Wiman, C. (2012, May 4). Dying into life: What faith reveals. *Commonweal,* 12-13.

Wuthrow, R. (2008). Religion. In P. H. Schuck & J. Q. Wilson (Eds.), *Understanding America: The anatomy of an exceptional nation* (pp. 275-305). New York, NY: Public Affairs Press.

Zehner, J. (2009). Systematic theology: Fundamental theology. In H. D. Betz, D. S. Browing, B. Janowski, & E. Jungel (Eds.), *Religion: Past & present: Vol. 4 of the encyclopedia of theology and religion* (pp. 291-292). Boston, MA: Brill.

Contributors

SUSAN ADAMS, PhD, is associate professor of counseling at Texas Woman's University in Denton, Texas. She received her doctorate in Counselor Education from Texas A&M University-Commerce in 2000. She has a limited private practice, with counseling specialties in grief and loss issues and working with adult survivors of past trauma and abuse. Adams is active in her professional organizations and has conducted more than 200 workshops locally, statewide, nationally, and internationally. She was invited to be the keynote speaker at the International Grief Conference in 2008 and 2010 and frequently presents at this conference.

DENISE BEVAN is a family and systemic psychotherapist and social worker and has worked in palliative care settings for 15 years, providing psychosocial and bereavement services. She has also worked as a family therapist in child and adolescent mental health services and worked in a community project as a birth-family therapist with parents who have children in foster care and who hope to restore relationships with these children. Her other interests are in staff care and self-care and, as such, she provides clinical supervision and reflective group support for counselors, therapists, and other professionals. Bevan's publications include exploring aspects of inequalities in dying and bereavement and the implications for service development.

STEPHEN R. CONNOR, PhD, is Senior Fellow to the Worldwide Palliative Care Alliance. He has 36 years of experience in hospice and palliative care. He is an international palliative care consultant to the Soros Open Society Foundation and research director for Capital Caring. Connor is a licensed clinical psychologist, researcher, executive, advocate, and author. He has published more than 80 peer-reviewed articles, reviews, abstracts, and book chapters on issues related to palliative care for patients and their families. He is the author of *Hospice: Practice, Pitfalls, and Promise* (1998) and *Hospice and Palliative Care: The Essential Guide* (2009).

REV. CHRISTOPHER W. COX, CSC, is a Catholic priest of the Congregation of Holy Cross. He received his BA and MDiv from the University of Notre Dame. He has primarily served as a parish priest in immigrant communities in Phoenix, Arizona; South Bend, Indiana; and currently, Santiago, Chile, where he is pastor of Parroquia Nuestra Señora de Andacollo.

JOSEPH M. CURRIER, PhD, is a licensed clinical psychologist and assistant professor in the Clinical Psychology Department at Fuller Theological Seminary. Before joining the Fuller faculty, he completed a clinical internship and doctoral fellowship at the Memphis VA. Since 2005, he has had an active program of research in the psychological and spiritual issues faced by persons exposed to loss and other potential trauma. Currier is the author of more than 30 peer-reviewed articles. His research addresses the role of constructing meaning and making sense of challenging life events. He mentors an active research team of clinical doctoral students; teaches courses in the areas of trauma, bereavement, and spirituality; and serves as a regular reviewer for several journals that publish in these areas.

JESSICA DREWRY, RN, BScN, is a Registered Nurse and has been working at the Hospital for Sick Children in Toronto[1] since graduating in 2008. She has worked in the NICU for 5 years and recently began work in the PICU. She has a strong passion for family-centered care and creating good palliative care experiences for her patients and their families. Her interests include international nursing and global health, and she plans to start her master's in global health policy in the fall of 2013.

JESSICA FAUST, MSW, RSW, has been a Registered Social Worker since 2007, when she graduated from the University of Toronto with a master's in social work. She began her career supporting children and families in the area of mental health. She joined the Hospital for Sick Children in Toronto in 2008 to practice medical social work and joined the NICU in 2009. As a social worker in the NICU, she provides adjustment, supportive resource, and bereavement counseling to parents and families. She also supports families as they transition from pursuing aggressive treatment to palliative care for their babies.

REV. RICHARD B. GILBERT, DMin, BCC, FAAGC, CPBC, teaches at Mercy College, New York, and is founding director of the World Pastoral Care Center. He is a Board Certified Chaplain and Anglican Priest, extensively published, and widely recognized for his leadership and support work in chaplaincy, pastoral care, and health care and bereavement. He has addressed these issues internationally and continues to advocate for strong chaplaincy presence throughout health care.

MIYOUNG YOON HAMMER, PhD, is assistant professor of Marriage and Family Therapy at Fuller Theological Seminary. Before joining the Fuller faculty in 2009, she practiced as a medical family therapist and was an adjunct faculty member at the Chicago Center for Family Health, where she maintained a private practice and taught workshops in the Families, Systems, and Health

---

[1] Several of the presenters work at the Hospital for Sick Children in Toronto, Canada. The hospital is also referred to by the name "SickKids" and is affiliated with the University of Toronto.

postdoctoral program. As a professor, she is passionate about mentoring her students in their clinical, professional, and personal development. Her primary clinical and research interest is understanding how practitioners shape and are shaped by the clinical encounter with their clients/patients.

LORI IVES-BAINE has been a registered nurse since 1989 and has worked at the Hospital for Sick Children in Toronto for 22 years. She completed her master's in nursing with a specialty in pediatrics and bioethics at the University of Toronto in 2009. She works as Palliative Care and Bereavement Coordinator in the Neonatology Program, helping families and staff and providing educational research in end-of-life care in the NICU. She works with a team of professionals who believe in helping families and each other. Her research interests focus on babies and their families and the impact of their care on caregivers.

ROOP JOHAL, MSW, RSW, is a social worker in the NICU at the Hospital for Sick Children in Toronto. She completed her master's in social work at the University of Toronto in 2004, with a clinical focus on medical social work. She has a keen interest in women's and children's health issues. She works with families in the NICU, providing adjustment, supportive resource, and bereavement counseling. Johal has worked with the neonatal population at three centers across Canada and has a keen interest in promoting parental health and well-being during neonates' hospitalization.

JATINDER KALRA, RN, BScN, has been a registered nurse since 1992 and has worked at the Hospital for Sick Children in Toronto for 8 years. She is pursuing her master's in education from Central Michigan University. She works at the bedside and as clinical instructor for students in the Perinatal Intensive Care nursing program at a local college. As a member of the End-of-Life Committee, she provides support to the staff in providing end-of-life care in the NICU. She is a valuable resource in legacy creation.

KATHIE KOBLER, MS, APN, PCNS-BC, CHPPN, serves as Advance Practice Nurse Leader of the perinatal and pediatric palliative care programs at Advocate Children's Hospital, Park Ridge, Illinois. She has been caring for medically fragile infants and children since 1985. She speaks and writes at the national level to promote the growth of pediatric palliative care, currently serving in leadership roles on the National Board for Certification of Hospice and Palliative Care Nurses, the National Pediatric Hospice and Palliative Care Collaboration, and the Alliance for Excellence in Hospice and Palliative Care Nursing.

KENT KOPPELMAN, PhD, graduated from the University of Nebraska, taught high school English and social studies, then earned his PhD from Iowa State University. He taught in the School of Education at the University of Wisconsin-La Crosse for 28 years. In 1988, Wisconsin's Department of Public Instruction selected him as Teacher of the Year. This achievement was followed by a family tragedy in 1989, when his son, Jason, was killed in a car accident. Koppelman described his experience with loss and grief in his first book, *The Fall of a Sparrow: Of Death and Dreams and Healing* (1994). He has written several other books. After retiring in 2007, he received the College of Human Sciences at Iowa State University's Virgil S. Lagomarcino Laureate Award to honor his "distinguished achievement in the field of education."

MICHAEL MARSHALL, MDiv, is the Anglican Chaplain at SickKids in Toronto. A priest with the Diocese of Toronto, he is a member of the Canadian Association for Spiritual Care and is the priest-in-charge at St. Andrew by-the-Lake, Toronto Islands. Marshall has been the liaison chaplain to the NICU at the Hospital for Sick Children in Toronto since 1996. His role has been a part of the developments in interprofessional practice in palliative, end-of-life, and bereavement care at the hospital. He works in other parts of the hospital but sees his primary role as chaplain in the NICU. He has spoken in the community about his work and about the importance of a ministry of listening and has taught theology students at Toronto School of Theology. Marshall has an interest in research that focuses on the spirituality of children, the impact of socioeconomic means on access to holistic care, and the impact of pastoral care in the context of medical practice.

ALYSON MAYNE, RN, has been a nurse for 21 years and has worked at the Hospital for Sick Children in Toronto for the past 13 years. She specializes in the newborn population in the NICU, where she is a strong advocate for family-centered care and adamantly believes in death with dignity. She is a member of the NICU's End-of-Life Resource Team.

JANET S. McCORD, PhD, FT, chairs the Edwin S. Shneidman Department of Thanatology at Marian University in Fond du Lac, Wisconsin, a graduate program in death, dying, grief, and bereavement. Under the direct supervision of Elie Wiesel, she focused her doctoral dissertation on Holocaust-survivor writers who killed themselves after the war, utilizing Shneidman's psychological pain theories to conduct literary psychological autopsies. She completed her training in Psychological Autopsy Investigation with the American Association of Suicidology, serves as secretary for the Association for Death Education and Counseling, and is a member of the steering committee for Prevent Suicide Wisconsin.

ROBERT A. NEIMEYER, PhD, is professor of psychology at the University of Memphis; he also maintains an active clinical practice. He has published 25 books, including *Techniques of Grief Therapy: Creative Practices for Counseling the Bereaved*, and serves as editor of the journal *Death Studies*. The author of nearly 400 articles and book chapters, Neimeyer is currently working to advance a more adequate theory of grieving as a meaning-making process. In recognition of his scholarly contributions, he has received the Phoenix Award: Rising to the Service of Humanity from the MISS Foundation and is a Fellow of the American Psychological Association.

DANAI PAPADATOU, PhD, is professor of clinical psychology in the Faculty of Nursing of the University of Athens. She is also the founder and president of a Greek nonprofit organization, Merimna, which provides pediatric palliative home-care services and bereavement support to children and families who encounter illness and death experiences. Her clinical experience, research interests, and publications focus mostly on issues related to health, psychology, pediatric palliative care, bereavement support, and healthcare providers' responses to the death of their patients. She co-edited the book *Children and Death* (1991) and recently published *In the Face of Death: Professionals Who Care for the Dying and the Bereaved* (2009). Papadatou is a member and past chair of the International Work-Group on Death, Dying, and Bereavement.

COLIN MURRAY PARKES, OBE, MD, FRCPsych, is Emeritus Consultant Psychiatrist to St. Christopher's Hospice, Sydenham and Life President of Cruse Bereavement Care. He is the author of *Bereavement: Studies of Grief in Adult Life* and *Love and Loss: The Roots of Grief and Its Complications* and editor of *Death and Bereavement Across Cultures* and *Responses to Terrorism: Can the Cycle Be Broken?* (all published by Routledge). He has numerous publications on the psychological aspects of bereavement, limb amputation, disasters, and other life crises, and he is on the editorial boards of the journals *Bereavement Care* and *Mortality*. Recent work has focused on prolonged grief disorder, traumatic bereavements (with special reference to violent deaths, armed conflict, and the cycle of violence), and the roots in childhood attachment of the psychiatric problems that can follow bereavement in adult life.

NICOLE PIZZINI, PhD, is a faculty member in the Department of Sociology and Criminal Justice at St. Ambrose University, Davenport, Iowa. She received her PhD in rehabilitation counseling education at the University of Iowa in 2008, with an emphasis on criminal justice and co-occurring disorders. Pizzini teaches both graduate and undergraduate classes in the areas of offender treatment, drugs and society, corrections, leadership and program planning, policy analysis, and stress and crisis management. She is an active member of several professional organizations and has presented at local, state, national, and international conferences on the topics of offender treatment, offender employment, treatment best practices, program development, and collaboration.

CONLEY M. POTTER Is a senior in high school, living near Madison, Wisconsin. This is the second book to which he has contributed. (He is coauthor, with Doug Smith, of *Spiritual Growth and Healing*.) Although he has been heavily involved in music and theater throughout high school—performing in close to 15 plays and musicals, playing piano, saxophone, guitar, and singing—he also has a strong interest in spirituality and a newfound interest in economics and finance. After high school he hopes to attend a major university where he can continue pursuing his many interests.

DOUGLAS C. SMITH, MA, MS, MDiv, is a healthcare consultant, trainer, and counselor. He has worked in diverse settings: hospitals, hospices, universities, social service agencies, and churches. A recipient of three master's degrees in three different disciplines, he teaches and counsels with a truly holistic perspective. He is known for embracing the physical, psychological, and spiritual dimensions of patients and clients. He has written several books, including

Caregiving: Hospice-Proven Techniques for Healing Body and Soul, The Tao of Dying, and *Spiritual Growth and Healing.* For more information, see www.dougcsmith.com.

HAROLD IVAN SMITH, PhD, is a grief specialist on the teaching faculties of Saint Luke's Hospital, Kansas City, Missouri, and the Carondolet Medical Institute in Eau Claire, Wisconsin. He is recognized as a Fellow in Thanatology by the Association for Death Education and Counseling (ADEC), receiving the Distinguished Service Award from ADEC in 2009. Smith graduated from the MidAmerican School of Funeral Service and earned his doctorate from Asbury Theological Seminary in Wilmore, Kentucky, and EdS from George Peabody College of Vanderbilt University. He speaks frequently to grievers and grief counselors and educators. He has spoken recently to the Minnesota, Kentucky, and New Jersey funeral director conventions. He has lectured in Vietnam, Taiwan, Switzerland, England, and Haiti. His writing has been published in *Illness, Crisis & Loss*; *Living with Loss*; *The Director*; *The Forum*; and other journals. His primary research is on borrowing narratives from the grief of U.S. presidents and first ladies. His *Griefkeeping: Learning How Long Grief Lasts* chronicles the grief of 16 presidents and 8 first ladies. He has facilitated Grief Gatherings, creative storytelling groups for grievers at Saint Luke's Hospital for 18 years. Books by Smith include *Borrowed Narratives, A Decembered Grief, A Long-Shadowed Grief: Suicide and Its Aftermath, ABCs of Healthy Bereavement, When You Don't Know What to Say, On Grieving the Death of a Father, Grievers Ask,* and *Grieving the Death of a Mother.*

ANDREA R. SULLIVAN has an undergraduate degree from Saint Mary's College, Notre Dame, Indiana, and a master's in divinity from the University of Notre Dame.

NEIL THOMPSON, PhD, DLitt, is an independent consultant, trainer, and author. He has held full or honorary professorships at four UK universities. He has more than 150 publications, including 32 books, many of which are best-sellers. He has been a speaker at conferences and seminars in countries around the world. Thompson is a Fellow of the Chartered Institute of Personnel and Development, the Higher Education Academy, and the Royal Society of Arts, and is a Life Fellow of the Institute of Welsh Affairs. He was previously the editor of *Illness, Crisis & Loss.* His website is at www.neilthompson.info